Tolley'
Factoring

A guide to factoring
practice and law

by
F R Salinger MC FCA

Tolley Publishing Company Limited
AN EXTEL GROUP PUBLICATION

Published by
Tolley Publishing Company Ltd
Tolley House
17 Scarbrook Road
Croydon
Surrey CR0 1SQ England

Typeset by Kerrypress Ltd
Luton, Beds., England

Printed in
Great Britain at
Heffers Printers Ltd
Cambridge

Foreword

Factoring is not only an important financial tool, it is also intensely interesting to the commercial lawyer, presenting some of the most difficult and fundamental questions of contract law, assignment and priority of competing real rights. It is therefore surprising that factoring has been so seriously neglected by English business and legal literature, and that there has been no full-length English text on the subject for the best part of a decade.

I was therefore delighted to learn that Mr Freddy Salinger was to repair this omission with a comprehensive description of the practice and law of factoring. I knew of no one better qualified to write the book that was so sorely needed. Freddy Salinger combines a vast experience of factoring with a legal knowledge of the subject possessed by few trained lawyers, an acute business sense and a remarkable ability to detect storm signals which are not visible to others and to take appropriate remedial action. He has played a leading role both in the development of factoring, national and international, and in the formulation of rules governing international factoring, particularly in relation to the International Factoring Customs of the Factors Chain International and the proposed Unidroit Uniform Rules for International Factoring.

In this excellent book the reader will find a detailed analysis of the structure and organisation of factoring, the procedures and documents used, and the many business and legal considerations that must constantly be borne in mind by those engaged in factoring transactions. I can warmly commend this book to all who are interested in factoring, whether as financiers, practising lawyers or academics. They will find it an invaluable guide to this fascinating and complex subject.

Roy Goode
Centre for Commercial Law Studies
Queen Mary College
May 1984

Preface

The last significant book on the subject of factoring in its modern sense, 'the factoring of trade debts', appeared here some eight years ago. Most of the published matter in the United Kingdom, before and since, has been by way of articles in professional and trade papers written or ghosted by executives of factoring companies or by professional journalists who may be trying to find a newsworthy angle.

Factoring in the United Kingdom arouses strong emotional feelings in factors, clients, professional advisers and the business community in general. A mention of the word to anyone who has had experience of its use will rarely elicit a dispassionate response either way. Professional advisers who have witnessed the penalties of its misuse seem to shut their minds to possibilities of its benefits and any evidence of its success. Factors, faced with evidence that in some quarters the word has an unfavourable connotation, will rarely accept the possibility that their own actions may have contributed to its reputation and will allege misunderstandings or even a dire conspiracy!

It is natural in these circumstances that executives in a young and exciting industry should become enthusiastic to the point of emotional involvement. 'Factoring is a disease!', said the wife of the chief executive of a factoring company, 'look at him—I have been talking to him for five minutes about our plans to entertain you this evening but he is still thinking about that complex problem you mentioned an hour ago!'

It is, therefore, unfortunate that we have rarely witnessed balanced, disinterested accounts of this most useful and strongly developing financial service. Perhaps it is the paucity of commentary by the academics that has created this gap. Indeed, apart from a few excellent treatises on the more arcane aspects of the law little has been written by the lawyers. (For example: R M Goode 'The Right to Trace and its Impact in Commercial Transactions' (1976) 92 LQR 547; D M McLauchlan 'Priorities—Equitable Tracing Rights and Assignments of Book Debts' (1980) 96 LQR 90; R M Goode 'Commercial Law' Penguin/Allen Lane, at p 858.) Accountants have appeared uninterested rather than disinterested.

The gap in the literature has been apparent to me for some time and I welcome the opportunity to fill it. Although I have worked in factoring for about twenty years, I have also spent some years in a professional office and in commerce and, as I am now approaching retirement, I believe that I am no longer tainted with the factoring disease. I feel that I can look back, and forward too, with a temperate mind and give an up-to-date account of the nature, uses (and misuses) and operation of factoring in the UK in all its various forms. It is hoped, therefore that this book will appeal to a much wider circle than factors and their clients; for the former it may be useful, in particular for those who are setting out on a career in the service. It should be of particular help to those who

Preface

are considering the use of the now expanding service and to present and potential professional and banking advisers in this field.

I have mentioned its various forms because there is much disagreement, even among factoring executives themselves, about what does or does not constitute factoring. This aspect is discussed in the introduction and for this reason a glossary of terms has been included as Appendix I.

Of necessity, a great deal of commercial law, especially that which relates to assignments and security rights, is included in this book. I have not attempted to deal at length with some of the more uncertain and esoteric points; nor have I dealt with Scottish law otherwise than to point to differences and possible areas of difficulty. Others are more qualified to deal with these. Factoring, however, entails relations between several parties and, as it is the law that governs these relations, the law must be stated in order to describe them. For this reason the law (as it applies to England, Wales and Northern Ireland) has not been separated out into a special section, but entwined as a thread throughout the whole book. However, having regard to the readers to whom the book is aimed I have assumed that they will have at least basic knowledge of commercial law and ordinary usages.

If I have been able to present a balanced and factual account on which the business and financial community may rely, then I will have filled the gap.

Acknowledgements and warmest thanks are due to my colleague Ben Hosh and my wife Ann; without the encouragement and helpful suggestions of both of them this book would not have been started.

I have received unstinted help from many of my colleagues and friends. My warmest thanks are due, in particular to Anne Gilbey who supervised the typescript and read the proofs, to Julie Young who managed to decipher my manuscript and created the typescript, to Brian Arculus and Sam Gale, with whom I discussed some of my ideas, and to Jo Stafford of Tolley who patiently corrected my solecisms and obscure patches and made the most useful suggestions on the lay-out and headings.

The book would not have been possible without a great deal of help from Edward Wilde of Messrs Wilde and Partners, Solicitors, London, on many aspects of English law and in particular those parts of the book that deal with collections from and the insolvency of debtors. In other areas of law I have been helped by John Campbell of Messrs Anderson and Gardner of Glasgow, Carroll G ('Peter') Moore, formerly General Counsel of William Iselin & Co Inc of New York and Heinrich J Sommer, Joint Managing Director of Diskont & Kredit AG of Dusseldorf.

I should like to express my sincere appreciation of the great interest *in factoring* shown by Professor R M Goode, OBE, Director of the Centre for Commercial Law Studies, Queen Mary College, London. I am grateful for his help and guidance over many years, on those aspects of commercial law which impinge upon factoring and on some of the more difficult matters on which I have touched in this book.

Finally, I wish to make two special points. First, as in my experience the factor is always, and the client usually, a corporate body, a purist might expect me to refer to each of them as 'it'; I hope, however, that I shall be forgiven for referring to each of them as 'he' for reasons of style. Secondly, my references to the law have been bedevilled by its rapid changes. No doubt there will be further changes between the time of the final typescript and publication, particularly in relation to insolvency law and I have been able to make several references to the White Paper—'A Revised Framework for Insolvency Law' (1984; Cmnd 9175). For the sake of brevity I have referred to these insolvency proposals as 'the White Paper' throughout the book. Otherwise the references to the law are as I understood it at 1 May 1984.

F R Salinger
Anglo Factoring Services Limited
Brighton
May 1984

Stop press The widespread use of retention of title provisions in terms of sale has been a matter of much concern to factors and their legal advisers. An analysis of this has been dealt with in Chapter 16 in which it has been suggested that the supplier's claim to the proceeds would be unlikely to stand up (even where the goods are clearly identifiable and sold on by the client in an unchanged form) unless the terms agreed between the supplier and the client unequivocally placed the client in a fiduciary capacity as regards the proceeds. A recent case, *In re Andrabell Ltd, The Times, 12 June 1984,* appears to confirm this view. In that case the supplier's claim failed because:

(*a*)   there was no provision for separate storage of the goods before they became the subject of a sub-sale; and

(*b*)   the terms contained no acknowledgement of a fiduciary relationship; and

(*c*)   the terms did not provide for a duty to account for the whole of the proceeds of the sub-sale irrespective of the amount owing by the purchaser to the supplier.

Contents

Page

Table of Statutes   xiv
Table of Cases   xv

1. **Introduction**   1
    The origin of factoring   1
    Developments in Europe and the United Kingdom   4
    The definition of factoring   7
    Establishing the rights to ownership of debts   9
    Factoring and the Consumer Credit Act 1974   10

    PART A : FACTORING USE AND PRACTICE

2. **The Nature of Factoring — The Full Service**   13
    A description of the full service   13
    The provision of finance for trade credit through the factoring
      service   15
    The commencement of the arrangement for factoring   16
    Termination of the arrangement   16

3. **The Nature of Factoring — Other Forms**   17
    Recourse factoring   17
    Bulk factoring   18
    Maturity factoring   19
    Invoice discounting or confidential factoring   19
    Undisclosed factoring   21
    Agency factoring   22
    Co-operation with credit insurers : recourse factoring or
      invoice discounting in conjunction with credit insurance   22
    Co-operation with banks : client/factor/bank arrangements   24
    Conclusion and new developments   25
    Table: factoring variants   26

4. **The Benefits of Factoring**   27
    The importance of good sales ledger administration   27
    The administrative service provided by factoring   29
    The benefit of protection against bad debts   30

Contents

Table: Credit insurance and factoring compared   31
The provision of finance without formal limit by factoring   34
Non-recourse factoring and the client's balance sheet   34

5.   **The Use and Misuse of Factoring**   36
The nature of true trade credit   36
Limitations on factoring use   37
Businesses for which factoring is highly suitable   39
Some effects of misuse of the service   40
Recognition of misuse can help image   43
Factoring and overtrading   43

6.   **Factoring and the Accountant in Practice**   45
The accountant as adviser   45
The accountant as auditor   48

PART B : THE RELATIONSHIP BETWEEN THE FACTOR AND
THE CLIENT

7.   **The Factoring Agreement : The Main Functions and Types**   50
Transfer of ownership of debts : the requirements of a valid
   assignment   50
Stamp duty considerations   53
Basic types of agreement   54
Lending on security distinguished from outright purchase   55
Facultative agreements   56
Whole turnover agreements   58
Sole traders and partnerships   60
Special considerations for Scotland   61

8.   **The Factoring Agreement : Other Terms and the Factor's Rights**   64

PART I : ANCILLARY PROVISIONS
Warranties and undertakings by the client : general   64
Warranties in connection with variations of sale contracts   67
Perfecting the factor's title and powers of attorney   70
Creation of trusts by client in respect of debts sold   71
Recovery of funds paid by debtor to client   72
Approved and unapproved debts   73
Recourse : the right to be repaid by the client
   for debts purchased   75
Transfer of ancillary rights   75
Provision for proof of delivery of goods by client   76
Inspection of client's records and accounts   77

PART II : FACTOR'S RIGHTS ON BREACH
AND TERMINATION OF THE AGREEMENT
Factor's rights on breach of warranty by client   77
Collateral security in case of client company   78
Termination of the agreement   80

9. **The Factor's Charges and Accounting Procedures**   83
    The administration charge   83
    Other charges for services   85
    Finance charges : method of calculation   85
    The client account : purchase price payable on collection   89
    The client accounts : purchase price payable after fixed
        maturity period   91
    Value added tax   93

10. **The Factor's Assessment of a Prospective Client**   95
    The nature of the business   95
    The terms and conditions of sale   96
    The financial position of the business   96
    Administration of sales records by client   97
    Assessment of credit risks   98
    Encumbrances on the debts   99
    Special sales   100
    Special consideration of credit risks   101

    PART C : THE RELATIONSHIP BETWEEN THE FACTOR AND
    THE DEBTOR

11. **Collection from the Debtor and the Debtor's Countervailing Rights** 103
    Normal procedures of collection   103
    Legal remedies as final resort   108
    The debtor's defences and counterclaims   111
    No positive liability of factor to the debtor   114
    Position of the factor arising from total failure of consideration 115
    Factor's liability for credit balances   116
    Position of the factor on insolvency of the client   118
    Crown set-off   120

12. **Insolvency of the Debtor**   122
    Receivership   122
    The factor's procedures in liquidation or bankruptcy of
        the debtor   124
    Factor's recourse for unapproved debts   126
    Recovery of value added tax   128
    Reservation of title in the client's terms of sale   128

13. **Contractual Terms Prohibiting Assignments**   130
    The pre-1978 view of the effect of terms prohibiting assignments   130
    The position since the 'Helstan' case   131
    The use of 'ban on assignment' terms   131
    The rationale for inclusion of terms prohibiting assignment   133
    Methods by which a factor may overcome the problem   134

14. **Other Terms in Contracts of Sale Affecting the Factor**   136
    Long term contracts   136

Contents

Cut-off clauses   138
Contracts for 'sale or return' or 'sale on approval'   139

PART D : CONFLICTS WITH THIRD PARTIES

15. The Factor's Conflicts with Other Assignees and Chargees   141
The factor's position vis à vis other assignees and chargees   141
The rule in *Dearle v Hall* : priority of charges   143
Waivers from the third party : a safeguard   144
Types of conflicting charges   146

16. The Factor's Conflicts with Other Claimants to Debts   151
'Romalpa' clauses   151
Goods released on trust receipt   156
The liens of a carrier   156
The rights of a mercantile agent   157

PART E : INSOLVENCY OF THE CLIENT

17. Receivership   158
Relations between the receiver and the factor   158
Factor's rights on appointment: general   159
Factor's position as regards existing debts   161
Position as regards debts coming into existence after
    the appointment   162
Continuation of the arrangement for factoring by the
    receiver   163
The position of the receiver subsequent to a winding-up order   163
Appointment of administrator proposed in White Paper   164

18. Winding-up and Bankruptcy   166
The effect of a winding-up by the court   166
The effect of voluntary winding-up   168
Bankruptcy of the client   169
Factor's rights on winding-up or bankruptcy of client   171

19. Miscellaneous Problems on the Insolvency of the Client   174
Credit balances on the debtor's account   174
Attachment of balance owing by the factor to the
    client by creditor of the client   175

PART F : INTERNATIONAL FACTORING

20. Systems for International Factoring   178
The 'two factor' system   178
Direct import factoring   181
Direct export factoring   182
Invoice discounting or undisclosed factoring for exports   183
Back-to-back factoring   184

21. **International Matters for Special Consideration** 186
The legal effect of international transactions 186
Transmission of funds in settlement of debts 189
Currency risks associated with international factoring 191
The International Institute for the Unification of Private
Law (Unidroit) 191
International factoring — the client's viewpoint 193

PART G : THE FUTURE

22. **The Legal Framework** 196
An alternative legal form of providing finance by
factoring 196
Lending on the security of the debts 198
A composite method of factoring 200

23. **The Influence of the Micro-Computer** 202
Data processing packages for small businesses 202
The provision of sales statistics by the factor 203

24. **Conclusion : The Growing Acceptability of Factoring** 204
Proved benefits to independent businesses 204
Need for codification of commercial law 204

APPENDICES
I. **Glossary of Terms** 209
II. **Checklist for Adviser** 214
III. **Checklist for Factor** 217
IV. **Specimen Facultative Factoring Agreement** 222
V. **Specimen Whole Turnover Factoring Agreement** 230
VI. **Client Account : Purchase Price Paid on Collection Date** 240
VII. **Client Accounts : Purchase Price Paid on Maturity** 241
VIII. **Export Factoring : 'Two Factor' System** 244
IX. **Export Factoring : 'Back-to-Back' Factoring** 245

INDEX 247

Table of Statutes

1873 Judicature Act
      s 25(6)   7.5

1878 Bills of Sale Act
      s 20   7.31

1882 Bills of Sale Act
      s 15   7.31

1882 Bills of Exchange Act
      s 29(1)   11.11

1889 Factors Act
      s 2(1)   16.4
      s 9   16.4

1891 Stamp Duty Act   7.8
      s 54   7.9

1914 Bankruptcy Act
      s 7(1)   12.5
      s 8   18.11
      s 10   18.11
      s 31   8.21, 11.27, 11.44,
                     11.45, 20.18
      s 37   18.9
      s 38(2)(c)   7.31, 18.10,
                            18.11
      s 40   19.6
      s 40(1)   12.7
      s 41   12.7
      s 43   15.2, 18.11
      s 43(1)   7.29, 18.10
      s 45   18.9, 18.11
      s 54   18.9
      s 56   18.11

1925 Law of Property Act
      s 136   7.5, 8.20, 11.14
      s 136(1)   15.6
      s 137   15.5

1947 Crown Proceedings Act
      s 35(2)   11.44

1948 Companies Act
      s 94   12.3, 17.2
      s 95   3.23, 7.14, 10.10
      s 95(1)   8.5
      s 95(2)(c)   7.15
      s 95(2)(e) 7.15, 8.5, 15.15
      s 223(a)   11.9
      s 223(d)   11.9
      s 227   7.20, 18.2, 18.3
      s 229   7.20, 18.2
      s 231   12.5, 18.1
      s 280   18.5
      s 283   18.5
      s 285   18.5
      s 285(2)   18.6
      s 293(1)   18.5, 18.7
      s 302   12.5
      s 317   8.21, 11.27, 11.44,
                            20.18
      s 322   8.39
      s 323   18.1
      s 325   12.7
      s 325(1)   19.6
      s 326   12.7
      s 369(2)   12.4, 17.15

1971 Powers of Attorney Act
      s 4   8.17

1974 Consumer Credit Act
                      1.28, 1.32
      s 8   1.29
      s 16   1.29
      s 145(8)   1.31
      s 146(6)(a)   1.30
      s 189(1)   1.29

1978 Finance Act
      s 12   12.15

1979	Sale of Goods Act		1981	Companies Act	
	s 18 rule 4	14.9		s 106	18.5
	s 25(1)	16.4		s 106(1)	18.7
	s 25(2)	16.2		s 106(2)	18.8
	s 30(1)	14.4			
	s 31(2)	14.4	1982	Insurance Companies	
	s 48(4)	12.21		Act	22.6
	s 51(1)	14.4		s 2(4)	22.7
	s 53(1)(*a*)	11.24		Schedule 2	22.7

Table of Cases

Airlines Airspares Ltd v Handley Page Ltd [1970] 1 AER 29	17.2
Aluminium Industrie Vaassen BV v Romalpa Aluminium Ltd [1976] 2 AER 552	16.2
Re Anchor Line (Henderson Bros) Ltd [1937] 2 AER 823	21.5
Attorney General v Cohen [1937] 1 KB 478	7.10, 7.12
Bolton v Mahadeva [1972] 2 AER 1322	14.3
Re Bond Worth Ltd [1979] 3 AER 919	12.19, 16.4
Borden (UK) Ltd v Scottish Timber Products Ltd [1979] 3 AER 961	12.19, 16.4
Business Computers Ltd v Anglo-African Leasing Ltd [1977] 2 AER 741	11.25, 14.3
Re Centrebind Ltd [1966] 3 AER 889	18.8
Chow Yoong Hong v Choong Fah Rubber Manufactory [1962] AC 209	1.11, 7.17, 9.9
Clark Taylor & Co Ltd v Quality Site Development (Edinburgh) Ltd 1981 SLT 308	7.38, 16.10
Re Cushla Ltd [1979] STC 615	11.44
Dearle v Hall (1823) 3 Russ 1	15.5, 15.9, 15.16, 15.19, 15.20, 16.5, 16.8
Gosling v Gaskell & Grocott [1895–9] AER Rep 300	12.3, 17.16
Government of Newfoundland v Newfoundland Railway Co (1888) 13 AC 199	14.3

Re Claim by Helbert Wagg & Co Ltd [1956] Ch 323 — 21.7

Helstan Securities Ltd v Hertfordshire County Council
[1978] 3 AER 262 — 13.1, 13.2

Hendy Lennox (Industrial Engines) Ltd v Grahame Puttick Ltd
[1984] 1 WLR 485 — 12.20, 16.4

Hoenig v Isaacs [1952] 2 AER 176 — 14.3

Holroyd v Marshall (1862) 10 HL Cas 191 — 7.24, 18.2

Holt v Heatherfield Trust Ltd [1942] 1 AER 404 — 7.4, 7.5, 15.5

International Factors Ltd v Rodriguez [1979] 1 AER 17 — 8.19, 8.22

Re Lind, Industrials Finance Syndicate Ltd v Lind
[1914–15] AER Rep 527 — 18.2

Lloyds & Scottish Finance Ltd v Cyril Lord Carpets
Sales Ltd and others (1979), HL (unreported) — 7.17, 9.9, 15.1

Manchester Ship Canal Co v Manchester Racecourse Co (1901)
2 Ch 37 — 15.16

In re Maudslay, Sons & Field [1900] 1 Ch 602 — 21.6, 21.8

Medical Defence Union Ltd v Department of Trade
[1979] 2 AER 421 — 22.7

'The Nanfri' [1978] 2 Lloyds Rep 132 — 11.25, 14.3

National Westminster Bank Ltd v Halesowen Presswork
& Assemblies Ltd [1972] 1 AER 641 — 11.29

Re Newdigate Colliery Ltd [1912] 1 Ch 468 — 17.2

Newhart Developments Ltd v Co-operative Commercial
Bank Ltd [1978] 2 AER 896 — 12.2, 17.2

North Western Bank Ltd v John Poynter Son
& MacDonalds (1895) AC 56 — 16.11

Olds Discount Co Ltd v John Playfair Ltd [1938] 3 AER 275 — 15.1

Re Peachdart Ltd [1983] 3 AER 204 — 12.19, 16.4

Re Pinto Leite & Nephew [1929] 1 Ch 221 — 11.25

Quinn v Leathem [1900–3] AER Rep 1 — 7.17

'The Raven' [1980] 2 Lloyds Rep 266 — 11.25

Roberts Petroleum Ltd v Bernard Kenny Ltd (in liquidation)
[1983] 1 AER 564 — 12.8

Rogers v Challis (1859) 27 Beav 175 — 7.24

Rolls Razor Ltd v Cox [1967] 1 AER 397 — 16.15

Roxburghe v Cox (1881) 17 Ch D 520 — 11.24, 14.3

Re Sass [1896] 2 QB 12 — 12.10, 12.14, 18.16

Shaw & Co v Moss Empires & Bastow (1908) 25 TLR 190 — 13.1

Siebe Gorman & Co Ltd v Barclays Bank Ltd [1979]
   2 Lloyds Rep 142   15.20, 15.21
Smith v Lord Advocate 1981 SLT 19   11.45
Sowman v David Samuel Trust Ltd [1978] 1 WLR 22   17.16
Swiss Bank Corporation v Lloyds Bank Ltd and others
   [1979] 2 AER 853   15.16, 15.21

Tailby v Official Receiver (1888) 13 Ap Cas 523   7.24, 18.2, 18.11
Thomas v Todd [1926] 2 KB 511   17.16

Wm Brandts Sons & Co v Dunlop Rubber Co Ltd [1905] AC 454   7.6, 8.20
Willingale (Inspector of Taxes) v International Commercial
   Bank Ltd [1978] 1 AER 754   9.9

Yorkshire Woolcombers Association Ltd [1903] 2 Ch 284   15.14, 15.20

Chapter 1

Introduction

1.1   Much has been written in the technical and financial press in the last few years about factoring and factors. However, many businessmen and their professional advisers still have only a vague, and sometimes incorrect, conception of the several forms of the service. Although the selling of trade debts to raise funds has been practised for as long as there have been historical records of business, it is only in recent years that the practice has come to be known as factoring. Confusion has been aggravated, first, by the continuing use of the expression 'factor' in its original sense of a mercantile agent selling his principal's goods on commission and, secondly, by the absence of agreement among factors themselves as to what is and what is not factoring. This question of definition is dealt with later in this chapter (see 1.19 below), after a short history of the development of factoring in its modern sense which may help towards an understanding of the service in all its forms (see 1.3–1.18 below).

1.2   This book is about factoring of debts in all its most usual forms. Of these forms the most complete service is an arrangement by which the factor purchases on a continuing basis all the debts of a supplier of goods and services (the client) to trade customers and by which the client is:

(*a*) relieved from the administrative tasks of keeping a sales ledger and collecting from the debtors; and

(*b*) protected against bad debts; and

(*c*) provided with funds.

This full service is described in Chapter 2 and the main variants in Chapter 3.

The origin of factoring

The beginnings

1.3   The use of a factor, in the sense of 'mercantile agent', by merchants and manufacturers is as old as any historical records of business. Owing to slow communications and transport of goods, a business selling in another territory had perforce to appoint such an agent to find customers, hold the principal's goods on consignment, sell and deliver the goods for the principal and collect the proceeds. This method of doing business developed strongly during the great period of colonisation by European countries from the sixteenth century onwards. The mother countries, being more developed than the colonies, sent increasing volumes of manufactured goods to the colonies and the exporters needed to appoint mercantile agents in the territories which they supplied. The system was especially marked on the eastern seaboard of the United States, where factors not only held stocks of goods (mainly textiles, clothing and related merchandise) for their principals in Europe and sold them on the principal's behalf, but also guaranteed payment as 'del credere' agents. Because of the great distances between centres of population in the US, local manufacturers also found it necessary to employ such factors.

Transformation to modern factoring

1.4   Later, as the factors prospered, they were able to make early payments to their principals before the customers settled. The factor substituted himself as one debtor of high credit standing for the individual customers of uncertain creditworthiness from whom the principal would otherwise have to collect. As communications improved it was no longer necessary for the manufacturer to send goods on consignment to a mercantile agent; goods could be sold by sample through the agent and despatched to the customer direct. The principals had felt comfortable relying on their agents who were well known to them and trusted and who would pay on shipment of the goods. They, therefore, wished to retain this aspect of the agent's service.

1.5   Thus, factoring in its modern sense was created. By purchasing the debts arising from the sale of goods by their principals the factors acquired the right to collect the debts as owners and this took the place of the factor's prescriptive right to collect as a mercantile agent. The factor, in the old sense, provided services under the headings of marketing, distribution, administration and finance. Modern methods of marketing and distribution, based on fast and efficient communications and transport, dispense with the need for services under the first two heads.

Early developments of modern factoring in the United States

1.6   The early factors in the US acted without a comprehensive framework of statutory law. They acted as mercantile agents under the common law. Factors' Acts, which validated the factor's lien on his principal's goods in his possession as security for commission owed to him and advances to the principals, were adopted by many of the states by the 1940's. When the transformation to modern factoring took place, the new relationship of the principal and agent as assignor and assignee had to be established by judicial decisions and precedent. By the 1930's this case law was fairly well established in New York and the New England states where most of the factoring houses were located. In the majority of such states case law required that notice of the assignment to be given to the debtor in order to secure the assignee against claims of third parties or of the countervailing rights of the debtor.

1.7   In the remainder of the country factoring companies had to rely on an even less certain foundation for their business. However, owing to the growing demand for the service in the 1940's, most of the commercially important states adopted statutes to provide for the assignment of debts both by way of outright sale and purchase and by way of security right. The validation was usually by one of three methods:

(*a*)   the registration of a security interest; or

(*b*)   reliance on a written instrument evidencing the assignment; or

(*c*)   the marking of the assignor's books of account.

The statutes normally validated assignments of future debts to secure fluctuating advances. They were the foundation for those parts of the Uniform Commercial Code (UCC) which deal with factoring and financing of trade debts (or 'accounts receivable' as they are referred to in the US). The UCC, which has been adopted by every state except Louisiana, has, it is believed, given a great boost to the provision of factoring in its widest sense in the US. Factors are now able to provide the service in confidence knowing exactly where they stand in most conceivable circumstances and what formalities are necessary to secure their full rights to the debts assigned to them. It is significant that the provision of these services has increased greatly since the 1950's.

Factoring in the United States now

1.8   However, in spite of this growth, factors in the US have not yet ventured far outside the trades and industries in which they have operated since their early times as mercantile agents. The traditions of factoring are in the textile and apparel industries and in related consumer goods trades. The reasons usually advanced for this conservatism rest on the methods by which US factors protect themselves against losses arising from the insolvency of debtors. Unlike their counterparts in the UK who rely, as an insurance company does, on a spread of risks or in some cases on credit insurance itself, the US factors rely on a thorough knowledge of the trade and in particular on up-to-date financial statements sent to them direct from larger debtors. In a trade in which factoring is usual and in which factors may readily give trade references to each other, it is natural that a purchaser on credit terms should be willing to give information to the credit granters to establish his creditworthiness. It is, indeed, not unusual for a US factor to refuse to accept the assignment of a debt within a factoring arrangement only because the debtor has refused to submit financial information.

1.9   In this environment the factors feel unhappy in breaking into trades with which they are not familiar. In unfamiliar trades they find it difficult to insist on the supply of information by debtors; they have no credit files built up from experience of many clients supplying the same debtor; and they have little knowledge of the usages of such trades. Some US factoring executives have expressed the view that the investment needed to acquire the credit information is not worthwhile and point to the losses sustained by factors who have ventured into new fields. In addition, as factoring is not readily accepted outside the traditional fields, marketing costs are higher. These problems are compounded by the poor profitability of factors in the US in recent years. The poor results are themselves the result of the same problems: restricting themselves to certain fields, the factors are competing with each other fiercely for a limited number of prospective clients and cutting their charges. Poor profitability arises from the restriction and the result is a reluctance to break out and thus risk their investment.

1.10   There have, however, been moves in recent years to develop factoring in more modern industries such as electronics and plastics and some US factors are looking to international trade. It will certainly be through these two developments, if they are vigorously pursued, that factoring will grow in the US. The UK and the rest of Europe and indeed most of the developed countries in the world have taken up factoring from its country of origin. Now it may be the turn of the US to learn from developments on this side of the Atlantic.

Developments in Europe and the United Kingdom

1.11   Although the United States is often referred to, not least by factors there, as the country of origin of modern factoring, many writers, including some in the UK, have traced its origin much further back in history. The reason for this is that factoring in the United Kingdom in all its forms, as described in Chapters 2 and 3, is derived from two sources: it is derived not only from the activities of US factors but also from certain continental practices relating to the financing of trade debts. The selling of debts to raise finance has been traced back to the beginnings of commerce. ('There are many ways of raising cash besides borrowing. One is by selling book debts . . .'; *Chow Yoong Hong v Choong Fah Rubber Manufactory [1962] AC 209.*) In England, such transactions were known in mediaeval times. Certainly, the practice of assigning trade debts, evidenced by copies of invoices, to a bank, either by way of sale or as security in order to raise money, has for many decades been practised in most countries on the continent of Europe. The practice has declined in recent years owing to the reluctance of the banks to provide for the resulting high administrative workload in their branches. It is doubtful if the taking of copy invoices has given the banks much in the way of security in countries where a notice to the debtor in some form (apart from other formalities) would be necessary to validate the assignment, and such arrangements have usually been effected in confidence without such notices. However, in the absence of a satisfactory means of taking security rights over trade debts and other circulating assets, such as has been available in England and Wales by means of a floating charge, the

European banker would no doubt have regarded the copy invoice as reasonable evidence that the cash equivalent of its face value would shortly be received by the borrower and enable him to repay the advance.

Invoice discounting in the early post-war years

1.12   In the early post war years, the influence of this continental practice of assigning trade debts evidenced by copy invoices may have been at work in England and have thus led to the establishment, by the early 1950's, of several large and many small invoice discounters in the City and West End of London. Many immigrants from Central Europe were experts in the very trades which were used to discounting their invoices with the continental banks. These trades included furniture and garment manufacturing. Seeing that this was an activity in which the British banks took little part and encouraged perhaps by the more liberal formalities for the assignment of debts in English equity, some of them were attracted to what appeared to be a gap in the financial services market.

1.13   The use of the expression 'invoice discounting' for the discounting of trade debts may, by analogy with bill discounting, have encouraged such financiers to assume that they were as secure as the holder of a negotiable instrument. But, whereas the holder in due course of a bill of exchange has the right to recover payment in full free from any countervailing rights of the acceptor or any third party claims, the assignee of a debt on open credit owns a pure intangible claim with no such special rights. Furthermore, the amount payable in respect of a trade debt is often not the face value of the invoice; a trade debt represents a balance, on an account, of debits for invoices and other charges and credits for payments (some of which may not be appropriated to specific invoices) and for returns and allowances. The invoice discounted may sometimes be free from such credits and payable in full but deductions of one kind or another (including large settlement discounts) are usual in these trades.

1.14   Losses were incurred by such financiers on the insolvency of clients by reason of recoveries of net indebtedness of sums less than the face value of invoices. Such a shortfall in recovery may sometimes have arisen through irresponsible invoicing by the client but more often through the deductions described in 1.13 above. As these arrangements were, after the continental usage, confidential and without notice to the debtor, and, as the recoveries before the client's insolvency were through the client and not direct from the debtors, the discounter would not be aware of the regular deductions until it was too late and recourse to the insolvent client would be nugatory.

The early entrants into the field in the United Kingdom

1.15   The attraction of taking the whole of a debtor portfolio of a client on a continuing 'whole turnover' basis, with notices to and direct collection from the debtors, encouraged the establishment of factoring by the early 1960's to take up the gap left by some of the discounters who had decided that the risk of loss was not compensated by the often relatively high discounting charges levied. At least one of the factoring companies established in those early days was based on the activities of an invoice discounter. The direct collection had the effect of keeping the factor aware at an early stage of disputes, deductions and counterclaims, so that immediate recourse could be effected, a pattern of such deductions established and security retentions maintained. The other source of modern factoring in the UK was the practice in the US described in 1.4–1.10 above. Even those who had developed the service out of invoice discounting tended to look to the US for guidance in practical operations. These early entrants into the field, for the most part partnerships between confirming houses and merchant banks, looked for businesses that were unable to obtain working capital from traditional sources. Although they advertised the service of collection and protection against bad debts, they tended to stress in their marketing the immediate and easy access to funds.

A contrast with the situation in the US

1.16   The early 1960's was a time when factors in the US, to whom all the early practitioners looked for guidance, were providing their services increasingly to businesses that had no use for the financial facility and were looking for administrative services and protection against bad debts. The reasons for this apparent paradox are not hard to find: the trades for which factoring had traditionally been used in the US were well served in the UK by a form of credit insurance developed on a much wider and more flexible basis than the US, and sales accounting and credit control were until fairly recently the 'Cinderella' of accounts departments. The benefits of these services were hard to sell and these early factors slipped into the easier practice of providing finance for those who did not meet the standards required by the banks. Very often this service, necessitating disclosure to customers, was accepted reluctantly.

Restraints on early growth in the UK

1.17   As a result of these developments and owing also to the entry into the field of some smaller companies, calling themselves factors, which did not provide the full service of an adequate sales ledger administration and protection against bad debts, the factoring service became known mainly as a provider of finance *of last resort*. Parallel with this development, some of the early factors being unable to make much headway in the traditional trades, offered factoring to companies of poor financial standing and in industries, such as the construction industry, in which recoveries on the insolvency of a contractor are questionable. There were even cases of the purchase by factors of claims represented by uncertified interim accounts under long-term building contracts, which amounts became valueless in the face of an uncompleted contract. It is unfortunate that some of these factors did not appear to grasp the fundamental difference between the circumstances in the US where factoring law and practice is reasonably certain under the influence of the UCC and the uncertain environment of developing case law in the UK. The losses suffered by this injudicious acceptance of unsuitable clients caused the closure of a few of the early factoring companies.

Interest of the clearing banks

1.18   The influences mentioned in 1.17 above severely restrained the growth of factoring until the entry of the clearing banks as owners of factoring companies towards the end of the 1960's and early 1970's. The access by the factoring companies, owned by or connected with banks with thousands of branches, to an enormous market gave a fresh impetus to the growth of factoring. However, the inclusion of factoring within the range of financial services, as a form of asset-based finance, rather than as an alternative to credit insurance and relief from accounting and collection of trade debts, had the effect of continuing to market the service mainly as a means of finance.

The definition of factoring

1.19   Before going further into the details of those services, it is necessary to consider the meaning of 'factoring' in its modern sense. In the United States, factoring is generally accepted as meaning the purchase only of trade debts owed on normal short terms without recourse and with notice to and direct collection from the debtors. It has been defined as follows:

'. . . a continuing arrangement between a factoring concern and the seller of goods or services on open account, pursuant to which the factor performs the following services with respect to the accounts receivables arising from sales of such goods or services:

1 Purchases all accounts receivables for immediate cash.
2 Maintains the ledgers and performs the other book-keeping duties relating to such accounts receivable.
3 Collects the accounts receivable.
4 Assumes the losses which may arise from any customer's financial inability to pay (credit losses).'

(Carroll G. Moore 'Factoring—A Unique and Important Form of Financing and Service'. The Business Lawyer, Vol XIV, No 3 1959.)

Although some practitioners in the UK accept only this narrower definition, factoring is accepted as including the following variations by others in this country. These variations, which will be dealt with in detail in Chapter 3, include buying the debts:

(*a*) with recourse to the supplier as regards credit losses; and/or

(*b*) without notice to the debtor or without relieving the supplier of goods or services from the task of administering the accounts of the debtors in his own books.

There is a definition in the Concise Oxford Dictionary which is still wider than the US definition plus these variations ('v.i.; buy at discount the debts owed to another, in order to profit by collecting them'). According to the Dictionary, factoring would thus also include;

—the purchase of debts owed by individuals in their private capacity;

—the purchase of instalment debts (normally referred to as block discounting);

—the purchase of debts arising otherwise than from the sale of goods or the provision of services in the normal course of business.

None of these, however, is generally accepted as factoring in the UK.

Differences recognised by UNIDROIT

1.20 This general difficulty of definition was considered by the study group set up by UNIDROIT (International Institute for the Unification of Private Law, Via Panisperna 28, 00184 ROME) in order to consider draft uniform rules for international factoring. The study group and observers, all of whom took an active part in the discussions, consisted of practitioners and academics from about a dozen countries. There were considerable disagreements over not only the definition of factoring but also whether the rules should apply to all forms or be more restricted. An example of these wide differences was a view which emerged that the purchase of a debt with payment of the purchase price only on its maturity (so that no finance was provided) could not be regarded as factoring. On the other hand, maturity factoring without recourse with the main purpose of protecting the client against bad debts, has constituted a large part of the business of US and UK factors in recent years. The conclusion reached in general terms was that only an arrangement which included at least *two* of the following services was factoring:

(*a*) finance;

(*b*) the maintenance of accounts;

(*c*) the collection of debts;

(*d*) protection against credit risks.

1.21   It was decided that the definition of factoring did not exclude the purchase of debts payable on long terms or by instalments, nor debts owing by individuals; nor did it exclude arrangements whereby collection was to be effected by the supplier. The reasons for this conclusion and how it was dealt with in the rules are described in Chapter 21 (see 21.18–21.22).

An even wider definition?

1.22   A further difficulty arises from the fact that future developments may show all these definitions to be too narrow in relation to one aspect. As described more fully in Chapter 22, there are moves afoot to change the basis of the service from the purchase of debts to the charging of the debts by the client in favour of the factor. If in the end result the same service is provided, does this mean that the arrangement should no longer be referred to as 'factoring'? The Concise Oxford Dictionary definition (see 1.19 above) deals with the matter only from the point of view of the factor. What really matters, however, is the end result for the client, i.e. what is the client getting in return for the profit given to the factor? With this in view this book will deal with the arrangements between a supplier of goods or services to trade customers and the factor, whereby, through the sale of trade debts to the factor by the client, the client obtains finance directly related to such debts or a sales ledger administration service or both, with or without protection against bad debts. The term 'factoring' will refer to any form of service as described above and individual variations will be referred to by the use of qualifying adjectival nouns (e.g. 'recourse factoring', 'maturity factoring') as described in Chapter 3. Where the narrower definition is required the arrangement will be referred to as the 'full service'. A Table explaining the variations is included in Chapter 3.

1.23   The inclusion in a book on factoring of a reference to the charging of book debts, as distinct from the sale and purchase of them, presents some difficulty because it overlaps to a large extent with the subject of banking. As such an arrangement has not yet been used in factoring in the UK, it will be dealt with only as a matter of the future developments of the service (see Part G).

Establishing the rights to ownership of debts

1.24   A large part of the book is devoted to the problems encountered by the factor in obtaining the ownership of a debt payable to him in full without any encumbrance either by way of defence or cross-claim on the part of the debtor or by way of claims of third parties. In theory this appears to be a simple matter; but the practical difficulties have been the cause of substantial losses to factoring companies. From the point of view of the potential client or his adviser this aspect, the factor's security, may not appear to be other than of academic interest; but the problems have created anxiety among some factoring circles and the client can obtain a good service at an economic price only if the factor has confidence in his ability to collect in full the sums laid out in payments to the client for the purchase of his trade debts.

Trend towards maturity factoring

1.25   Naturally, when factoring is used only for the administration of the sales ledger and the collection from debtors with or without protection against bad debts but without the finance included in the full service, the factor need not be too concerned with this aspect (this is normally called 'maturity factoring'—see 3.7–3.8). If a debt purchased by a factor on this basis is not to be paid owing to a debtor's countervailing rights or a third party claim, the factor will have ample opportunity to exercise his right of recourse. In most cases he will not have paid for the debt so that the recourse becomes a mere book entry.

1.26   At present there is a trend towards the adoption of factoring on a maturity basis as a pure service without finance. The trend appears to have developed largely from the needs of small businesses in times of great uncertainty regarding the solvency of even well-established debtors rather than from a change in marketing emphasis by the factors themselves. The full service includes finance and, of the eight variations mentioned in Chapter 3, only two relate to factoring without a financial facility. It is however possible that this book, which seeks to dispel some of the misconceptions about factoring and to bring into the open some of its misuses, may have some influence on the proper use of the service in all its forms.

1.27   However, in spite of the growing practice of maturity factoring, the service unconnected with any financial facility, the widespread use of factoring and invoice discounting *in all its forms* for finance demands a full exposition of this problem and its solutions. To those who are considering the use of maturity factoring, or advising on its use, those parts of the book that deal with the factor's security must be read with this in mind: to the majority of business people and to most clients, in spite of the growing use of maturity factoring, factoring still means finance.

Factoring and the Consumer Credit Act 1974

Licence for consumer credit business normally not necessary

1.28   It was indicated in 1.19 above that, to be acceptable as factoring in the UK, an arrangement for the sale and purchase of debts should relate to debts payable otherwise than by instalments. Almost invariably each debt factored in the UK is a debt which, by the relevant contract of sale or service, is payable in one amount on a specific due date. For this reason normal factoring contracts are not regulated by the Consumer Credit Act 1974. By Article 3(1)(*a*)(i) of the Consumer Credit (Exempt Agreements) Order 1977, 'the Act shall not regulate a consumer credit agreement . . . being . . . any agreement for fixed sum credit under which the number of payments to be made by the debtor does not exceed four . . .'. As a result it is not usual for factors to be licensed for consumer credit business as such; but some factors consider it necessary to be licensed for ancillary business, as described in 1.30 below.

1.29   A regulated consumer credit agreement will, however, exist where the debtor is an individual or partnership, the creditor is an assignee of the original creditor and the creditor provides the debtor with credit not exceeding £15,000. By Section 8 of the Act, as amended by the Consumer Credit (Increase of Monetary Limits) Order 1983, a 'regulated agreement' is an agreement (not being an agreement exempted by Section 16) by which the creditor provides credit to an individual not exceeding £15,000. The definition of 'creditor' in Section 189(1) of the Act includes an assignee, and that of an 'individual' includes a partnership. It is not unusual for factoring transactions to relate to the purchase of debts which arise from credit granted by the client (the original creditor) to sole traders and partnerships amounting to less than £15,000. None of the exemptions listed in Section 16 are likely to apply. As a result of the foregoing, if it is possible that the factor will accept the assignment of debts payable by five or more instalments, a licence for consumer credit business may well be necessary.

Ancillary credit business (Part X of the Act)

1.30   It is normal for factors to obtain licences for the following activities, because of the exclusion of *assignees* from the exemption for the regulation of these businesses by Section 146(6)(*a*) of the 1974 Act:

(*a*) debt adjusting;

(*b*) debt counselling;

(*c*) debt collecting.

Many factors would also consider it desirable to obtain a licence for credit brokerage in view of possible introductions by their staff to associated companies (such as hire purchase or leasing companies) carrying on consumer credit or consumer hire business.

1.31   It is not considered necessary, however, for factors to obtain a licence for the business of a credit reference agency. According to Section 145(8) of the Consumer Credit Act, such an agency is 'a person carrying on a business comprising the furnishing of persons with information relevant to the financial standing of individuals, being information obtained for that purpose'. The credit information obtained by factors is obtained for their giving of credit approvals, i.e. for specifying to what extent the fac' or will be prepared (i) to provide finance by way of early payment for the debts purchased, or (ii) to accept the credit risk, or (iii) for both reasons. Such information is not, in the ordinary course of business, obtained for the purpose of furnishing it to clients.

1.32   *Introduction*

1.32   The above is a brief summary of the position of factors under the Consumer Credit Act 1974. It will be noted that, provided that they are licensed for the ancillary business mentioned, the Act is unlikely to impinge to a great extent upon their operations. Accordingly, no attempt has been made in this book to analyse or explain the provision of the Act in any more detail.

Part A
Factoring Use and Practice

Chapter 2

The Nature of Factoring—
The Full Service

2.1　This chapter describes the full factoring service by which the client obtains not only finance but by which he is also relieved of the task of administering his sales ledger and is protected against bad debts. The chapter also describes the practicalities of beginning and ending the arrangement. The variants in which one or two of the elements of the full service are absent are described in Chapter 3.

A description of the full service

2.2　Factoring, in its full form, is a continuing relationship in which the factor purchases substantially all the trade debts of his client arising from sales of goods or the provision of services to trade customers as they arise in the normal course of business. The client in return for agreed fees and finance charges is thereby relieved:

(*a*) from the need to administer and control a sales ledger and collect amounts payable from his customers; and

(*b*) from losses arising from the inability of a customer to pay; and

(*c*) from the provision of trade credit to his customers, to a substantial degree (see 2.7 below).

Factoring is usually described as a service to the client by way of sales accounting, collection, protection against bad debts and finance. It is apparent, however, that as the ownership of the debts passes to the factor, largely without recourse, the service performed by the factor is for himself. By transferring ownership of the debts, the client has divested himself of the need for these services.

Transfer of ownership of the debts and factor's administrative duties

2.3 The transfer of ownership of the debts is normally accompanied by:

(*a*) the submission to the factor either of copies of invoices representing the debts sold; *or*

(*b*) the submission of originals to the factor for onward transmission to the debtors, accompanied by copies for retention by the factor.

The debtors are instructed that debts have been assigned to the factor (see 2.10 below), to whom alone payment should be made, normally by means of a notice on each invoice. As the debts have been purchased outright by the factor, and as payments are to be made direct to the factor, it is the factor's responsibility to keep and administer the sales ledger and to collect from the debtors.

2.4 The factor, in turn, is responsible to the *client* for the purchase price of the debts assigned. The purchase price is normally the amount payable by the debtor after the deduction of any discount or other allowance and after deduction of the factor's charges. The factor will credit the account of the client in his records with such purchase price of debts sold and as a corollary the client may charge all his sales to one account—that of the factor. The client will now look to the factor alone to collect the proceeds of his sales.

Protection of the client against bad debts: factor's 'approval'

2.5 To the extent that the factor has given *approval* of the debts, he purchases debts without recourse to the client if the debtor becomes insolvent. The client thus receives full protection against bad debts provided that he does not sell to any debtor not approved by the factor or to an extent greater than the approval given (see 8.24). The approval may be given in one of two ways:

(*a*) by the approval of individual orders and by giving limits on regular accounts of monthly or weekly sales, usually referred to as 'shipment limits'; or

(*b*) by the approval of an overall limit of credit on each debtor account.

In the case of (*b*) the client, in the absence of sales ledger records, must receive sufficient feedback of information to enable him to know whether any order received or delivery of goods or provision of services will result in an excess over the approved limit.

Disputes between client and debtor, deductions and credit notes

2.6 Factors do not accept responsibility for the following:

(*a*) the acceptance by the customer of the goods or services of the client; and

(*b*) the compliance by the client with his responsibilities to the customer; and (*c*) the accuracy of invoices and credit notes issued.

Factors also expect that the debts sold to them are free from any rights of set-off or counterclaims from the customers. Should any query or dispute be raised by a debtor on a demand for payment by the factor or any deduction be made on payment (e.g. by way of unauthorised discount), the client should be notified immediately and given an opportunity to dispose of the matter. In the absence of agreement between the client and the debtor, the disputed or queried indebtedness will be charged back to the client and the debtor notified of its reassignment. Naturally, the factor will require to have submitted to him either copies or originals (for onward transmission) of credit notes issued to debtors, so that he can adjust the debtors' accounts accordingly and reduce the amount payable to the client for the value of debts purchased.

The provision of finance for trade credit through the factoring service

2.7   By making a prepayment of a substantial part of the purchase price of each debt *as soon as it is created and purchased*, the factor provides for most of the trade credit requirements of the client's debtors. Some factors make such a prepayment by way of an advance secured by their right to set it off against the full purchase price when due, whereas others provide for prepayments by part payments of the purchase price itself. The effect is exactly the same in each case. The factor will make a *retention* of part of the purchase price of each debt so that in aggregate he will hold a sufficient balance to provide for any amount to be charged to the client by way of recourse for the non-payment of an unapproved or disputed debt. However, the balance credited for the purchase price of debts purchased less the retention may normally be drawn by the client by way of prepayment at twenty-four hours notice.

The factor's retention

2.8   The retention is calculated by some factors as a percentage of the total value of all debts outstanding. Other factors calculate the retention as a percentage of debts purchased which have not yet become overdue beyond an agreed maturity date based on the average period of credit expected to be taken in the trade or industry concerned. A third method is to retain the aggregate of the equivalent of the unapproved debts outstanding and a percentage of the approved debts. Whichever method is used it is usually open to the factor to retain, in addition, the equivalent of any disputed debts or deductions mentioned in 2.6 above. The retention will be released and the balance of the purchase price paid to the client either on payment of the relevant debt to the factor or, where a maturity system is in operation (see 9.21–9.23), on the maturity date provided that the debt is not disputed. The percentages of general retention normally vary from 15% to 25% where an additional retention (equivalent to unapproved debts outstanding) is made, and otherwise from 20% to 30%. The percentage will depend largely upon the factor's expectation of credit notes to be issued, recourse for disputes and deductions and, in the latter case, for unapproved debts.

The commencement of the arrangement for factoring

2.9   Having entered into an agreement with a factor the client will, at the outset, normally advise all his debtors by letter of the arrangement and inform them that only by paying to the factor will they discharge their obligations for goods or services supplied. The factor will then consider the creditworthiness of all the existing and prospective customer accounts so that he may be in a position to give approval of the debts to be sold to him.

2.10   It is usual in the UK for factors to purchase all debts outstanding on the starting date to avoid the debtors having to pay some part of the account to the client and some part to the factor. For the purchase of debts in existence at the starting date of the agreement, the client will bring his sales ledger up-to-date to the day before the starting date, send statements of account to his customers bearing notices of the assignment by which payments are directed to the factor and send copies of the statements to the factor. From the details on these copy statements, the factor will credit the account of the client with the aggregate value of the debts less the charges and will debit each of the debtor accounts. Some factors (even when providing the full service) will require that all debts in existence at the starting date should be subject to full recourse even though they are within the approved limit. Others will provide for the full protection up to the approvals given for such debts provided that they are not seriously overdue. In any event the client will be given a facility for prepayments subject to the usual retention (as in 2.8 above).

Termination of the arrangement

2.11   Arrangements for termination of factoring are usually by an agreed period of notice by either party in the absence of the insolvency of the client or a material breach of the agreement. Although all factors provide that after the termination date no further debts are to be sold by the client, arrangements for dealing with the oustanding debts vesting in the factor vary considerably. Some factors provide for a repurchase of such debts by the client whilst others will collect such outstanding debts. In many cases, however, no further payments will be made to the clients until the factor has recovered all the funds he has laid out by way of early payments. (See further 8.40–8.43.)

Chapter 3

The Nature of Factoring—
Other Forms

3.1   There are many variations of the full service described in Chapter 2 and
those that are well known are considered in this chapter. The variations
are as follows:

—Recourse factoring (see 3.2–3.4 below);

—Bulk factoring (see 3.5–3.6 below);

—Maturity factoring (see 3.7–3.8 below);

—Invoice discounting, otherwise known as confidential factoring (see
3.9–3.13 below);

—Undisclosed factoring (see 3.14–3.15 below);

—Agency factoring (see 3.16–3.17 below);

—Recourse factoring or invoice discounting in conjunction with credit
insurance by the client (see 3.18–3.21 below);

—Tripartite client/bank/factor arrangements (see 3.22–3.23 below).

The chapter ends with a paragraph indicating the recent development of
another variant of factoring. A Table showing which services are
included in each of the variations listed above will be found on page 26
to help make the differences clear.

Recourse factoring

3.2   As the name implies, 'recourse factoring' provides finance for the client
together with a sales ledger administration and collections, but no
protection against bad debts. The factor has full 'recourse' (the right to
have payment guaranteed or the debt repurchased by the client) for
debts unpaid for any reason, including insolvency of the debtor. Thus,
the variation is effected by the simple expedient of providing that in
respect of every debt purchased by the factor he shall have the right to
sell it (or part of it) back at its full invoice value (or be guaranteed
payment in full by the client) to the extent that the debtor shall not have
settled it by an agreed period after invoice date. The period often agreed
is three months or ninety days from the end of the month in which the

invoice is dated. Such a period postulates that in many trades and industries, in which the normal usage is for payment to be due at the end of the month following that of the invoice, the factor must collect payment within two months of the due date or the recourse may be effected. It is usual to provide that the factor will refrain from exercising his right of recourse for a specified further period on payment of an additional charge by the client. In such a case, however, the factor may require that an additional retention be maintained against the purchase price of further debts purchased so that in effect the client will have repaid the amount paid by the factor against, or on account of, the purchase price of the unpaid debts.

3.3   Thus, in respect of debts that are seriously overdue, the client may continue to receive the collection service (see 2.3) but the finance for such debts may be withdrawn. If the debt becomes irrecoverable the recourse is then finally exercised. In all other respects, the service, in particular as regards retentions, disputes and deductions, the start and termination, is as described in Chapter 2. Approvals of credit are given by the factor on debtor accounts for the purpose of specifying the amount of finance available against them, or as an advisory service to the client, or for both reasons.

3.4   Unlike the position in the United States and some continental countries where the purchase of debts with full recourse is regarded as the lending of money on the security of the debts (accounts receivable financing), recourse factoring in the UK is treated as the outright purchase of the debts notwithstanding the recourse element. The debts assigned to the factor are recorded in his books and balance sheet as in his ownership, and not in the balance sheet of the client.

Bulk factoring

3.5   'Bulk factoring' provides finance to the client but no administrative or protection service. However, unlike invoice discounting (see 3.9 below), it includes directions to debtors to pay direct to the factor. As virtually all factoring is carried out on a 'whole turnover' basis with the submission to the factor of batches or schedules of debts in bulk, this term could be applied to all forms. However, it is usually used to denote the form for which the Germans use the more descriptive term 'Eigen Service—Factoring' ('Own Service Factoring'). This form of factoring is further removed from the full service in that the factor, although requiring that directions be given to the debtors to pay direct to him, takes no responsibility for the administration or collection of the debts and the factoring is fully on a recourse basis. The purpose of the arrangement is purely for financing the trade credit requirements of the client's debtors and the notice to them to pay the factor is to improve the factor's security. The service provided is, therefore, no more than that obtained by means of invoice discounting (see 3.9–3.13 below).

3.6   As the client has the task of administering the sales ledger on behalf of the factor, to whom the ownership of the debts has been transferred, it is necessary for the factor to remit to the client daily details of remittances received from debtors. In view of the resulting administrative costs to the factor, the latter's charges tend to be similar to those made for recourse factoring but without the compensating benefit to the client of an administrative service provided by the factor. In other respects the arrangement is similar to recourse factoring (as described in 3.2–3.4 above). This system is used where the client's pattern of trade consists of a large number of small debtor accounts but he does not meet the standards in financial standing or administration required for consideration of an invoice discounting arrangement. However, although the foregoing is the usual nature of bulk factoring, at least one leading factoring company provides this service on a non-recourse basis, subject to approval of debtor accounts. This service (i.e. bulk factoring with protection against bad debts) has otherwise been referred to as 'agency factoring' (see 3.17 below) and it will be so referred to in this book.

Maturity factoring

3.7   'Maturity factoring', increasingly used by smaller businesses as an alternative to credit insurance, comprises full administration of the sales ledger, collections from the debtors and protection against bad debts. The arrangement is that of the full service (as in Chapter 2) but without the facility for prepayment by the factor to the client and, accordingly, no finance charge is levied. The factor's remuneration consists only of a fee related to the value of debts purchased by him. Payments for the debts purchased are made either:

(*a*)   after a fixed period (based on expectation of the average period of credit to be taken by debtors—the 'maturity period') from either invoice date or the date of the transfer of the debts to the factor and the submission of copy invoices; *or*

(*b*)   on receipt of payment from each debtor or, in respect of approved debts, the earlier insolvency of the debtor.

3.8   The system in 3.7 (*a*) above offers obvious attractions to the client in that he may calculate his clash flow in advance as soon as sales are effected to approved accounts. On the other hand the factor, in the absence of any finance charge, will tend to make a liberal estimate of the maturity period and in many cases will reserve the right to adjust it in accordance with actual experience from time to time. As an alternative under this system, some factors, although paying on a fixed maturity date, will make a finance charge or allowance on the basis of a comparison of the actual collection period with the agreed period. The second method has the advantage of flexibility in allowing for changes of terms of payment by the client and requests to the factor for allowing latitude to debtors.

Invoice discounting or confidential factoring

3.9   For those clients who need finance for the trade credit requirements of their debtors but no administrative service or protection, another service is provided extensively by factors. By the simple expedient of releasing the client from the need to notify the debtors to pay direct to the factor and by providing that all debts sold to the factor should be subject to full recourse, factoring is changed to a purely financial service sometimes referred to as 'confidential factoring' or, more commonly, 'invoice discounting'. In the early days of invoice discounting, debts represented by individual invoices were sold to factors. This system gave rise to some difficulties: it was not always possible for the client to pass on to the factor the payment for the invoice in its original form as the payment might be made after deductions for cross-claims or combined with payment on other invoices (see 1.13–1.14).

3.10   In recent years, the service of invoice discounting has more usually been provided on a 'whole turnover' basis. The client maintains the sales ledger and collects from debtors on behalf of the factor to whom the ownership of the debts had been transferred. A typical invoice discounting arrangement would work as follows:

(*a*) On the starting date the client sends the factor a complete aged list of debtors (see 4.3(2)(*f*)) and the balance of all the debts listed is credited to the client's account, less the factor's charges.

(*b*) Within twenty-four hours the client may draw against that credit, subject to a retention equivalent to the amount of any debt which is not eligible, in addition to an agreed percentage (normally 20%) of those debts within the limits. The ineligible amounts are those in excess of agreed credit limits or those overdue for more than the agreed period (normally three months).

(*c*) Each week, the client sends to the factor a note of total sales, discounts taken and returns; and he may draw up to the agreed percentage of the net amount plus the balance of debts settled during that week.

(*d*) All payments received from debtors are banked direct to the factor's bank. A three part paying-in book is used so that the factor may be notified of remittances paid in by use of the third copy of the paying-in slip.

(*e*) At the end of each month the client sends to the factor an up-to-date aged list of debtors and a copy of the control account. The factor will reconcile his records with this and adjust the retention for the ineligible debts.

Some factors however, also require the submission of copy invoices but do not normally record them individually unless the arrangement is restricted to specific debts or debtors.

3.11   In order to protect the factor when the client's administration is in disarray or he becomes insolvent, it is usual for the factor to have the right to notify the debtors of the assignments and instruct them on behalf of the client to make payment direct to him. In the event of such disarray or insolvency, the factor would require the submission of individual invoices and credit notes and take over the management of the ledger.

3.12   Although little in the way of service, save for finance, may be provided, it is not unusual for the factor to charge a fee related to the value of the debts purchased in addition to a finance charge. The rationale for such a fee is that it is a commitment fee for the provision of finance without formal limit and related only to the aggregate of debts owed by creditworthy debtors. In addition, the client receives advice on the administration of the sales ledger and credit control.

3.13   In these arrangements the factor normally requires that he should be at liberty to inspect the ledger and supporting documentation periodically.

Undisclosed factoring

3.14   The term 'undisclosed factoring' is sometimes applied to an invoice discounting arrangement whereby the factor will provide protection against bad debts to a limited extent by specifying that an agreed percentage (normally 80%) of any approved indebtedness shall be *without recourse* as regards credit risks. The arrangement limits the protection to such a percentage so that the client, who maintains the ledger and collects from debtors, has some incentive to carry out these duties with efficiency.

3.15   The undisclosed factoring arrangement is in general the same as for invoice discounting (see 3.9 above) save that approved debts that become three months overdue are not ineligible for the financial facility nor added to the retention. Only the excesses over credit approvals are ineligible and not the percentage (normally 20%) within such approval that are with recourse. In addition to the finance charge, a fee related to the value of debts purchased is charged. In view of the service provided, this will be more substantial than in the case of invoice discounting. It is usually provided in such an arrangement that, when any debt becomes seriously overdue by an agreed period, the debtor should be notified of the factor's interest in all amounts owing by the debtor and that the factor should be able to effect collection direct. By this means the factor should be able to 'flush out' disputed items that are to be recoursed. The arrangement provides confidential finance which is not repayable by the client, provided the right goods have been delivered to the right customer and the invoice correctly compiled. There can, however, be difficulties caused by the provisions relating to seriously overdue accounts. If a good customer account becomes seriously overdue, the client will be reluctant to disclose the factor's interest and the factor will then require to come 'off risk'. In this way, some accounts may come 'off' and 'on risk' periodically or the debtor may be harrassed by having to pay the factor and then, when the overdues have been cleared, again to pay the client. On the whole, in spite of these difficulties, the service meets the needs of some larger businesses in trades where factoring is not yet entirely acceptable and as a developing service some refinements may be introduced in order to meet this problem.

Agency factoring

3.16   The term 'agency factoring' has two distinct meanings. By the first meaning, which has largely fallen into disuse, it is a method by which confidential finance may be provided together with protection against bad debts, and with or without the administrative service. There have been several variations of this arrangement under which the debts are assigned to a company with a name similar to that of the client and that company acts as agent for the factor. The company is owned by the factor. The agency company, to which the debtors are instructed to pay, may be managed by the factor, or by the client, depending on whether or not the client requires the factor to carry out the administrative service. This practice, which is in any event less in evidence now than some fifteen or twenty years ago, seems from one aspect commercially unacceptable. The factor is, in effect, trying to conceal the fact of the assignments, while at the same time seeking to rely on them for his security. An error on the part of a debtor in paying to the client, instead of an assignee of similar name, could theoretically give rise to the possibility of the debtor having to pay a second time on the client's insolvency. The debtor would then feel, with some justification, that he had been intentionally misled. The decline in the practice seems to have stemmed from the more recent developments in invoice discounting and undisclosed factoring as described above.

3.17   The expression 'agency factoring' is now more often used in another sense. At least one factoring company uses it for factoring services which comprise finance and protection against bad debts but without the administration of the sales ledger and collection of debts. The administration and collection is carried out by the client, in effect, as agent for the factor in whom the responsibility for these matters rests by reason of his ownership of the debts. Thus, agency factoring in this sense is bulk factoring (see 3.5 above) with the addition of protection against bad debts (as described in 2.4).

Co-operation with credit insurers: recourse factoring or invoice discounting in conjunction with credit insurance

3.18   For some clients who do not wish to accept the protection afforded by the full service (see Chapter 2) or undisclosed factoring (see 3.14 above), but prefer to rely on a credit insurance policy, co-operation between the factor and credit insurer may be arranged. First, a service almost equivalent to the full service can be provided by the combination of recourse factoring (see 3.2 above) and credit insurance; and, secondly, as an alternative to undisclosed factoring, finance without any borrowing can be provided confidentially by the use of invoice discounting (see 3.9 above) with credit insurance. However, in both cases, unless the factor undertakes to administer the policy, the client will not have the full benefit of relief from administrative burdens which is provided by the full service. Furthermore, in many trades served by factors, domestic credit insurers normally provide only 75% or 80% cover up to approved limits. This compares with the full amount of protection up to the approvals given by the factor which is included in the full factoring service. It is also quite usual in these days for there to be an arrangement by which small debts (say up to £500) are not covered.

3.19   The administration of the policy includes the reporting of seriously overdue accounts and debtors in difficulty, declarations of turnover and the obtaining of adequate information to justify credit on new accounts. In the case of invoice discounting, the client would in any event expect not to be relieved of administration (see 3.9 above). Further, as the alternative of undisclosed factoring normally provides only 80% protection, the combination of invoice discounting with credit insurance can provide all that undisclosed factoring provides. The factor, in such arrangements, may be able to refrain from exercising recourse back to the client in respect of seriously overdue accounts and look for recovery of his prepayments direct from the insurer.

3.20   An assignment only of the benefits of the policy of credit insurance affords the factor little protection because:

   (*a*)   most policies provide that, for a claim to be admitted, the debt must rank in the insolvent estate in favour of the insured (the factor's client); and for security reasons the factor will not wish to reassign the debt to the client; and

   (*b*)   the factor cannot be certain that the client has complied with the policy conditions (e.g. reporting seriously overdue debts); and

   (*c*)   the insurer imposes certain requirements on the insured as regards credit control and collections and may not have recognised the factor's right to carry out some of these functions; and

   (*d*)   if the client becomes insolvent, the administrator would have no incentive to submit a claim to the insurer so that the factor could recover under the assignment of the policy.

3.21   The combination of invoice discounting or recourse factoring with credit insurance should, therefore, be carried out by either of the following methods:

   (A)   By a factoring endorsement to the client's policy, such as is issued by the Export Credits Guarantee Department, by which the factor's ownership of the insured debts, his right to prove in any debtor's insolvent estate and his obligation to collect the debts are recognised. The factoring endorsement must be combined with an assignment of the benefits of the policy.

OR

(B) By having the policy issued to the *client and the factor jointly* for their respective rights and interests. In such a case the factor's rights to the ownership of the debts and to administer the ledger would be recognised. Additionally, the advantage of this arrangement is that the factor may submit claims on the policy, as an insured person. However, as a joint insured the factor has responsibilities as well as rights. In particular he is liable for the premium if this is not paid by his client. It is probably advisable, as between himself and his client, for the factor to take the responsibility for reporting overdue accounts, making declarations and paying the premium and to charge his client accordingly. In this way, he can be certain that all these formalities are up-to-date.

Most factoring agreements include a provision by which, on the assignment of a debt, all related rights of the client, including rights under credit insurance policies, are transferred to the factor. All that should be necessary then is for notice to be given to the insurer. Insurers, however, for reasons best known to themselves, prefer the assignment to be evidenced on their own forms and it should be no hardship for the factor and the client to comply with this requirement. (See 8.28–8.29.)

Co-operation with banks: client/factor/bank arrangements

3.22 Arrangements are sometimes made on a tripartite basis among a factor's client, the factor and a bank, by which a financial facility is provided direct to the client by the bank to take the place of prepayments by the factor. In outline the co-operation between the three is as follows:

(*a*) The prepayment facility is at the option of the client. If the client does not elect to take this choice, he draws the purchase price of each debt only on maturity as described in 3.7–3.8 above.

(*b*) The result of the arrangement in (*a*) will be that the amount owed by the factor to the client from time to time for the debts purchased will be approximately equivalent to the debts owed to the factor by the debtors; and as far as his own records are concerned, the client has substituted for the myriad debtors of uncertain standing one debtor of high standing—one that will pay a substantial part of what is owed at call.

(*c*) By assigning that one debt to the bank the client may provide the bank with security for its advances to take place of the prepayment facility.

3.23   A typical arrangement on these terms would work as follows:

(1)   The assignment to the bank is registered under the Companies Act 1948, s 95. The assignment document may be drafted to constitute a fixed charge on the indebtedness.

(2)   The client gives the factor irrevocable instructions by which all amounts payable by the factor to the client, for the debts purchased by the factor, are to be paid to the bank.

(3)   On instruction from the client, the factor will report to the bank periodically (say—weekly) the amount that may be drawn from the factor by the client by way of prepayment for the debts purchased. Such reports may include the basis on which the availability is made up, i.e. the amount of assigned trade debts outstanding at the time and the amount of unapproved and disputed debts within that total.

(4)   The bank uses these reports as a basis for part or all of its lending and for the level of the facilities available from time to time.

(5)   As the factor's finance charges for early payment are fixed above the equivalent interest charge of the bank, the client will be unlikely to take prepayments from the factor. The reasons for this probable election by the client are:

(i)   that any prepayment must go direct to the bank, and
(ii)   that any such prepayment will reduce the amount shown on the factor's availability report to the bank and thus the bank's facility.

(6)   As all payments by the factor will be made to the bank, it will be able to control the level of the facility from time to time.

Conclusion and new developments

3.24   The above are the most common variations of the full factoring service. There are wide differences of nomenclature and a reference to the glossary in Appendix I may dispel some of the confusion caused by them. There are also other variations some of which are pending and others of which are being developed to meet the varying needs of the business community. One of these merits special mention. A well known finance house has developed an alternative to credit insurance by an arrangement by which the client's debts are purchased confidentially without notice to the debtors and without recourse to the client. When used purely as a credit protection facility, the client is paid the purchase price of any debt sold only in the same circumstances as those in which he would have made a claim on his insurer under a policy of credit insurance. The Table overleaf shows the services provided by the different factoring variants.

Table: Factoring Variants

	Availability of Finance	Protection Against Bad Debts*	Notices to Debtors	Sales Ledger Administration	Collections	
Full Service	A	A	A	A	A	Any of these may be referred to as: 'Notification Factoring' OR 'Disclosed Factoring'
Recourse Factoring	A	N	A	A	A	
Bulk Factoring	A	N	A	N	N	
Maturity Factoring	N	A	A	A	A	
Agency Factoring	A	S	U	S	N	
Invoice Discounting	A	N	N	N	N	Alternatively: 'Confidential Factoring' OR 'Non-Notification Factoring'
Undisclosed Factoring	A	S	N	N	N	

*Any form which includes this element may be referred to as *non-recourse factoring*.

Key: A = Always provided
U = Usually provided
S = Sometimes provided
N = Never or rarely provided

Chapter 4

The Benefits of Factoring

The importance of good sales ledger administration

4.1　The concentration of the minds of the members of the accountancy profession on financial accounting under the Companies Acts, management accounting, current cost accounting and some more recondite branches of the subject seems to have created a myopia in relation to the importance of good sales ledger accounting. This chapter, which deals with the benefits of the full factoring service and some of its variants, starts with a recapitulation of the importance to a business of this part of the function of a normal accounts department. Without an emphasis of its importance, the benefits of having the function carried out in an efficient way by experts will not be fully appreciated. Furthermore, although the accounting for sales is carried out by the factor in the full service (see Chapter 2) and recourse factoring (see 3.2), certain aspects on which sales accounting relies, such as the preparation of source documerιs, are still carried out by the client. In this connection a successful factoring arrangement depends on a partnership between an efficient factor and an efficient client.

4.2　Apart from compliance with the statutory requirements of the Companies Acts, the object of sales accounting should be:

(*a*)　To enable the company to have a clear idea of the amount of credit outstanding to each customer and in total and its ageing (i.e. its analysis by age of due date or invoice date).

(*b*)　To enable the company to submit clear and accurate statements to its customers.

(*c*)　To provide those responsible for credit control and collections with up-to-date data upon which to act and make decisions.

4.3　To achieve these objects the sales ledger and the source documents must be promptly prepared, up-to-date and accurate. The following are some important guidelines to be followed.

(1)　**Source documents (e.g. invoices, despatch notes):**

(*a*)　In order that invoices may represent accurately the amount payable for each item of sales delivered or services rendered a system must be in force to ensure that invoices are raised only in

27

accordance with the agreed terms and conditions of each accepted order on delivery of the relevant goods.

(*b*) Invoices must be raised promptly on the completion of each order (or part of order where the customer agrees to pay for each delivery as it is made).

(*c*) The responsibility for the authorisation of the issue of credit notes must be clearly defined and credit notes should be issued promptly when agreed; debtors often hold up large payments whilst waiting for a credit note for a small sum.

(*d*) Periodic reports and analyses of credit notes issued should be available to management as a check on the acceptability of goods and the efficiency of the administration.

(2) **Sales accounting:**

(*a*) Postings of invoices, credit notes and cash should be effected daily. If not, the sales records are not up-to-date and the objects referred to in 4.2 above are not achieved.

(*b*) Journal entries (i.e. any entry not supported by a payment, invoice or credit note) should be effected only on the authority of a senior official. This is just as necessary as the authorisation of credit notes.

(*c*) There should be an analysis of journal entries, or those of substantial size, for management.

(*d*) The sales accounts should be kept on an 'open item system' rather than by balance brought forward. The open item system shows all outstanding invoices and unallocated cash, credits and adjustments. The other system shows a balance brought forward each month which may include a number of old disputed items or deductions and these may not be brought to light for months or even years.

(*e*) It is important that there should be a discipline to ensure that allocations of cash to invoices are kept up-to-date and that unallocated cash and credits are kept to the minimum.

(*f*) An accurate and up-to-date aged balance report (i.e. a listing of outstanding debts analysed by reference to due date) should be produced promptly at least at each month end and examined by a senior official. The report should show also disputes and unallocated credits and cash so that management may monitor those items which may indicate inefficiency in the accounts or sales department.

4.4   The level of credit notes and disputes is an indication of the efficiency of the system and, more important, of the quality of the product. Good credit control can save finance charges and credit control can only be as good as the information fed to it, that is by the sales ledger and early notification of disputes.

The administrative service provided by factoring

4.5 The requirements of a sales ledger system as indicated in the preceding paragraph can rarely be provided in a small business at an expense consistent with the income of the business. Even the advent of micro computers with small business systems will not necessarily produce the high quality of reports required. Indeed, some of the software in common use for sales accounting does not even provide an open item system (see 4.3(2)(*d*) above). Apart from the data processing system necessary to provide such efficient management information there is a requirement for experienced personnel to keep correct allocations of cash up-to-date and for the strict control by management of unallocated cash and credits. The full factoring service provides complete relief from the need to collect from debtors, in addition to the relief from the need to keep and administer sales accounts. In many small businesses the task of collection is taken on by management or other personnel on a part-time basis, because the employment of a full-time credit controller would not be justified. The collection of the debts and the task of keeping the credit period taken by debtors to a minimum without prejudicing customer relations is a skilled task.

4.6 By means of the full factoring service or recourse factoring, even the smallest business has access to some of the most experienced people in this field and management of business is relieved from the aggravating burden of supervising these duties. Even where a full-time credit controller might be justified by the size of the business, the use of the factor means that there is constant attention to this aspect of business without interruptions caused by holidays and sickness. To many small and medium-sized concerns the cost of factoring is outweighed by the facility to dispense with the sales accounting and collection functions alone even without taking into account the benefit of protection against bad debts (provided by the full service) and the availability of finance.

Ancillary services

4.7 In addition to the relief from sales accounting and collection many factors provide their clients with regular returns such as monthly aged listing of debts, showing details of unallocated cash and credits and disputed items and regular listings of approved credit limits; some factors also provide regular reports of aggregate sales to date over specified periods. Owing to their computer based accounting systems many factors can also provide analyses of sales according to the individual requirements of clients. These analyses, for example, may be by area, product or salesman. However, there is one aspect in relation to sales analyses which seems to be worthy of further development and this is covered in Chapter 23.

The benefit of protection against bad debts

4.8   Surprisingly, credit insurance or the protection offered by factoring in its non-recourse variants, have not always been considered as a natural service to be adopted by a business selling on credit terms in the same way that fire insurance is a *sine qua non* for any business owning property. It is surprising because it is quite usual for businesses to insure items of current or shifting assets against risks of rare disasters; but, when in the normal circulation of working capital that capital is invested in assets of highest value with profit value added, no consideration may be given to protection against disasters which are happening many times each year. In 5.14 it is postulated that it is no part of factoring (or indeed of credit insurance) to indemnify a business for the usual run of small losses which are in effect part of the cost of running a business in certain trades and industries. These regular losses must be absorbed within the cost structure of the business and recovered through selling prices. This fact is recognised by credit insurance companies which have increasingly excluded such losses from cover by means of minimum retentions for the account of their insured or thresholds within which no cover is available on any single account. Some factors have now followed this line by agreeing with clients that small losses up to an agreed figure should be borne by the client even in a non-recourse arrangement.

4.9   It is the major unexpected losses that damage or even destroy businesses. Apart from the notorious cases, well publicised in the press, the recession which started in the early 1980's has resulted in the failure of many large and medium-sized companies, until then considered to be undoubted for credit. It is rare in such a case not to find several suppliers who have been taken by complete surprise. Following many years of inflation, such debts, suddenly found by suppliers to be irrecoverable, have increased considerably in value (even without growth in real terms) and have outpaced the ability of such suppliers to provide bad debts reserves or even to retain profits. Even if a bad debt reserve sufficient to cover an unexpected large loss has been created it is doubtful if such reserve will be represented by an investment in a fund of liquid resources sufficient to replace the lost cash flow. The interruption of cash flow, when the expected payments do not arrive, may cause considerable strain on the supplier, who will have to bear additional finance charges. His losses will arise not only from the bad debt but also from loss of work-in-progress and of a sales outlet. It is not unusual for a supplier to fail in such circumstances; this is often described as the 'domino' effect of business failures.

4.10   Credit insurance and factoring have their cost, but in each case it is a predictable budgeted cost and it relieves a business from the need to set aside resources to provide for such losses. By spreading the incidence of the very occasional loss over a long period the services provide the client with the facility to absorb the cost from their normal gross profit margin and to avoid any sudden interruption in cash flow.

4.11   The choice between the use of credit insurance or of factoring for this aspect of the factoring service alone—debt protection—must depend very largely upon the type and size of the business and whether or not the additional services included in the full service, undisclosed factoring or maturity factoring are required. The following are some of the differences between a typical credit insurance arrangement and a typical non-recourse factoring agreement (that is to say: the full service, maturity factoring, undisclosed factoring and—in its second sense— agency factoring):

Table: Credit insurance and factoring compared

	Credit insurance	*Factoring (non-recourse)*
Cost:	A premium calculated on gross sales value (i.e. before deducting credit notes). Likely to be considerably less than the equivalent factoring charge.	An administration charge calculated on gross sales values. Charge covers the full administrative service and a commitment fee for the financial element (if these are provided).
Exclusions:	No premium is payable on sales to debtor accounts on which no approval has been given nor on sales to government departments, nationalised industries and local authorities which are excluded.	Normally no exclusions.
VAT:	Arrangements may be made to exclude the VAT element in sales on the grounds that it is recoverable in some cases of debtor insolvency; as a result no premium is payable on this element.	Administration charge payable on sales value including VAT.
Cover:	Normally varies between 75% and 80% according to trade. Exceptionally up to 90%.	Normally 100%.
Contracts or work in progress cover available:	In certain trades and industries.	Not normal.

4.11 *The Benefits of Factoring*

	Credit insurance	Factoring (non-recourse)
Limits:	Permitted limits of outstanding indebtedness approved on major debtors. Insured required to justify credit granted for smaller amounts either by experience or information.	Either (*a*) by permitted limits of indebtedness outstanding for the time being on each customer, or (*b*) by individual order approvals and limits of monthly deliveries (shipment limits).
Time of indemnity for credit losses:	Claims payable 30 days after debt has been confirmed by the administrator of an insolvent estate or, in the absence of insolvency, within 6 months after protracted default. (Normally this is deemed to occur 3 months after due date or, where the due date has been postponed with the insured's consent, the extended due date.)	Purchase price of debt (or balance after any pre-payment) payable on a fixed maturity date or in some cases on commencement of insolvency or deemed insolvency.
Salvage:	After cancellation of limit, notification of financial difficulties or insolvency (whichever is earlier) all recoveries divided rateably between insured and uninsured portion of indebtedness.	After cancellation of limit it is normal that all recoveries are appropriated in priority to the approved part of any debt. After insolvency dividends may be applied rateably.
Disputes:	No responsibility to pay if debt unpaid owing to dispute; but in respect of insured debt insurer remains on risk and will accept liability if: (*a*) dispute settled in favour of insured; and (*b*) failure to pay subsequently arises from debtor insolvency.	Factor may come off risk altogether if debt is disputed.
Time limit:	Insurer comes off risk altogether 6 months after termination of policy which is not renewed.	No time limit, but in some cases factor may come off risk on insolvency of client.

	Credit insurance	*Factoring (non-recourse)*
Administrative service:	Collections on difficult accounts if required.	Services may include full sales accounting, routine collections, feedback of information.
	Credit approvals given by endorsement to policy.	Credit approvals given by letter and position confirmed periodically (mainly monthly) on lists of debtors showing exact position on each debtor account.
Administrative task for client:	Declarations of turnover; declarations of seriously overdue accounts; submission of applications for credit limits (in some cases with details of history of debtor payments).	Normally submission of copy invoices and credit notes and requests for approval on new debtors only.
Additional costs:	Fees for collections; charges for maintained credit limits.	None in respect of approved debts.

4.12   For certain trades and industries where losses from uncompleted contracts or work-in-progress are almost as important considerations as credit losses there is little doubt that, in the absence of the need for the other elements of the factoring service, credit insurance will be more suitable than factoring. An example of this is the advertising industry wherein agencies are most concerned about their liabilities for uncancellable space bookings on the insolvency of a client. In such cases, if credit insurance can provide more suitable cover and if the other aspects of factoring are required, arrangements may then be made for recourse factoring combined with credit insurance.

4.13   However, for smaller and medium-sized businesses in most industries, the relief from the administration of a credit insurance policy and the automatic collection by the factor of all debts (including the difficult cases) make the additional cost of factoring well worthwhile. In addition the full payment of approved amounts on a fixed maturity date or the commencement of insolvency, without the formalities of the submission of a claim and the obtaining of confirmation from a liquidator, trustee or receiver, is the service that is most suitable for such businesses. The cash is available to them at the point when it is missed. For many larger concerns that require only protection against catastrophe and need no administrative assistance, credit insurance can provide an answer that is not normally available by means of a factoring arrangement.

The provision of finance without formal limit by factoring

4.14   The finance available from the full factoring service and all its variants (save for maturity factoring—see 3.7) can be available automatically against the sale and delivery of acceptable goods to creditworthy customers. Although some factors specify that the prepayment facility is at the factor's discretion, many provide an automatic prepayment facility against approved undisputed debts which will remain in being until the termination of the factoring arrangement. Such a facility provides a businessman with the means to plan growth on the basis of adequate working capital without having the cost, trouble and uncertainty of having to establish facilities and limits by the production of statistical and accounting information.

4.15   Even for those who may expect to finance their planned operations by traditional means, the additional facility of being able to liquidate trade debts on demand provides the possibility of the immediate exploitation of business opportunities. For example, the additional facility may be used:

(*a*)   To make bulk purchases on better than usual terms;

(*b*)   To obtain substantial discounts by making early payments to suppliers;

(*c*)   To accept a larger than usual order in spite of the working capital that may be necessary to finance the resultant credit;

(*d*)   To allow extended terms in exceptional cases.

The availability of finance on this basis is of particular benefit to those who have the necessary products and market to grow faster than resources from traditional means allow. Factoring will allow them to avoid the restraint on their growth that is normally imposed by the necessity of having to produce the profits to support an application for traditional means of finance before achieving the turnover from which those profits would emerge.

Non-recourse factoring and the client's balance sheet

4.16   The preceding paragraphs have considered the principal benefits to a client who uses the full service or some of its variants; but there is yet another benefit of financing by the means of selling debts rather than borrowing. This benefit, which is not yet fully recognised, arises from the fact that the purchase of debts and payment for them removes them from the balance sheet of the client. If debts are sold to a factor and a substantial part of the purchase price is drawn and used to reduce short-term borrowing or other short-term creditors, then, to the extent that the purchase price has been drawn and so used, both current assets and current liabilities will have been reduced. This has the effect, in the normal circumstances in which current assets exceed current liabilities, of improving the current ratio. For this reason factoring and its variants are often referred to as 'off balance sheet' finance. However, this accounting arrangement will only be effective if the debts sold have been purchased without recourse to the client. If the arrangement is *with* recourse there will need to be a note of the contingent liability in the accounts and this will detract from the effect.

4.17   It may be that the client does not wish for protection against bad debts and is unwilling to pay the price for it, and to meet this situation there is an arrangement that may be made for absence of recourse in another sense: in such an arrangement the factor would not take responsibility for any particular debt for any particular amount, but specify that he would have no right of recourse in respect of all debts outstanding at any particular time greater than the normal retention. In other words, the factor would look only to the debts to recover the prepayments made and if there were to be a shortfall overall he would have no rights against the client. For example, if the prepayment facility were to be 80% (less the factor's charges) and the retention 20%, then in the event of the full amount having been drawn and the insolvency of the client, the factor would be able to exercise recourse up to 20%, but no more, for his inability to recover for any reason. The recourse up to 20% would be set against the retention. The accounts of the client would show the 20% retention under 'debtors' after deduction of a bad debt reserve relating to all of the outstanding debts. However, there would be no contingent liability to repay the factor any of the prepayments; thus the 'off balance' sheet nature of the arrangement is retained. The expression 'non-recourse' purchase of debts has been heard in this connection and as more large companies wish to improve their balance sheet ratios we may hear it more often in the future.

Chapter 5

The Use and Misuse of Factoring

The nature of true trade credit

5.1   No description of factoring would be complete without a consideration of trade credit, the granting of which is a necessary concomitant of the sales of most businesses which supply trade customers; and factoring was devised to facilitate the granting of such trade credit. The importance of trade credit, that is to say the credit granted by a business concern to other business concerns, is often overlooked owing to the absence of clear statistics and the more frequent concentrations of minds on the other main forms of credit—bank credit and consumer credit. However, the part played by it in the commercial life of the country cannot be overstated; as long ago as 1959, in evidence to the Radcliffe Commission on the working of the monetary system, it was stated that the amount of trade credit outstanding was estimated at any one time to be 2.5 to 3 times that of bank credit and that, consequently, a moderate change in the period of trade credit allowed or taken would have a disproportionate effect on the reliance of business on the banking system.

5.2   The true historical nature of short term trade credit is that it is the means of financing the movement of goods to buyers who, by selling them on to sub-purchasers, will be able automatically to liquidate the credit granted to them. Such onward sales may be of their goods in their original form or incorporated into others. Factoring was developed to fill the requirements of suppliers of goods for the granting of true short term trade credit to their customers; therefore, the service is most suitable for the suppliers of raw materials, components and consumer goods. These goods can be made, sold and forgotten; the debts arising from their sales can stand by themselves and be fully collectable in the absence of the supplier; and unlike goods which are sold to a user as capital equipment they are not often subject to substantial after sales service or back-up. In the succeeding paragraphs of this chapter it is proposed to show the reasons for this limitation on the use of factoring. The undoubted benefits available to the user in the right circumstances have been set out in Chapter 4. As there is a demand for a debtor-related service in the capital goods industries, a service to provide this may be developed; this will be dealt with later in the book (see 22.9–22.12).

Limitations on factoring use

From the point of view of the client

5.3   This chapter deals in the main with forms of factoring *other than* maturity factoring, that is to say, those forms in which a financial facility by way of prepayment (for the debts purchased) is included or in which bank finance is available. The objections to the use of a factor in the circumstances mentioned below are not to be seen only from the factor's viewpoint—which will be influenced by his requirement to be able safely to recover the prepayments made. From the user's point of view as well the service may in many cases not live up to its promise: the difficulties in dealing with other than straightforward collections which result from the provision of self-liquidating trade credit as described above in 5.1–5.2 above will very often create the following problems:

(*a*)   An expensive service;

(*b*)   The interruption of cash flow on the withholding of prepayments owing to normal queries;

(*c*)   Further delays when the client and debtor are involved in delicate negotiations over their contracts (e.g. the modifications of special purpose machinery, for which payments are often the subject of discussions between engineers).

5.4   Plant and machinery is often sold on terms that provide for percentages of the purchase price to be paid (i) with the order, (ii) on delivery, (iii) on commissioning and the balance as a retention; these terms are designed to provide finance for the client by payments made as early as it is safe for the customer of make them without his giving up his security relating to the suitability of the plant. Similar contracts in the building industry provide for interim payments on architect's certificates; until certification, a debt arising from such a contract is not suitable for factoring because the supplier cannot warrant its validity and the major requirement for the financing of building operations is the period up to certification. (See 5.5(3) below.)

From the point of view of the factor

5.5   The following are some examples of businesses *not* generally considered suitable for use of the factoring service.

(1)   *Capital equipment sold to the ultimate user*
The user of capital equipment will be able to liquidate the credit taken for its purchase only by the profits generated by its use and by depreciation absorbed by the sale of the products of its use. It is apparent that short term trade credit taken by a purchaser of equipment in such circumstances will put the purchaser in little better position after the normal period of such credit—say 60 or 90 days—than he was when the equipment was delivered. Either the buyer should have funds to make the investment straight away and

pay cash or he should finance it by instalment credit or leasing whilst the equipment is paying for itself by its use. Very often any normal short term credit taken for the purchase of such equipment will be a period for commissioning, testing and perhaps modification and it is no function of factoring to fill in such a period. Furthermore, such equipment sales will normally be subject to contractual obligations on the part of the seller for maintenance over an extended period. A factor making prepayments for debts arising from such transactions may be in a difficult position on the insolvency of his client; the debtor will be reluctant to pay for equipment for which there is no after sales service. There are many in the field of finance who regard any type of indebtedness, provided that it is created in the normal course of business of a supplier of goods and services, as an ideal form of security to provide for the recovery of advances to the supplier. In a straightforward factoring arrangement, however, the factor's means of recovering the funds laid out in the purchase of a trade debt lie in the trade debt itself. Therefore, to be secure the factor must ensure that the debts that he purchases will be paid, without substantial cross-claims from the debtor, in the absence of any support from his client. Where debts result from the sale of capital equipment, unlike a banker financing such debts by means of a charge which provides for the appointment of a receiver on the supplier's insolvency, the factor rarely has the means to provide the back up by way of after sales service. In the case of suppliers of small items of capital equipment, such as office machinery or vending machines, factoring is sometimes sought to deal with the problem of accounting for service calls. Invoices for service payable in advance cannot be factored safely even on a maturity basis. If the factor has collected, in the absence of the provision of any service by the client, the debtor may well have the right to recover the amount paid; and, if the factor has parted with the purchase price of the debt to the client who has failed, he will find himself in some difficulty. (See 11.32–11.34.)

(2) *Long term contracts*
Similar considerations apply to goods sold or services supplied under long term contracts which provide for invoices to be issued and payments made periodically during the course of the contract. If the client fails before the contract is completed the debtor will have some redress for failure of the client to complete. This will affect the factor's ability to recover any debt arising out of such an unfinished contract (see 14.2–14.5).

If the client fails at an early stage in the contract the counterclaim for damages may be substantial in relation to the factor's claim and may even be enough to extinguish it. (As regards the ability of the debtor to set off a counterclaim, see 11.23–11.30.) It should not be inferred that debts arising under long term contracts are never suitable for factoring; but if they are to be included in a factoring arrangement the factor should ensure that they are subject to a 'cut-off' clause (see 14.6–14.8). In practice the monitoring of a client's contracts to this extent can be difficult; but, where such contracts are likely owing to the nature of the trade, the factor may well be able to make arrangements for the inclusion of such a provision in the client's standard terms. Otherwise the uncertainty of recovering on the failure of the client may result in such an increase in the factor's retention that any arrangement other than maturity factoring (i.e. no prepayment) will be unworkable.

(3) *Contracts in the construction industry*
These have been briefly touched upon in the introduction to this chapter. The remarks in (2) above regarding long term contracts apply to this type of contract with the additional difficulty for the factor that the usages of the industry and the type of contracts in common use preclude the provision of a 'cut-off clause' (see 14.6–14.8). In practice, on the insolvency of a contractor or sub-contractor in this industry, debts represented by interim invoices can be recovered only while work proceeds; this means that on the insolvency of the client the continuation of work must be by the administrator of the estate and it is unlikely that such an administrator would continue a contract in order to enable the factor to recover the debts he has purchased. Even in cases where a sub-contractor under a 'supply and fix' contract has made arrangements for the supply and fixing to be deemed to be separate contracts (so that payment is to be made by the main contractor or user on supply of the goods irrespective of the fixing) experience has shown that in practice the debtor will be reluctant to pay until fixing is completed. As a result protracted legal proceedings for recovery of a debt for the supply only may be necessary. Final accounts for payment may in most cases consist mainly of retentions to be released only after it has been established that the work is entirely satisfactory many months later; as such, following the insolvency of the client, they may never be released in the absence of rectification of any faulty work.

For these reasons, only in the rare circumstances when the client's contracts provide for one invoice and one payment on completion of the work, will factoring be suitable for contractors or sub-contractors in this industry. There may, however, be cases where the possibilities described later may provide a solution (see 22.9–22.12).

Businesses for which factoring is highly suitable

5.6   Apart from the maturity service, the full service and the variations in its present form should ideally be used for (i) true trade credit, and (ii) for goods that can be made, sold and forgotten and for services that are completed and invoiced in one amount; it should thus be used for businesss in which, in accordance with normal practices, all the client's obligations under contracts of sale are completed by invoice date. Factoring may be considered for those businesses that sell or supply services in such a way that invoices are rendered before completion of the contract only if a 'cut-off' clause can be provided for in each such contract (see 14.6–14.8). In addition, and exceptionally, suppliers of smaller and standard items of capital equipment selling through distributors may be suitable for these services. A consideration of the origins of factoring in the United States gives support to these limitations on its use: factoring was developed from the activities of mercantile agents and is naturally suited to those sections of trade and industry which would be likely to consider the use of a mercantile agent or distributor in a strange market.

5.7   From a description of the benefits of the factoring service given in Chapter 4, it will be apparent that the full service, maturity factoring and agency factoring (in its second sense) are particularly of benefit to businesses developing new products and markets. The full service (see Chapter 2), recourse factoring (see 3.2–3.4) or invoice discounting (see 3.9–3.13), may be of substantial benefit in particular to businesses that are expanding rapidly or have marked seasonal needs. The suitability of these services in particular circumstances will be more fully described in 6.1.

Some effects of misuse of the service

5.8   The results of using factoring in any of its forms (other than maturity factoring) in the wrong circumstances bring disservice not only to the client but to the factor also and sometimes even the debtor. In the foregoing paragraphs it has been demonstrated that a factor will have difficulty in finding himself secure in providing his services to certain industries. It has also been postulated that such feeling of insecurity will result in a poor service to the client, a restriction in prepayments and even a complete interruption to the client's cash flow. To the client the resulting disservice is apparent; the difficulties may cause an aggravation of the deficiency of working capital which may have initially caused its management to look to factoring. The business may well have embarked on planned growth on the understanding that the agreed percentage of sales would be available on despatch of its products; but, owing to its being unable to warrant that it had completed all its obligations under its contract of sale, it may then find that prepayments by the factor are withheld only because, in accordance with trade practice, there may be much to be done after invoice date.

5.9   An example of such a position might arise in sales of goods for export to a confirming house or export merchant in the UK; the goods may well be invoiced on despatch from the client's premises, but the debtor will only pay when the client can pass to him a bill of lading. If shipment of the goods is delayed *sine die*, either the factor will find himself having paid for a debt without final due date or the client's prepayment will be withheld. In such a case the client should be made to understand that factoring can only fill the gap between bill of lading and payment.

Factoring finance used for capital expenditure

5.10   A similar situation of frustrated expectations for both client and factor
may arise when factoring is used as a means of financing capital
expenditure. The additional funds generated by the prepayments made
available to the client become locked up in fixed assets. The business is
then in the position of being paid regularly for a large part of its sales
immediately on despatch of the goods but will continue to take the
normal period of credit from its suppliers. If the business had strained
resources before the new investment and the start of factoring, the
growth will still be inhibited because no new working capital has been
provided and the investment in the new fixed assets will not be able to
pay for their keep. If the business was financing comfortably before the
new investment any downturn in trade will now cause delays in
payments to creditors: prepayments for a reduced level of sales will not
be sufficient to cover expenses and creditors previously incurred at a
higher level of trade. This is a classical overtrading situation (see further
5.18 below) in which the growth of the business must continue
indefinitely and any downturn avoided at all costs if financial difficulties
are not to be met. The position can be avoided by using factoring with a
financial facility for the purpose for which it was designed—to increase
working capital—and by financing the capital investment by medium
term loans, leasing or capital.

Disregard of responsibility to accept recourse

5.11   A particular form of difficulty may arise from a misunderstanding of the
client of the nature of recourse factoring, bulk factoring or invoice
discounting without the added safeguard of credit insurance. It has been
known for a concern, with the type of business for which factoring is
quite suitable, to enter into such a recourse arrangement without full
regard to the recourse provisions, and to use the prepayments in such a
way that the funds would be removed from working capital. The result is
that, when the factor exercises his right of recourse, no funds are
available to repay the prepayments; and the factor must perforce make
deductions from further payments in order to recover what is due to
him. Thus, the planned cash flow may not materialise and the client may
find himself in difficulty. It is situations such as this that cause
professional advisers to dissuade their clients from using factoring in
any of its forms; a not uncommon complaint is that a factor will make
his prepayments but that the balance of the purchase price seems to be
delayed indefinitely owing to the setting off of recourse against it.
However, it is not the factoring arrangement that is wrong, it is the
misuse of the funds generated and the failure of the client to understand
that the funds provided under a recourse arrangement are not 'non-
returnable cash'. Such arrangements are the equivalent in substance,
though not in form, of the borrowing of money on the security of the
debts and should be treated as such in financial planning.

Client's failure to achieve profits

5.12   Factoring is no saviour of an unprofitable business of which the working capital has been lost by reason of trading losses. In such cases factoring in any of its forms will be taken on purely for the funds generated by it. The charges of the factor may not be recovered by reduced administration in such a case and the extra cost may well increase the losses. The usual result is to defer the ultimate failure so that when it does occur the assets available for creditors have been further dissipated. Time and again recourse has been made to a factor in such circumstances for what has become known as 'last resort finance'. Only if the factor can clearly see that the business is returning to satisfactory profitability should he accept such a proposal; it is then that the extra breathing space may be of value. Otherwise, on the failure of the business, no credit will reflect on the factor nor on the adviser who suggested the arrangements to the management.

High incidence of after sales service

5.13   Even maturity factoring may be misused. The entry into a maturity agreement by a supplier of goods with substantial after sales services and with agreements for periodic service calls with a view to reducing the office administration may in fact cause additional problems by the intervention of a third party—the factor—in the multitude of queries arising. It is often the case that the administrative problems are not those associated with credit control or sales accounting but arise from service queries and warranty claims.

Factoring no panacea for debtors of poor quality

5.14   Businesses that sell traditionally to trades and industries in which the expectation of bad debt losses is exceptionally high will not find a solution to this problem through factoring or credit insurance. These services can only spread the costs of such losses horizontally, across their many clients or insured, and by time over a period of years; they cannot therefore, subsidise such a business in its regular high incidence of losses. Losses, other than those that are exceptional, have to be absorbed by a high margin of profit. The result of the use of maturity factoring on normal terms in such circumstances will be a severe disappointment with the level of approvals. If the full service is used by such a business there may also be disappointment at the level of prepayments; if a financial facility is required recourse factoring or invoice discounting with a low percentage of prepayment agreed at the outset may be the best solution.

5.15   It is for this reason that in offering the full service or maturity factoring for such trades or industries factors sometimes provide that a specific limited amount (say £250 or £500) of any loss should be on a 'with recourse' basis notwithstanding any approved limit. In this way the usual run of small losses must be absorbed by the client's profit margin;

this arrangement is similar to the damage excesses, normally a part of any motor insurance policy.

5.16   Prospective clients in trades in which long credit and latitude by suppliers are established usages should not expect that a factor can reduce the average period of credit taken by overturning such accepted practices. Although factors are experts at credit control and collections and may often considerably improve the collection period they can expect to do no better than such trade practices allow.

Recognition of misuse can help image

5.17   Factoring can only benefit by a thorough consideration of its proper use and the difficulties caused by its misuse as described above. Much of the poor image of factoring has been caused by the pressure of the owners of factoring companies in insisting on quick returns from managements; this in turn has persuaded managements into sometimes accepting the wrong type of client in the wrong circumstances for the wrong reasons. Only by a full ventilation and discussion of the misuse of the services can the undoubted benefits and value of factoring and some of its variations be brought to the attention of the business community and professional advisers. The problems have never arisen from the very nature of the service; only from its misuse.

Factoring and overtrading

5.18   The benefits of factoring, the relief from administrative burdens and bad debt losses and the availability of finance linked to sales volume without formal limit, are especially valuable to and appreciated by businesses which are growing vigorously. This attraction to factoring, and especially to the financial service provided by factoring and several of its variants, by the newer growing industries has led to allegations, not least among bankers, that the financial service provided is a cause of overtrading. To take such a view is a false syllogism; because many who are overtrading turn to factoring, factoring is not on that account a cause or encouragement to overtrade. Certainly, as demonstrated earlier, factoring in any form will not help those who are already overtrading in the classical sense: selling on shorter terms than they are buying so that growth is imperative at any cost (even at a loss) to keep the business alive. Indeed, if any form of factoring with finance is used in such circumstances and the funds generated used for investment in fixed assets, then the difficulties may be aggravated (see 5.10 above).

5.19   Overtrading in its widest sense is usually taken to mean the carrying on of a business which is too large for the resources available for its support. The availability of funds without recourse to the extent of 75% or 80% of debts created by the sale of acceptable goods to creditworthy customers should enable a business to plan for growth with the resources automatically available. Thus, provided that the resources generated are used wisely as working capital to finance profitable sales and creditors are paid in due time, the growth may take place without overtrading. The factoring facility will provide the basis for achieving increased profits, which themselves can form the basis for the raising of additional resources. It seems that a more potent cause of overtrading is the reluctance of traditional providers of capital and lenders to provide a business with the necessary resources until profits have been earned and ploughed back and a healthy net asset position achieved. In this way businesses are tempted to try to achieve the profits without the resources to support the necessary sales volume. Factoring will break into this vicious circle, providing the necessary resources in the first place so that the increased sales may be achieved and profit earned.

5.20   However, the key to the avoidance of overtrading is the non-recourse element in the full service, undisclosed factoring, agency factoring (in its second sense) or a combination with credit insurance. With such a service the client has no need to provide for the increasing contingent liability for recourse as trading grows. Also the service must be provided for a business of the kind for which it is suitable, as described in Chapter 4.

Chapter 6

Factoring and the Accountant in Practice

The accountant as adviser

6.1   The most usual forms of factoring and related services as provided by some of the main factors in the United Kingdom have been described in Chapter 3, and in Chapters 4 and 5 some indications were given as to the considerations to be taken into account by a professional adviser in considering the use of the service by his client. It is important that the adviser should not be swayed at the outset by some of the obloquy regarding the services; such unfavourable reports have often been based on ill-informed and emotional reactions to experiences of the service's misuse. On the other hand the adviser should carefully analyse the benefits predicated of the service by the factor with whom he is negotiating.

Choosing the right service

6.2   First, the adviser should question whether he has looked to factoring as a solution to his client's problems or purposes only because he can think of no other service that will avail and not because the particular service selected is that which is most suited to deal with them. In particular, if he is looking to factoring in any of the circumstances described in 5.3–5.17, the dangers and disadvantages should be taken into account. The most usual circumstances in which care should be taken is the case of a business which has dissipated its working capital by losses over a long period and is grasping at a straw (see 5.12).

6.3   Secondly, it is necessary to select the variant of the service that is most suitable. For example:

(*a*)   Finance for growth alone for a well-established company with adequate reserves, a well spread portfolio of debts or an existing credit insurance policy, may well be satisfied by invoice discounting alone (see 3.9–3.13).

(*b*)   A company whose expansion requires the exploitation of new markets may be better served by the full service (see Chapter 2), so that the unfamiliar risks and usages are dealt with by a factor with experience in the particular sector of trade or industry.

(*c*) Finance for a fast growing business in its early years postulates the full service so that it can plan for growth confidently knowing that it will not be set back by bad debts or cash flow problems caused by poor administration of collection from debtors.

6.4   Thirdly, cash flow forecasts and other financial projections should be made to show a comparison of the position of the business with and without the use of factoring. The adviser will probably not be justified in recommending factoring for the traditional reasons for its use unless, (i) the service will enable the business to achieve additional profitable sales, and (ii) the additional profit will outweigh the cost of the service not recoverable through savings in administration and expected credit losses. There may, however, be other reasons for the prospective use of factoring. Examples of such reasons are:

(*a*) In the case of *maturity factoring* an alternative to the employment of sales ledger and/or credit control staff. (In some circumstances it has been demonstrated that the charge for maturity factoring for a relatively small business will be no more than the resulting saving of staff costs, without taking into account the protection against bad debts provided.)

(*b*) For a small business (say with an annual sales volume not exceeding £1m) the full service or maturity factoring may be an alternative to credit insurance (see 4.13).

(*c*) The wish to rely on a more certain and permanent means of finance than a facility which may be repayable on demand in any circumstances.

(*d*) The requirement for a stand-by facility to take advantage of special circumstances such as bulk purchases at a large discount.

(*e*) To provide working capital in the case of a management or leveraged buy-out.

6.5   Fourthly, in making these forward projections the adviser should never assume prepayments to the full limit at all times. Those who have used factoring most successfully have never budgeted for the use of the financial facility to the full; as a result difficulties arising from a shortfall from planned sales or other reductions in cash flow may be overcome without acute problems and additional expense. Furthermore, the possible restrictions on the finance available arising from sales to uncreditworthy customers or the failure of a customer to accept the goods or services invoiced must be taken into account.

Choice of factor

6.6   The adviser, having decided on the particular services required, should then give careful consideration to the choice of factoring company.

Many prospective clients do not request sight of the factoring companies' standard contracts until they have made decisions in principle to accept the service. This is a mistake: first, because contract terms vary very widely, particularly in details which may not have been covered in the negotiations; and, secondly, at the stage of acceptance of terms it is difficult to obtain from the factor any concessions on standard provisions. At an early stage in negotiations when competitors are still in the field such concessions may be available. Some of the more important points to be considered in reviewing the factoring contract are as follows:

(*a*) The basis for calculation of the administration or service charges and whether or not there are any additional charges to be made when a debt becomes seriously overdue (sometimes called a 'refactoring charge', see 9.6).

(*b*) The basis of calculation of the finance charge for prepayments and, in particular, the point at which the charge begins to accrue—e.g. is it at the date when a prepayment cheque is despatched to or automated transfer initiated for the client or on receipt of cleared funds by the client?

(*c*) The final due date for the purchase price of debts sold to the factor—a fixed maturity date or when payment is received by the factor.

(*d*) If a maturity date system is to be in operation, the provisions for adjustment of the period in the light of experience.

(*e*) In the case of the full service, maturity factoring, undisclosed factoring or agency factoring, the arrangements for approval of debts (i.e. whether by credit limits or approval of orders—see 2.5), the provisions for cancellation of approvals and the allocation of recoveries after cancellation. In this connection, unless the factoring agreement provides for the purchase or sale of all trade debts coming into existence during its term (rather than for the offer of trade debts and their acceptance by the factor), it should be appreciated that the factor normally has the absolute right to refuse to purchase the indebtedness represented by any invoice offered to him (see 7.18).

(*f*) In the case of the full service or any of the variants which include a financial facility, the certainty of the facility. It should be noted that some facilities for prepayments give the factor wide discretion either to reduce the prepayment percentage or to increase retentions.

(*g*) Arrangements for termination other than in the event of the insolvency of, or material breaches of the agreement by, the client; the consideration of this aspect should include an enquiry into the continuation of the financial facility during any period of notice and the arrangements for payment of the balance of purchase price after termination.

Summary of adviser's role

6.7   It comes to this: the adviser should ensure that the service is the right one for his client's aspirations, provided by a company whose contract and method of operation fulfill his client's requirements and that the service will be used to promote profitable business. (A 'Checklist for Adviser' is included as Appendix II.)

The accountant as auditor

6.8   The use of the full service, recourse factoring or maturity factoring by his client can be of assistance to the auditor if the service is provided by a reputable company. Factors make full and clear returns showing the unpaid balance of the purchase price of debts owing to the client. Such returns show details of unapproved debts and others liable to be recoursed. As a result, the auditor should be relieved of most tasks in relation to the sales, including, where factoring is on a non-recourse basis, the consideration of reserves for bad debts. Most factors are especially diligent in notifying their clients of queries by debtors and disputes; in this way deductions on payment by debtors and other events, that may give rise to the issue of credit notes, are brought to the attention of both the client and his auditor at an early stage.

6.9   Owing to the outright purchase by the factor or discounter of his client's debts, in the way that all the variants of the service are carried out at present, the client's balance sheet will show only the *net* amount of the unpaid balance of the purchase price of the debts sold. This amount should appear as a debtor under the heading of 'current assets'. The balance will be the amount of the debts purchased by the factor and outstanding at the balance sheet date less amounts paid by the factor for or on account of the purchase price of such debts and less the factor's charges.

6.10   The outstanding debts themselves will naturally appear in the balance sheet of the factor. It seems necessary to state these self evident facts, which apply no less to invoice discounting and undisclosed factoring as to full factoring and the other variants, because experience has shown that many accountants have prepared factored clients' accounts in a way that would imply that the financial service is the lending of money on the security of the debts. For the legal position of the current practice, see 7.1–7.6: in the UK, unlike the position in the United States and some continental countries, even recourse factoring or invoice discounting are treated as the outright purchase of debts and the position should be shown accordingly. This treatment is likely to continue unless the provision of these services is made by lending against the security of debts as postulated in Chapter 22.

6.11   On the analogy of accounting for discounted bills of exchange, it is contended that the client's accounts should include a note of the contingent liability in respect of debts liable to recourse; in the full service and other non-recourse arrangements such debts are those which are not approved owing to their being outside credit limits authorised by the factor. A suggested wording for such a note might be:

'There is a contingent liability not exceeding £...... in respect of debts realised but unrecovered.'

The amount of the contingent liability should presumably include amounts liable to recourse for the issue of credit notes for returns and allowances and in particular for disputes already notified by the factor, unless a provision for such items is created and deducted from the debt owing from the factor to the client.

Part B

The Relationship between the Factor and his Client

Chapter 7

The Factoring Agreement: The Main Functions and Types

7.1   In this chapter and the next the legal relations between the factor and his client are considered. The process of transferring the ownership of the debts purchased by the factor is set out here and in the next chapter the remaining rights and obligations of the parties to a factoring contract are described. The agreement (or contract) for factoring or invoice discounting (in all its forms—see Chapters 2 and 3) governs the relations between the factor and his client. It contains in detail the obligations of the client to the factor particularly in relation to the warranties and undertakings that the client must give to the factor. It also, naturally, contains the factor's obligations to the client particularly regarding the time when he must pay for the debts he has purchased and the broad limits within which administrative arrangements for the general conduct of the factoring services may be agreed from time to time.

Transfer of ownership of debts: the requirements of a valid assignment

7.2   The principal demand of the *client* is that the agreement should make provision for the payment to him of the purchase price of the debts sold in such a way and at such a time that he will receive service, by way of finance and/or relief from administration and bad debts, that has been predicated of the arrangement during negotiations for its use. The *factor's* principal requirement is that the ownership of the debts which he purchases should be transferred to him in such a way that his rights to collect the full sum owing are absolute and unencumbered.

Effective assignments

7.3   Debts such as those which fall within the scope of an arrangement for the full service or any of its variants, belong to a class of property known to lawyers as 'choses in action'. These are pure intangibles; broadly speaking they are assets the ownership of which cannot be enforced by physical possession and the transfer of which cannot be effected by delivery. The transfer of ownership of debts is usually completed by an assignment, an agreement by the creditor to transfer the debt to another party and the latter's agreement to take the transfer without necessarily having the consent of the debtor. In order to consider how the transfer of ownership is effected in any form of factoring (as described in Chapters 2 and 3) it is necessary to consider the way in which an effective assignment may be made and the incidence of stamp duty. Common law would not recognise the transfer of ownership of such pure intangibles except by means of a novation requiring the consent of the debtor; the common law courts were influenced (i) by what they considered to be the personal character of the obligation of the debtor, and (ii) by the fear of the purchase of dubious claims at a large discount by wealthy people resulting in the flooding of the courts with contentious litigation.

Historical background

7.4   Although courts of equity recognised such assignments, proceedings for the recovery of debts had to be pursued in the common law courts. As a result it was necessary for the assignee to recover from the debtor by using the assignor's name and, if the latter refused to co-operate, to obtain an order for the assignor so to do from a court of equity before starting proceedings in the common law court. Since 1873 when the Judicature Act combined the administration of the common law courts and the courts of equity this cumbersome procedure has been unnecessary provided that all three parties, the debtor, the assignor and the assignee, are before the court. If the assignor co-operates in the action the assignor and assignee will be joint plaintiffs in the action; if he does not, then the assignee must proceed against the debtor and the assignor as joint defendants. (*Holt v Heatherfield Trust Ltd [1942] 1 AER 404*).

Assignments in statutory form: legal assignments

7.5   Furthermore, since the Judicature Act 1873, assignments of debts or other legal *choses in action* have received statutory recognition. [*Section 25(6)*]. The provisions were substantially re-enacted in 1925 [*Law of Property Act 1925, s 136*]; a formal assignment in accordance with the statutory provisions is normally referred to by factors as a 'legal assignment' in order to distinguish it from an assignment in a form always recognised by equity. It will be so referred to here. The requirements of a **legal assignment** are substantially as follows:

(*a*) it must be in writing under the hand of the assignor; and (*b*) it must be *absolute* (i.e. it must be an outright sale or mortgage of the whole debt and not an assignment of part of it or by way of a charge); and

(*c*) express notice in writing must be given to the debtor.

The legal assignment is complete upon the notice being received by the debtor. (*Holt v Heatherfield Trust Ltd*, as above). The rights of an assignee under an assignment in this form are subject to equities having priority; this is germane to the question of competing interests dealt with in Chapter 15. Subject to this, the effect is to transfer all legal rights in relation to the debt assigned to the assignee including the right in his own name alone (i) to take action through the courts for recovery from the debtor, and (ii) to give a good discharge.

Equitable and legal assignment compared

7.6   Any assignment of a debt or other legal *chose in action* which does not fulfil these requirements will be valid *in equity* provided that the intention of the parties is clear and value given. Such an equitable assignment need not be in writing. Notice to the debtor is not a necessary prerequisite to the transfer of ownership; but notice is important in relation to competing interests and the debtor's countervailing rights. (See 11.30 and 15.5.) Such an assignment may be of part of a debt only or by way of a charge. However, whether an assignment is legal or equitable, provided that the substance of the transaction is for the outright sale and purchase of a debt, such assignment will have the effect of transferring the ownership absolutely. The statute has in no way detracted from the efficacy of equitable assignments and the position in relation to them remains exactly as it was before 1873. (*Wm Brandts Sons & Co v Dunlop Rubber Co Ltd [1905] AC 454, at p 462*). The difference is mainly procedural; the assignee has the right to sue in his own name alone for recovery from the debtor only if the assignment is legal. Otherwise the proceedings should be in the joint names of the assignee and the assignor. On the face of it, it would seem therefore that a factor providing the full service or any other variant under which he was responsible for collections would make arrangements for a legal assignment in every case so that he would be in a position to proceed in his own name without having to join his client in the action. Such procedures would make for speed and simplicity.

7.7   The incidence of stamp duty however (see 7.8–7.11 below), makes it difficult to establish legal assignments (or indeed any assignment evidenced individually by a written document) under a continuing arrangement such as factoring or any disclosed variant of it; and in the case of undisclosed or invoice discounting the absence of notice to the debtors precludes their establishment. Furthermore, factors' arrangements with their clients now normally provide for speedy recourse to the courts even where the assignments on invoice date are effective in equity only.

Stamp duty considerations

7.8   Stamp duty, a charge to which is imposed by the Stamp Duty Act 1891, as amended by subsequent Finance Acts, is a duty on *instruments* and not on transactions. Accordingly, if a transaction can be conducted without an instrument, then there can be no liability to the duty. Most deeds under seal are liable only to a flat rate duty of 50p and agreements under hand, other than those for which specific provision is made in the statutes, are not liable.

7.9   An assignment of a debt is a conveyance or transfer of property and any instrument evidencing such a conveyance or transfer is liable under the Act to *ad valorem* duty. [*Stamp Duty Act 1891, s 54 and 1 Sch*]. The duty is levied according to the consideration, which in a factoring transaction will be the amount payable by the debtor less the factor's charges, i.e. not substantially less than the amount invoiced. The rate of duty is 1% subject to an exemption which, with effect from 20 March 1984, relates to any independent transaction whereof the consideration does not exceed £30,000 (based on the 1984 Budget proposals). However, in order to qualify for the exemption the instrument must include a certificate of value by which it is certified that the transaction represented by the instrument does not form part of a larger transaction or series of transactions in respect of which the aggregate consideration is of greater value. Thus, all linked transactions must be aggregated for the purpose of qualification for the exemption. The signature on the certificate is that of the assignor.

7.10   In a factoring transaction where an individual debt, previously assigned in equity in the absence of a written instrument, is assigned in writing the factor normally signs on behalf of the client by the authority of a power of attorney. At one time such an assignment was considered to be an individual transaction and a certificate of value was added. Now the prevailing view is that it should be regarded as linked together with all the other assignments, whether written or not, under the factoring agreement. It is therefore most unlikely that a written assignment in an arrangement for factoring can qualify for this exemption. (For an analogy see *Attorney General v Cohen [1937] 1 KB 478, at pp 490/491*.)

7.11   Even in the absence of a written instrument to give effect to the assignment of each individual debt in an arrangement for factoring, consideration must be given to the stamping of the factoring agreement itself. A contract or agreement providing for the sale of any equitable estate or interest in any property whatsoever is chargeable to *ad valorem* duty. On the face of it, as a factoring agreement under which debts are assigned in the absence of a written assignment must provide for the equitable sale of the debts, such an agreement would appear to be liable. However, instruments are stampable on execution and an *ad valorem* duty cannot be charged at the date of the execution of the factoring agreement (provided that this date precedes the starting date) because at that time it is not possible to calculate the value of the debts to be assigned, the consideration and, consequently, the duty. In such an event the document, if under seal, would be liable to a 50p stamp as a deed.

Basic types of agreement

7.12   It is apparent that, if it is necessary that an assignment should be in writing in order that it should be recognised as a legal assignment, in relation to every legal assignment there will be an instrument which (subject to the exemption referred to in 7.8 above) will be liable to stamp duty. Attempts have been made in the past to provide for legal assignments to be effected on every sale by the client as soon as goods are delivered or services completed without the incidence of stamp duty, but these arrangements are of doubtful validity. The method usually adopted was to structure the agreement to provide (apart from the normal ancillary provisions described in Chapter 8) for the client to offer the debts to the factor as they arose and for the factor to have the absolute right to accept or decline each debt offered. By this method the agreement does not provide for the actual transfer of ownership of the debts, this being effected by the individual offers and acceptances. The agreement thus becomes a *master agreement* giving effect to the terms by which all the prospective assignments will be regulated. By arranging for each offer to cover debts of an aggregate value of less than the exemption limit then in force, it was hoped to apply the exemption to every written assignment. The doubt about the exemption from stamp duty of this arrangement arises from the premise that, as the master agreement provides that all trade debts arising in the business of the client must be offered, the factor has an option to purchase every such debt and, accordingly, the master agreement links all the transactions. (*Attorney General v Cohen*, as above).

7.13   It is now generally considered that in order to avoid the incidence of *ad valorem* stamp duty in an arrangement for factoring *one of two methods of vesting the debts in the factor must be adopted*. Both methods avoid the use of a document to evidence the assignment. The methods are:

(*a*) An agreement, by which debts are offered to the factor and accepted by him on a 'facultative' basis, as explained in 7.18, is used; but it is provided that in the absence of an acknowledgement the offer is deemed to be accepted. Thus, the offer document itself does not evidence the assignment.

(*b*) An agreement on a 'whole turnover' basis (see 7.23 below) is entered into by which *inter alia* every trade debt of the client in existence on the starting date and which comes into existence subsequently during its term is to be sold by the client to the factor and vests in the factor as soon as it comes into existence without further formality.

In the case of (*b*), as the agreement is executed before the start of the arrangement no debts are in fact assigned at that time and, accordingly, if it is a deed under seal it will attract only a 50p stamp. However, as the transfer of ownership takes place without a document evidencing the assignment, the factor will have an equitable assignment only (see 7.6 above), unless his ownership of any debt is subsequently formally perfected. During the currency of the agreement it is necessary for the client to notify the factor of debts which have been sold to him and are vested in him. Such notifications are considered not to be stampable; they are not 'conveyances or transfers' as the debts have already vested in the factor by virtue of the factoring agreement. Special considerations in relation to this form of agreement are necessary if it is entered into with an unincorporated client (see 7.29–7.32 below).

Lending on security distinguished from outright purchase

7.14   It is important to distinguish the normal basis for factoring by the outright purchase of debts from the lending (as by bankers) on the security of them. Although, as described later in 22.1–22.8, it would be possible to provide the full service and its variants with financial facilities by means of lending money on the security of a fixed charge on the client's book debts, at present normal factoring arrangements are based on the sale and purchase of the debts and the vesting of them in the factor. As a result of the outright sale and purchase, the debts cease to be the property of the client and, in the case of a client incorporated under the Companies Acts, there is no way of registering a security interest in them such as there is in the United States under the Uniform Commercial Code. (UCC, s 9–401/408). The arrangement certainly does not constitute a charge because the ownership has passed to the factor; consequently no registration is necessary or would be acceptable to the registrar under Section 95 of the Companies Act 1948.

7.15   In view of this absence of registration and as the lending on security of book debts and the purchase of them, together with prepayments, appear to be very similar in substance, it is most important that the distinction should be kept firmly in mind by the factor when dealing with an incorporated client. If the arrangement for prepayments of the purchase price of debts sold to the factor were held by the courts to be a mask for the lending on the security of specific book debts it might be held to be registerable under Section 95(2)(*e*); and if it were considered to be the lending of money against a general assignment of all existing and future book debts it would be registerable under Section 95(2)(*c*) on the analogy of the required registration as if it were a bill of sale in the case of a sole trader or partnership (see 7.30 below).

7.16   In either such event, the factor would be unable to recover in competition with the rights of a creditor or liquidator as he would be considered to have an unregistered charge as security for his advances. Where invoice discounting or bulk factoring are the services provided and the client not only guarantees payment of the debts sold to the factor but also collects them for him, there is, in particular, a very fine line between the purchase and a loan on security. It is therefore as well for the factor to ensure that, in all his documentation and communications both with the client and the outside world, his words are compatible with the outright purchase of debts. Words such as 'advance', 'loan' or even 'interest' should be eschewed in favour of 'prepayment', 'early payment' and 'discount'. Furthermore, as the normal test of a security right (as opposed to outright purchase) is the inclusion of an 'equity of redemption' (the right of the chargor to have revested the asset charged on repayment of the loan), the factor should never give his client the absolute right to repurchase any of the debts sold to the factor. He should be able to demonstrate that the substance of the transaction as well as the form is that of the purchase of debts.

7.17   The courts have almost always accepted that the agreement between the parties drawn up by their lawyers have reflected their true intentions. (For example, see: *Chow Yoong Hong v Choong Fah Rubber Manufactory [1962] AC 209; Lloyds & Scottish Finance Ltd v Cyril Lord Carpets Sales Ltd and others (1979), House of Lords (unreported)*.) It may well be, however, that in some future case arising from any kind of factoring arrangement, in particular invoice discounting or bulk factoring, the court may decide in accordance with the substance of the transactions as evidenced by communications between the factor and his client. For every case that is heard is not necessarily a reproduction of an earlier case on which precedent may be based; in this connection as long ago as 1901 Lord Halsbury said: 'a case is only authority for what it actually decides'. (*Quinn v Leathem [1900–3] AER Rep 1, at p 7*).

Facultative agreements

7.18   Most factoring agreements (for any of the forms of factoring described in Chapters 2 or 3) provide, as regards the vesting of the debts in the factor, only for the offer by the client and acceptance or rejection by the factor of each debt as it arises. This is based on factoring in the US and on typical arrangements for the block discounting of instalment and hire purchase agreements. The difference from a typical block discounting arrangement is that in an arrangement for factoring the client is, by the master agreement (see 7.12 above), obliged to offer every trade debt. As the factor is not obliged to accept, he has in effect an option to purchase every such debt; thus the arrangement is **facultative**.

7.19   From the point of view of the factor's security the advantage of this type of arrangement is that he has the absolute right to decline to purchase any debt; he could decline where his obligations in respect of any debt offered were onerous to a degree that outweighed the advantages of ownership. Examples of this are:

(*a*) Where the agreement commits the factor to prepay a fixed percentage of the purchase price of every debt, whether approved or unapproved, and the factor does not wish to commit further funds owing to his assessment of the client's financial position.

(*b*)   Where the relations between the client and a debtor are such that many of the invoices owed by the debtor are subject to dispute or query so that collection procedures are administratively difficult and expensive.

Such a refusal to accept a debt offered might also be effected to avoid the factor's liability to pay for a debt within an approved limit when the debtor had become a poor credit risk. This might occur if the factor had learnt of a change in the fortunes of the debtor after the client had delivered goods to that debtor and invoiced them but before the offer by the client to sell the debt. It is doubtful if any reputable factor would use this device for such a purpose; the detraction from his reputation for providing the equivalent of credit insurance would probably be a more serious matter to him than the loss of a bad debt.

7.20   The disadvantage to the factor of the facultative type of agreement arises from the fact that the debts do not vest in him by virtue of the agreement itself. Thus, if a client enters into an agreement of this type with factor 'A' and;

(*a*)   declines to offer to factor 'A' some of the debts arising in his business; or

(*b*)   charges them to a bank, by way of fixed charge, without offering them to factor 'A'; or

(*c*)   assigns them to factor 'B' without offering them to factor 'A',

then, in any such case, factor 'A' can do no more than claim damages for breach of the master agreement. As the debts do not vest in factor 'A', he has no proprietary rights in relation to them (see Chapter 15). Where, however, the debts are offered to and accepted by the factor and have also been charged or offered elsewhere the priority rules described in Chapter 15 apply. Furthermore, if a client company is wound up by the court, any debt accepted by the factor after the presentation of the petition on which the order is based, or any earlier resolution to wind up, will not vest in the factor. (*Companies Act 1948, s 227 and 229*, and see Chapter 18. See also 'Tolley's Liquidation Manual', paragraph 5.29.) For, at present, these events constitute the commencement of the liquidation; the proposals in the White Paper on Insolvency are that the winding-up order should be the relevant date. This would at present apply even if the debts had been offered to the factor beforehand. Similar considerations will apply in the case of the bankruptcy of an unincorporated business and these are dealt with in Chapter 18.

7.21   Whether or not the appointment of a receiver under a floating charge created by the client, or crystallisation of such a charge in any other manner, would prevent further debts vesting in the factor would depend on the precise details of any priority or waiver agreement between the holder of the charge and the factor. Most such waivers (as they are usually referred to) provide that the factor's rights shall have priority only in relation to debts actually vesting in the factor before crystallisation. Thus, in the case of a facultative type of agreement, debts in existence at the date of crystallisation not accepted by the factor (even though offered) may not vest in the factor in such an event.

7.22   An advantage sometimes claimed for this form of agreement is that it enables the factor to take legal assignments of all debts offered to him. However, it seems likely that considerations of stamp duty preclude this possibility (see 7.8–7.11 above). Furthermore, as some factors who use this type of agreement provide for no written acceptance of offers but deemed acceptance after a number of days without refusal, the delay in acceptance may have the effect of giving to the administrator of the insolvent estate the rights to debts which, if accepted promptly in writing by the factor, would have vested in him (see 7.13(*a*) above). A specimen facultative factoring agreement is set out in Appendix IV.

Whole turnover agreements

7.23   A type of agreement was evolved in the UK to provide the factor with the greatest possible degree of protection against competing interests in the debts purchased, or purported to be purchased, in the absence of legal assignments. In the agreement itself it is provided that all the debts arising in the course of the client's business, or in a certain part or division of it or of a certain category (e.g. in certain markets), will be sold to and purchased by the factor. It is further provided that such debts vest in the factor without any further formality. For convenience an agreement of this type is referred to as a **whole turnover** agreement.

7.24   Upon the first credit by the factor to the account of the client of the purchase price of any debt falling within the scope of an agreement of this type or the first payment in respect of such purchase price, there is constituted an equitable assignment of all future debts to which the agreement relates. Following the date of such a credit or payment the factor's rights to all such debts are absolute in equity. Equity treats that as done which ought to be done. See R M Goode 'Some Aspects of Factoring Law', J B L 1982, May p 242, published by Stevens & Son Ltd. Professor Goode adds a footnote:

> 'Before this date, the agreement is a mere contract. This is because equity does not decree specific performance of a contract to pay money; *Rogers v Challis (1859) 27 Beav 175*; so that for the agreement to be specifically enforceable, and thus to constitute an equitable assignment, the consideration must be executed, i.e. the creditor or purchaser must actually have laid out his money; *Holroyd v Marshall (1862) 10 HL Cas 191*. However, a single credit or payment suffices for this purpose, as this type of factoring agreement is an indivisible contract for the global sale of receivables, not a series of separate transactions.'

(See also *Tailby v Official Receiver (1888) 13 Ap Cas 523*.)

7.25   Thus, even in the absence of any further act by the client or any notification to the factor of the existence of the debts by the client's sending in copy invoices, the factor may himself take possession of such debts by sending notices to the debtors and demanding and taking proceedings for payment. If the client does not co-operate the factor may join him in the proceedings or effect a legal assignment on behalf of the client by the authority of a power of attorney (see 8.14). It is contended that there is no *miniscule scintilla* of time in which a debt, after its creation by the delivery of goods or the performance of service, vests in the client; the prevailing view is that they vest in the factor immediately upon coming into existence.

7.26   Such agreements also preclude the disadvantages to the client of his having to face the possibility that his factor may exercise his right to refuse any debt offered without his having to give reasons therefor. It is normal, however, in this type of arrangement for the factor to specify that prepayments of the purchase price of debts sold to him up to the agreed percentage will relate to approved debts only. It is in this way that the factor protects himself against having to make further funds available to a client in whom he may have lost confidence or in respect of debtors whose credit he has come to doubt or where relations between the client and the debtor have deteriorated and disputes may be expected.

7.27   Where a credit approval has been given it is normal for the factor to stipulate in a whole turnover agreement that any cancellation of it will apply only to deliveries of goods effected after notice of such cancellation. Once the debt has been created, it vests in the factor automatically. The factor is, therefore, committed to the ownership of it and to pay for it as an approved debt even if he has not been notified of its existence before his cancellation of the relevant approval, provided that the notification came in reasonable time.

7.28   From the point of view of the factor's rights on the insolvency of the client, this type of agreement has advantages. All debts created up to the commencement of winding-up (or possibly even afterwards) and prior to crystallisation of any charge over book debts created by the client or withdrawal of a waiver by a chargee will vest in the factor notwithstanding the absence of any notification by the client by way of sending in any copy invoices. This aspect is dealt with more fully in Chapter 15. The factor with this type of agreement also has a better chance of establishing the priority of his rights over those of a chargee in relation to a charge taken after the commencement of factoring (see 15.17 and 15.23). A specimen whole turnover agreement is set out in Appendix V.

Sole traders and partnerships

Registration of assignments

7.29   It is provided by Section 43(1) of the Bankruptcy Act 1914, that a general assignment of all existing and future book debts or any class thereof by an individual or a partnership is void against a trustee in bankruptcy of the assignor as regards such debts as are unpaid at the commencement of bankruptcy unless the assignment is registered as if it were an absolute bill of sale. This provision does not apply to an assignment of book debts due from specified debtors or growing due under specified contracts. In view of this exception from the rule there is no need for registration of the assignments under a *facultative* type of agreement nor of that type of agreement itself. All the debts assigned are specified.

7.30   However, registration is required of the *whole turnover* type of agreement as described in 7.23–7.28 above if entered into with a sole trader or partnership. The agreement is not a bill of sale but the Bankruptcy Act provides that it should be registered 'as if it were' such. The procedure normally adopted is as follows:

(*a*) Two copies of the agreement are executed by the factor. The copies are for the client and the factor. It is desirable for the factor to execute first because of the short time limit for registration.

(*b*) Both copies are executed by the client in the presence of a solicitor, who prepares a further photocopy of it.

(*c*) The solicitor makes an affidavit in which he affirms that the agreement has been executed before him and that he has explained the meaning and effect of the general assignment to the client. The photocopy of the agreement is attached to the affidavit as an exhibit.

(*d*) The executed copies are stamped with a 50p stamp, if they have been executed as deeds.

(*e*) The affidavit with exhibit is filed at the bills of sale registry of the High Court in London within seven days.

In the absence of registration the factor may expect that on the bankruptcy of his client he will lose not only all debts outstanding at the date of the receiving order, but also all debts which were outstanding at any earlier commencement date of the bankruptcy. This may be the date of the earliest available act of bankruptcy. Some of these debts may indeed already have been settled to the factor and the whole of the purchase price paid to the client (see also 18.11).

Reputed ownership in cases of bankruptcy

7.31   In the early days of factoring in the UK some advisers to those who were establishing factoring companies gave careful thought to the 'order and disposition' or 'reputed ownership' clause of the Bankruptcy Act 1914

(Section 38(2)(*c*)). By this provision all goods at the commencement of bankruptcy in the possession, order or disposition of the bankrupt, in his trade or business with the consent of the true owner in circumstances that he is the reputed owner, vest in the trustee in bankruptcy. The clause exempts *choses in action* other than trade debts due or growing due. From the factor's point of view it had been considered by some that in view of this provision any form of factoring with prepayments could not be safely provided for a sole trader or partnership. If the business failed the factor would lose the debts to the trustee. Such debts might include debts already paid to the factor before he was aware of the bankruptcy (see Chapter 18). At best he would be an unsecured creditor for his prepayments. It is, however, now generally accepted that an assigned debt is in the possession, order and disposition of the sole trader or partnership only so long as no notice has been given to the debtor. (See 'Williams & Muir Hunter on Bankruptcy', 19th Edition, at p 305.) Therefore, any form of factoring, that provides for such notices, can be provided for sole traders or partnerships with reasonable safety for the factor as regards this statutory provision. The question remains as to the position where no notice has been given before the commencement of bankruptcy in invoice discounting or undisclosed factoring arrangements. It seems possible, but by no means certain, that registration as described above of a whole turnover agreement would serve to exempt debts assigned under such an agreement from the 'order and disposition' or 'reputed ownership' provisions. [*Bills of Sale Act 1878, s 20*]. This section remains in force as regards absolute, but not conditional bills of sale [*Bills of Sale Act 1882, s 15*], but the section cannot be taken as an undoubted authority. The factoring agreement, being an agreement to assign future debts, is not an absolute bill of sale; it is merely to be registered 'as if it were' one.

7.32 In view of the uncertainty, in the absence of notice to the debtors, invoice discounting or undisclosed factoring would seem to be unsafe for the factor. Even trust property may be affected by the doctrine of reputed ownership; therefore any trust provisions in a factoring agreement, as described in 8.18–8.19, would be unlikely to assist a factor. (See 'Williams & Muir Hunter on Bankruptcy', at p 267.) For these reasons and in view of the uncertainty regarding the effect of registration on these provisions, the provision of invoice discounting or undisclosed factoring for unincorporated business is unusual by any method. However, in the White Paper on Insolvency, it is proposed that these provisions should be repealed. Such a change in the law will enable factors to provide these services on the basis of the same criteria as for corporate clients.

Special considerations for Scotland

7.33 The absence of any doctrine of equity in Scotland makes for special difficulties in relation to clients domiciled there. In order that the ownership of a debt should be transferred effectively in Scotland it is necessary that:

(*a*)   there should be a written assignation which is broadly similar to a written assignment in England; and

(*b*)   the assignation should be intimated to the debtor by means of a written notice.

It is therefore not possible safely to rely upon the normal whole turnover type of agreement which provides for the debts to be assigned equitably. On the insolvency of the client the administrator of the estate will be able to claim that the debts have not been effectively vested in the factor. On the other hand reliance on written assignations under a facultative type of agreement, with intimations to the debtors, would be effective to vest in the factor debts in respect of which such formalities had been completed before the commencement of liquidation of a corporate client or sequestration of an unincorporated business. However, the latter arrangement would have the effect of bringing the assignations within the scope of the Stamp Duty Act 1891 as instruments liable to *ad valorem* duty subject to any possible exemption as fully described in 7.9 above.

7.34   For these reasons efforts have been made to find ways of vesting debts in the factor without the need for assignations and intimations. One method which has been successfully adopted is to provide that in relation to every debt sold by the client to the factor the beneficial ownership should vest in the factor but that, in the absence of an assignation, the client should hold the debt on trust for the factor. The factor, under a power of attorney in the factoring agreement, will have the right to execute an assignation of any debt and intimate it to the debtor on behalf of and in the name of the client (see 8.14–8.19). However, he will do this only if it is absolutely necessary (e.g. to take proceedings against the debtor in his own name).

7.35   As the trust is not affected by liquidation or sequestration, any debt in relation to which a trust has been created prior to the commencement of such insolvency will remain in the ownership of the factor. As in England, trust property is not available to the trustee or liquidator of an insolvent firm or company.

7.36   The factor's rights to the debts as against the claims of a receiver appointed by the holder of a floating charge should be governed by a waiver agreement between the holder and the factor. The priority rights in the absence of a waiver would appear to be similar to those which apply in England and Wales (see Chapter 15).

7.37   In the absence of any rules of equity in Scotland it is not possible to take a fixed charge on a debt in the absence of an assignation nor to have a valid assignation of a debt which has yet to come into existence. For this reason fixed charges on book debts to secure banking advances to corporate customers are not taken in Scotland. Therefore although the system described above may be used with either a facultative type of agreement or a whole turnover agreement the advantage of having the debts vest in the factor without formality under the whole turnover type will be absent.

7.38   In order that a trust on these lines should be validly created it is necessary for the client to do something in relation to the debts which would be the equivalent of the delivery of the subject of a trust by him to an independent trustee. (*Clark Taylor & Co Ltd v Quality Site Development (Edinburgh) Ltd 1981, SLT 308*). The instruction to pay, sent to the debtor in a disclosed factoring arrangement, would probably suffice. This is a reason for the factor to prefer disclosed factoring in Scotland. There can be no trust until the debt is in existence and some act has taken place in connection with the debt which clearly denotes the trust's creation. In the absence of such an act there is no vesting of beneficial ownership; all that the factor has is a contract which may give him the right to damages for breach, but no more, on the insolvency of his client. The normal method adopted, apart from the instructions to the debtor, is for the agreement to provide that the submission of copy invoices to the factor and his crediting the client with the purchase price or payment on account of it will evidence the creation of a trust in relation to the debts represented by such invoices.

7.39   The system may be used for any of the variations of factoring including invoice discounting or undisclosed factoring. However, if any instruction is given to the debtor that payment should be made to the factor as soon as the trust is created, the debtor will be put on notice not to pay a subsequent assignee.

Chapter 8

The Factoring Agreement:
Other Terms and the Factor's Rights

8.1 Although, from the factor's point of view, the most important function of the factoring agreement is to ensure that the debts purchased vest in him (as considered in the previous chapter), there are a number of ancillary provisions which are essential to his security. These are provisions for recourse to the client on breach of warranty and provisions for perfecting the factor's title and rights to debts purchased and to the proceeds of them. From the client's point of view, too, there must be provisions for ensuring that in respect of approved debts there should be no recourse, so that he may be assured of receiving the administrative service and of protection in respect of such debts. All these matters are dealt with in the succeeding paragraphs. The client's other main requirement from the agreement is that arrangements for paying to him the purchase price of the debts sold to the factor should be satisfactory. The usual provisions for this aspect are dealt with in Chapter 9.

Warranties and undertakings by the client: general

Warranty of value and validity of debt

8.2 When purchasing debts represented purely by invoices raised by the client, with no acknowledgement of indebtedness by the debtor, the factor requires adequate assurances of the validity of such debts. It is normal, therefore, for the factoring agreement to provide that the offer (under a facultative agreement – see 7.18) or the notification by the sending in of a copy invoice (under a whole turnover agreement – see 7.23) will constitute a warranty by the client of the value and validity of the debt. The warranty will normally provide that:

(a) the goods which gave rise to the debt have been delivered or the services completed and that they conform to a contract of sale or services between the client and the debtor; and

(b) the invoice represents a valid collectable debt of the amount stated and that it will be paid without any dispute or deduction by the debtors; and

64

(c) the debt offered or notified to the factor is free from any cross-claim or right of set-off by the debtor and any encumbrance in favour of a third party (see Chapters 15 and 16).

Factors will normally rely on this undertaking and purchase debts relating to goods as soon as they have been despatched to the debtor (see 8.30 below).

Warranty regarding contract terms

8.3   The factor will normally also expect the client to warrant that any debt sold arises out of a contract of sale or services which provides that:

(a) the terms of payment are no more liberal than those which the factor has approved; and

(b) the payment by the debtor is made in a currency approved by the factor.

In the absence of such provisions, the extension of credit by the client to the debtor may increase the factor's credit risk; and the invoicing in a depreciating currency may cause his inability to recover the full purchase price of debts sold to him. It is also desirable from the factor's point of view that the client should ensure, and warrant, that his contracts of sale should be governed by English law (or Scottish law in the case of a client domiciled in Scotland). If, by reason of the bargaining power of a foreign debtor, the contract must be that of the debtor's country then the factor should accept and approve the debt only if the commercial law of that country is such as to provide adequate rights and remedies to an unpaid creditor.

Warranty to disclose

8.4   Although the credit protection element of a factoring agreement is analogous to a policy of credit insurance, a factor does not have the protection that an insurer has by reason of the insurance policy belonging to a class of contracts that are *uberrimae fidei*. Under such contracts it is assumed that one party (in the case of insurance the prospective insured) is in possession of most of the material facts regarding the subject matter of the contract; accordingly, that party is obliged to make a full disclosure of such facts. Failure to do so makes the contract voidable at the option of the other. A factoring agreement is not a contract *uberrimae fidei*. In order to place himself in a position equivalent to that of a credit insurer the factor should require a warranty from the client that, both before making the agreement and during its currency, the client has and will disclose any fact or matter known to the client which might influence the factor's decision in approving any debt. Such a warranty might also apply to any fact or matter which might influence the factor in making further prepayments in circumstances in which he is not obliged to do so.

Warranty against subsequent encumbrances

8.5   In order to avoid a conflict with the holder of any security right affecting book debts (see Chapter 15), the factor should require a warranty from the client that he has not granted, save as disclosed to the factor, and will not during the currency of the agreement grant any charge, disposition or other encumbrance, that affects or may affect the debts falling within the scope of the agreement. Naturally, any factor dealing with a prospective incorporated client should search the Companies Registry for any such security right. However, such a search cannot be conclusive. Some examples of security rights which may affect a factor's rights to debts purchased and which would not be revealed by a search at the outset of factoring are set out below:

(*a*)   A charge registerable under Section 95 of the Companies Act 1948 may be executed before the start of factoring but properly registered (within twenty-one days of execution) afterwards.

(*b*)   Several forms of security rights which may affect book debts are not registerable under this section. Examples of such forms in England are:

   (i)   equitable rights to debts created by the sale by the client of goods purchased with reservation of title or released to the client on a letter of trust; and

   (ii)   a charge on debts other than book debts; and

   (iii)   the deposit of a negotiable instrument by way of pledge.

(*c*)   A charge affecting book debts may be executed by a company and registered during the currency of the factoring agreement. Although factors normally search periodically (say every six months) such a charge may escape the factor's notice for sufficient time to create a conflict with the holder.

(*d*)   An unregistered charge on book debts given by a company to secure indebtedness may in fact be good as against the claims of a factor. Failure to register a charge on book debts has the effect, so far as security on the company's property is concerned, of making the charge void against any liquidator or creditor of the company. [*Companies Act 1948, s 95(1), (2)(e)*]. In normal circumstances a factor is not a creditor.

(*c*)   The client having sold trade debts to the factor under a factoring agreement may transfer the same debts to a third party by absolute assignment. Such an assignment would not be subject to registration (except in the case of an unincorporated business as described in 7.29–7.31). Although in most cases a factor's rights would prevail, particularly if his notice had been given to the debtors first, the factor must rely also on the good faith of his client.

Undertaking to co-operate in recovery proceedings

8.6   Where the debts vest in the factor by an equitable assignment and it is necessary for him to take legal proceedings for recovery it may be necessary for him to join the client or to use his name (see 11.14–11.16). A further undertaking required from the client is that he will co-operate with the factor in recovery procedures, whether through the courts or otherwise. Furthermore, in the case of invoice discounting, undisclosed factoring, agency factoring or bulk factoring, the factor requires the client to undertake to act promptly and efficiently in the collection of debts; the client, having sold the debts to the factor, is collecting them on his behalf.

Warranties in connection with variations of sale contracts

8.7   Having sold and delivered goods in accordance with a contract of sale, correctly invoiced them and sold the resultant debt to the factor, the client may seek to vary the contract of sale. This might occur if the debtor asked the client to take some goods back and the client was disposed to agree. If this occurred on a large scale with a number of debtors, the factor might be put in a position where he would be unable to collect from the debtors all that he had paid on account of the purchase price of debts sold to him. In their arrangements with their clients factors recognise that credit notes must be issued. In every business errors occur and to a limited extent the wrong goods or faulty goods may be delivered or invoices be incorrect. However, the conscious decision to vary a contract should not be made by a client without the consent of the factor, once the debt arising out of the contract has vested in the factor. The factor will expect an undertaking from his client not to vary or cancel any contract in such circumstances.

Credit notes

8.8   Some factors require that no credit note should be issued to a debtor without their consent; the client is required to send the original credit note to the factor who will then approve it and send it on to the debtor or reject it. A factor may also require, in combination with such an arrangement, that notices of the assignment of debts sold to him include an admonition by which the factor seeks to exempt himself from responsibility for any credit note not approved by him. However, in practice many factors consider that such arrangements are unnecessary except in relation to a very few clients in rare circumstances. It seems administratively cumbersome to deal with all clients on this basis for the sake of protection in a few cases. Furthermore, the admonition on the invoice may be of little effect because the true rights of the debtor in his relations with the factor depend on the facts of the case as described in Chapter 11 ('Collection from the Debtor and the Debtor's Countervailing Rights'). The credit note is not conclusive evidence of these facts. In order to protect himself in those rare cases in which experience of his client's business has shown that it is necessary, most factors would make provision for such arrangements for the approval of credit notes by him to come into operation only on notice being given by him to the client. However, as indicated above, such a provision may be of little effect except as a sanction to dissuade the client from breaching his undertaking not to vary or cancel any contract with his debtors.

Reduction in value of debts

8.9   The reduction or extinguishing of the value of a debt sold by a client to a factor can occur otherwise than as described above, i.e.

(*a*) by a mistake in the despatch of goods or the provision of services; or

(*b*) by a change in the amount by a conscious act by the client.

It may be caused by an established agreement between the client and the debtor for the giving of discounts or allowances by the client based on the value of goods taken by the debtor during a stated period. The credit note issued for such a quantity discount, although a small percentage of total sales, may be large in relation to the debt outstanding at the time of its issue. The client will be obliged to disclose such a potential detraction from the value of the debts. It may well, then, be necessary for an extra retention to be held by the factor to provide for this.

Disputes and counterclaims

8.10   The reduction in the debt value may also be caused by a serious dispute or disagreement between the client and the debtor relating to the quality or quantity of the goods sold, the performance of the service, the amount invoiced or whether or not there is a set-off available to the debtor relating to some other account. The factor will expect an undertaking from the client in the factoring agreement:

(*a*) to notify him promptly of any dispute; and

(*b*) to dispose of the matter in an efficient and prompt manner; and

(*c*) to repay (normally by deduction from the next payment by the factor to the client) any prepayment made in respect of the debt in question; and

(*d*) if the dispute is not resolved in a reasonable period (say two months) to repurchase the debt.

Notification of disputes by client

8.11   It is apparent that many disputes will be notified to the factor by the debtors, often by a laconic note on a debtor statement returned to the factor, before the client is aware of any difficulty. However, in some cases debtors appear to be reluctant to communicate such matters to the factor, who may be unaware of the problem for a few weeks until his collection procedures start to bite. It is essential that the factor should be aware of such disputes at an early stage so that:

(*a*) he may get an early indication if the quality of his client's products or administration is deteriorating; and

(*b*) he may avoid a situation arising in which the items to be repurchased by the client mount up beyond the point where they can be absorbed by the aggregate retention on current account.

If, when aggregated with other items to be recoursed, the disputed debts exceed such retention the client will probably be unable to repurchase all the debts to be recoursed; in a normal arrangement for factoring the client will have no cash flow from sales other than from the factor, and the factor will not be obliged to make further payments in such a situation. Thus, failure to notify such disputes and difficulties is regarded by factors as a serious breach of the factoring agreement.

Reassignment of disputed debts to client

8.12 The right to have the disputed debt repurchased by the client, to reassign it and to give instructions to the debtor to pay any amount payable in respect of it to the client should be exercised by a factor only *in extremis*. The former widespread practice of factors in exercising this right as soon as possible has brought reluctance on the part of important purchasers of goods and services to be supplied by the factored clients. From the debtor's point of view he would be faced with an administrative nightmare. Following instructions at the outset of factoring to pay all debts arising from the client's supplies to the factor the debtor would receive periodic instructions that individual amounts on the account were to be paid to the client. The factor should exercise this right only when the position has been reached that the debt should be written out of the sales ledger and transferred to a suspense account. He can protect himself by providing that a disputed debt, though previously approved, becomes unapproved and ineligible for prepayment. In the event that a prepayment has already been made in respect of a debt subsequently disputed, the prepayment may be recovered by an additional retention against further amounts payable for debts purchased thereafter.

8.13 It is sometimes suggested that factors rely on groundless allegations from debtors to evade credit risks; the factor, it is said, may regard such allegations as disputes and exercise either the right of recourse or the provision that a disputed debt shall become unapproved. This is a difficult grey area. There is no doubt that a factor needs protection against inability to recover debts not accepted as valid by the debtor. On the other hand, the client may consider that he is being unfairly prejudiced by a specious query on the part of the debtor. It seems that the fairest method of dealing with such occasional difficulties is to take legal proceedings against the debtor in the name of the client and for the factor to agree to remain on risk if judgment is obtained in the absence of a valid defence. In the event of a liquidation or bankruptcy of the debtor before such proceedings are completed, the admission of proof of debt by the liquidator or trustee might be accepted as conclusive. If the debtor raises a defence to the action the costs should be borne by the client.

Perfecting the factor's title and powers of attorney

Undertaking by client to execute necessary documents

8.14   The reasons for the vesting of debts in equity only were described in Chapter 7. It was concluded there that for most practical purposes a legal assignment of debts purchased was unnecessary save procedurally for debt collection. However, it is important that the factor should have the right to have his title to the debts purchased perfected in this way so that he may take proceedings against any debtor in his own name alone and without the possible need to join his client. Furthermore, it is sometimes considered advisable to have *legal* assignments of debts, which were previously assigned equitably, in order to defeat claims by third parties, such as those who have supplied the client on the basis of reservation of title (see 16.2–16.9). The execution of assignations to perfect the factor's title may be considered advisable, for instance, where a Scottish client is likely to become insolvent so that the factor may notify both English and Scottish debtors of an assignation or assignment; a notification of the trust arrangements (described in 7.34) would, it is believed, only detract from prompt collection as it would tend to send debtors to consultation with lawyers. The factoring agreement, for these reasons, normally contains an undertaking by the client to execute such documents as may be necessary to perfect the factor's title to the debts purchased. Such provisions normally stipulate that any such assignment should be at the expense of the client (except in the case of non-recourse factoring where it relates to the recovery of an approved account).

Factor to have power of attorney

8.15   It may be necessary for the factor to act quickly without having to call upon his client to deal with these formalities. In the case of an insolvent client, an officer with authority to sign may not be available nor may the administrator wish to co-operate. Therefore, it is normal, either within the factoring agreement itself or by a separate document, for the factor and the directors and other officers of the factor to be appointed jointly and severally to be the attorney or attorneys of the client for the purpose of executing any such document. In this way the factor may effect a legal assignment or assignation in his own office and give notice or intimation to the debtor without delay. Such powers normally include the authority:

(*a*)   to institute or defend proceedings in the client's name; and

(*b*)   to complete and endorse negotiable instruments in the name of the client where such instruments relate to factored debts.

8.16   The latter authority is necessary because many debtors, even after notice of the assignment and repeated reminders from the factor, continue to make cheques payable to the client even when they send them to the factor. In the absence of such an authority the factor would have to send the cheques to the client for endorsement and return. Such a delay would increase the credit risks and the finance charges payable by the client. In fact some factors have streamlined this arrangement even further by making arrangements with their bankers to accept for their accounts cheques made payable to their clients without endorsement. This is done on the basis of an undertaking by the factor that:

(*a*) any such cheque is the factor's property and is in settlement of a debt that vests in him by virtue of a factoring agreement; and

(*b*) the factor will indemnify the bank in respect of any claim or loss occasioned by this arrangement.

Alternatively, arrangements may be made for the client to authorise the bank to accept for the credit of the factor's account cheques made payable to the client. However, as a back-up provision, the power of attorney including the right to endorse, is normally considered a necessary safeguard even where such procedure is employed.

8.17   Any such power of attorney should be stated to be **irrevocable**. Where an irrevocable power of attorney is given to secure a proprietary interest the power is not to be revoked:

(*a*) by the donor unilaterally without the consent of the donee; or

(*b*) by the death or, in the case of an incorporated donee, by its winding-up or dissolution.

[*Powers of Attorney Act 1971, s 4*].

Thus, with an irrevocable power of attorney in the factoring agreement the factor may continue to perfect his title to debts, already vested in him, and to negotiable instruments after the bankruptcy, liquidation of or the appointment of a receiver to his client.

Creation of trusts by clients in respect of debts sold

8.18   Paragraphs 7.33 to 7.39 dealt with the arrangements in Scotland whereby, in the absence of a formal assignation, the client held any debt sold to the factor in trust for the factor. Similar provisions are sometimes made in factoring agreements for English and Welsh clients to catch the debts that for some technical reason may fail to vest in the client equitably. The most usual reason put forward for such a provision is the not uncommon practice of local authorities, government departments and nationalised undertakings by which, in their purchase contracts, their suppliers are prohibited from assigning any amount payable which arises from such a contract. There is some uncertainty whether an assignment, valid between assignor and assignee, can be created in contravention of such a contract term prohibiting it. This difficult question is more fully analysed in Chapter 13.

8.19   Such a trust provision in a factoring agreement (other than for a Scottish client) is at present unusual and has probably never been tested. However, a provision which is invariably included in all factoring agreements is that by which any payment received by a client from a debtor in respect of a debt vested in the factor is to be held in trust for the factor. The factoring agreement usually provides that any such remittance received by the client is to be handed on to the factor immediately upon receipt in its original form and to be held in trust in the meantime. The efficacy of such a provision has been confirmed in case law. (*International Factors Limited v Rodriguez [1979]* 1 AER 17, and see 8.22 below.) The importance of providing for a trust on these lines is evidenced by:

(*a*) the relatively large number of debtors who continue to make payment by cheques payable to and sent to the clients; and

(*b*) the fact that in the case of invoice discounting or undisclosed factoring it is necessary for the client to make all collections on behalf of the factor.

Recovery of funds paid by debtor to client

8.20   Once a debt has been assigned to a factor and notice has been given to the debtor, the latter is obliged to pay the factor. Payment to the client will not discharge the debtor's obligations in respect of the indebtedness and the factor is entitled to recover the debt direct from the debtor by a second payment. This is so whether the assignment is legal or equitable. In the case of a legal assignment the statute makes this clear. [*Law of Property Act 1925, s 136*]. In the case of an equitable assignment 'all that is necessary is that the debtor should be given to understand that the debt has been made over by the creditor to some third person. If the debtor ignores such a notice he does so at his peril'. (*Wm. Brandts Sons & Co v Dunlop Rubber Co Ltd [1905]* AC 454).

8.21   The factor will have no need to demand the second payment from the debtor if he can obtain the remittance from his client in accordance with provisions described in 8.19 above or a payment from the client in lieu of it. In general a factor will be reluctant to rely on his right to the second payment because, where the first payment was made by an oversight, the debtor may react unfavourably and decline to purchase from factored suppliers in the future. This will be so even where the factor may have good commercial reasons, as well as the legal right, to rely on this right; an example might be when he has warned the debtor repeatedly not to pay to the client. In view of this reluctance, even if the client has not complied with trust provisions and has taken a payment from the debtor and mingled it with his own funds or paid it into an overdrawn account, the factor will make every effort to recover from the client. While the arrangement for factoring continues, the factor may well be able to deduct the amount of the payment from his subsequent payments to the client. It is usual for any factoring agreement to provide for the set-off of amounts due to the factor from the client, on any account, against amounts payable by the factor to the client. Furthermore, in the absence of such a provision equitable set-off should be available to the factor and, in liquidation or bankruptcy, statutory set-off. [*Bankruptcy Act 1914, s 31; Companies Act 1948, s 317*]. In the event of the insolvency of the client the trust provisions would be effective in favour of the factor. However, if, in insolvency, there are no amounts payable by the factor to the client available for set-off and the payment from the debtor has lost its identity (e.g. because it has been paid into an overdrawn account) so that the trust provisions no longer apply, then the factor will not be able to recover from the client save to the extent of his proof as an unsecured creditor. (See R M Goode, 'Some Aspects of Factoring Law', J B L 1982 September, at p 410.)

8.22   A factor was successful in one such case in recovering from a solvent director of a client company in liquidation despite the absence of a personal guarantee or indemnity. In that case the director caused the client company to pay into that company's bank account a cheque, made payable by a debtor to the client company and sent to it, in respect of a debt which had been sold to the factor. The factoring agreement contained a trust provision on the lines of that described above which was known to the director. The director was held to be liable to the factor in tort. It was no defence that the director had acted on behalf of the company nor that the factor could avoid a loss by obtaining a second payment from the debtor. (*International Factors Limited v Rodriguez* [*1979*] *1 AER 17*).

8.23   When a client has received a payment from a debtor in respect of an assigned debt and, contrary to any trust provisions in the factoring agreement, paid the proceeds into his own bank account it may in some circumstances be possible for the factor to recover from the bank. If the banker was fully aware by reason of actual notice (as in most circumstances he would be) that his customer (the factor's client) was obliged to or had in fact sold every trade debt to the factor, he might be liable to the factor for the proceeds either:

(*a*) as a constructive trustee; or

(*b*) on a common law claim for money had and received.

It is not clear in such circumstances if the banker would be able to rely solely on the protection of Section 4 of the Cheques Act 1957, which gives the banker protection in relation to the collection for a customer of a cheque to which the customer's title is defective. (R M Goode, *op cit*, p 412).

Approved and unapproved debts

8.24   In recourse factoring, bulk factoring or invoice discounting an 'approved debt' is a debt which is eligible for the prepayments of a percentage of its purchase price (see 2.4). Some factors refer to such debts as 'eligible' to differentiate them from debts that are approved for credit. In all forms of factoring in which the service of protection against bad debts is included (e.g. the full service, maturity factoring or undisclosed factoring) then an approved debt is a debt which is not liable to be recoursed purely because the debtor is unable to pay owing to insolvency. For either purpose the approval can be given:

(*a*)   by specifying a permitted limit for each debtor within which the aggregate indebtedness in respect of that debtor is approved; or

(*b*)   by giving approvals of debts arising from specific orders received by the client from his customers; or

(*c*)   by specifying a limit of deliveries of goods in each month that will qualify for approval; or

(*d*)   by a combination of (*b*) and (*c*), or of all three methods.

Whichever method is used it must be spelled out clearly in the factoring agreement so that the client is aware of the precise extent to which he is protected or may be financed depending on the type of agreement. Many factors, in addition to notifying their clients of the limits approved from time to time, send periodic reports showing the indebtedness of each debtor and the extent to which it is approved. The agreement must also provide for the position on reduction or cancellation of a limit. In this respect it is usual for the client to be held covered within the limits for any deliveries made up to the time of notification of such reduction or cancellation.

8.25   In the case of limits of deliveries for each month, any amount delivered in excess of a monthly limit may remain unapproved and with recourse notwithstanding payments against earlier amounts. On the other hand in the case of a limit of outstanding indebtedness, a payment against the account may serve to reduce *pro tanto*, or to extinguish, an excess. In either case it is usual to provide that on cancellation of the limit (usually on account of adverse credit information or difficulty in obtaining payment) any unapproved amount will remain so and any payment will be allocated in priority to the approved part, notwithstanding any contrary appropriation by the debtor.

8.26   It is sometimes provided that on notification of a dispute or cross-claim by a debtor, the debt shall become subject to recourse even if it has previously been approved. The rationale for this provision is that the dispute may drag on for some time and increase the credit risk to the factor (see also 8.13 above). Such a disputed debt would in any event be subject to recourse. The provision will enable the factor to retain the debt and avoid annoyance to the customer by its transfer back and forth. At the same time the factor will be protected.

Recourse: the right to be repaid by the client for debts purchased

8.27   The provisions for recourse to the client are usually arranged by one or other of the following methods:

(*a*)   by specifying that the debts subject to recourse according to the agreement are guaranteed by the client as to payment on due date (or some later date) or any earlier notification of a dispute; or

(*b*)   by specifying that those debts are to be repurchased by the client on such dates.

Factoring agreements necessarily provide *which debts* are subject to recourse. In the case of recourse factoring, invoice discounting or bulk factoring it will be all of them (see Chapter 3). In the case of any form of factoring that provides credit protection, it will be those that are not approved or are subject to the client's breach of warranty. In all cases it should normally be provided, in one way or another, that the factor shall not be responsible for settlement discounts wrongly deducted. It could be postulated that it is not necessary to provide for recourse for such items because, if the deduction is not accepted by the client, then it amounts to a dispute. However, in many cases the debtor merely fails to pay what is a relatively small sum and it might be difficult in the absence of a communication from him to allege to the client that there is a 'dispute'. A factor should not accept responsibility for settlement discounts, whether allowable or not, in view of the small margins available from the charges levied (see Chapter 9).

Transfer of ancillary rights

8.28   With the transfer of ownership of any debt there should also be transferred to the factor all the client's other rights in relation to that debt. There should be a specific provision to this effect on the factoring agreement. Such ancillary rights include:

(*a*)   the benefit of any third party guarantees (e.g. from the debtor's parent company or directors); and

(*b*)   the benefit of any credit insurance policy (see 3.18–3.21); and

(*c*)   the right to receive returned goods; and

(*d*)   all other rights under the contract which gave rise to the debt.

8.29   In an agreement which has not terminated the right to receive returned goods will be waived. The factor does not wish to be burdened with such goods; he is able to charge the deduction from the value of the assigned debt, normally represented by a credit note, from the retention or his next payment to the client. However, in a situation of impending insolvency it may be important to him to seize and sell such goods. This may be the case where a client has failed and the volume of returned goods has exceeded the factor's retention, so that the unrecovered payments made to the client (the funds in use) exceed the payable outstanding debts vesting in the factor. It is normally provided in the agreement that such goods should be stored separately and marked with the factor's name. In a deteriorating situation the factor would withdraw his waiver of this provision and arrange for a member of his staff to visit the client's premises and monitor the control of such goods.

Provision for proof of delivery of goods by client

8.30   A factor accepts and pays against evidence of the existence of debts produced **solely by the seller** (his client), unlike a discounter of bills of exchange or a block discounter of instalment credit agreements. The bill discounter has the acceptor's signature; the block discounter that of the debtor or hirer. It is for this reason that a factor keeps a substantial retention even in respect of debts which he has approved for credit and in respect of which the risk of a bad debt cannot be recoursed. It is the risk of failure of the *customer* to accept the goods or invoice that renders the retention necessary. In view of such retentions, factors may normally dispense with the need for independent verification of the existence of the debt and its value as accepted by the debtor. Indeed, in order to provide a good service to a client who is in need of the finance generated by the arrangement, factors normally accept responsibility for debts assigned to them, both as regards the credit risk and for prepayments, as soon as goods have been despatched. Exceptions are sometimes made in the case of goods originating overseas sold by a UK client to a UK debtor in circumstances in which the goods are to be despatched direct from overseas to the debtor. In such a case the factor may accept the offer or notification only upon the goods being placed in transit to the debtor in the UK. The indeterminate period of shipment from overseas may be unacceptable as increasing the credit risk and, possibly more importantly, the proportion of debts vesting in the factor representing goods which the debtor has not had an opportunity to inspect. However, in any case the factor is relying to a large extent on his client's competence and integrity. The size of his retentions will reflect this and the natural percentage of rejection experienced in the trade. As an ultimate precaution the factoring agreement will provide for the factor to be able to stipulate the submission of proof of delivery, or even of acceptance of the goods or service, in respect of a particular debt or generally. Such a provision will be brought into effect by the factor normally only in the event of threatened insolvency of the client or a severe loss of confidence by the factor; for instance it may be brought into effect if there has been a persistent record of invoicing before despatch or other incompetence in the despatch of goods or the raising of invoices by the client. The coming into effect of such a provision would normally require the holding back by the client of copy invoices until a receipt for the goods (or in the case of services, for example, a signed time sheet) can be obtained. It has the effect, therefore, of severely slowing down the client's receipt of prepayments from the factor.

Inspection of client's records and accounts

8.31 It is usual for any factoring agreement to include provisions whereby:

(*a*) the client is obliged to submit to the factor copies of his annual accounts and other financial statements produced; and

(*b*) the factor is allowed to inspect the accounting records, together with supporting documents, of the client at the client's premises.

The provision for the submission of accounts in some cases may extend to monthly or quarterly management accounts, and to require their production if they are not otherwise produced. By monitoring the client's progress with these submissions, the factor may not only be in a position to safeguard the security of his unrecovered prepayments but also to advise his client as to the beneficial use of the finance and services provided. The provision for the inspection of records and documents sometimes includes only such records and documents as relate to the debts sold or to be sold to the factor. They would include copy invoices, orders, proof of delivery, remittance advices and correspondence with debtors. However, some factors require the right to inspect any of the books, accounts, records and correspondence that they may in their discretion require to see. The reasons for such inspection are described later in 10.18.

PART II: FACTOR'S RIGHTS ON BREACH, AND TERMINATION
OF THE AGREEMENT

Factor's rights on breach of warranty by the client

8.32 The effect of a breach of any of the foregoing warranties by the client will in many cases mean the inability of the factor to recover all the debts assigned to him, or some or one of them. The detraction from the factor's rights to recover may affect **all** the debts if, for example, the breach of warranty relates to a prior encumbrance on the debts unknown to the factor. On the other hand, it may affect only one or some of the debts if the breach of warranty relates to the delivery of goods not in accordance with a valid contract of sale. In any case of such inability to recover in full, the factor must be able to recover from the client.

8.33 The normal provision in the factoring agreement is for such debts to be subject to recourse (as described in 8.27 above) either specifically or by the bringing into effect of a guarantee by the client or by stipulating that such debts will rank as unapproved. The client will in most cases have little if any cash flow from his transactions in the normal course of business other than through the factor; whether on a facultative or whole turnover basis, the arrangement normally extends to virtually all the client's sales. The recourse, therefore, cannot normally be effected by payment to the factor by the client. The factor must have the right in his agreement to set off any recourse against amounts payable to the client in respect of the purchase price of any debts sold to him. This set-off is normally effected, in the case of maturity factoring, against the purchase price of the particular debt which is the subject of the recourse; payment of the purchase price will not be due until maturity. Where any amounts have been paid on account of the purchase price of the debt to be recoursed, then the set-off must be effected against the unpaid portion of the purchase price of other debts vesting in the factor – the factor's retention.

8.34   In some cases the level of the retention (normally between 15% and 30%) may not be sufficient to absorb all the recourse. The factor must for this reason retain the right, in the event of material or persistent breaches of the agreement, to withhold prepayments or even all payments to the client. Factors normally monitor closely the level of potential recourse by watching the level of disputes, the issue of credit notes and of deductions by debtors for discounts; and it is quite usual for the factor to have the right to adjust the retention to provide for material increases in the level of recourse. In the case of recourse factoring, bulk factoring or any other form in which prepayments are made on the basis of a percentage of total debts, as opposed to a percentage of approved only, then the factor must also watch carefully the level of potential recourse arising from debtors which are poor credit risks. Where prepayments are made in respect of approved debts only, the retention of the full amounts of unapproved debts will provide adequate cover for recourse for such poor risks.

8.35   In a typical factoring agreement it is also provided that, in the event of serious breaches of warranty, the factor may terminate the agreement immediately by notice and make no further payments until he has recovered all the funds he has laid out by way of prepayment. However, in the event that the level of recourse and potential recourse exceeds the retention, such a course will rarely be helpful to the factor; as a result of the termination, there will vest in him no further debts the purchase price of which might have been available for set-off. In most cases it will be considered advisable to keep the agreement in effect and to persuade the client to improve his administration and remedy his persistent breaches. (Termination of the agreement is considered in 8.40 below.)

Collateral security in the case of client company

Personal guarantees

8.36   In many cases a factor, at the outset of a factoring arrangement with a *limited company*, may take some form of collateral security to protect him in the event of recourse exceeding his retention. Such protection will be necessary when a client becomes insolvent and the business ceases to operate. In such a case there will be no further amounts payable by the factor to the client against which to set off the excess recourse; no further debts will be created. The normal form of collateral security takes the form of personal guarantees and indemnities from directors or shareholders of corporate clients. Such personal backing to the obligations of the client company is very often given in case of small companies which are managed by their shareholders. The rationale for such a requirement by the factor in a full factoring arrangement and accepted by most businessmen is that the factor, in most cases, will need to rely on such a guarantee and indemnity only if the client company breaches the warranties given to such an extent that recourse exceeds the factor's retention. This is particularly the case where prepayments are to be made in respect of approved debts only. The avoidance of such personal responsibility is in the hands of the management itself; in running the business efficiently the management should ensure that the right goods are sent to the right customers and correctly invoiced and that the resulting debts are not encumbered by third party rights or cross-claim by debtors, except as advised to the factor.

Restricted personal guarantees or indemnities

8.37 A full personal guarantee and indemnity given for such purposes would normally secure for the factor full recovery of prepayments made by him to the client to the extent that they were not recoverable for any reason from the debtors or by set-off against the retention. Although it would probably not be contemplated by the parties at the time of execution, the surety would extend to cases in which the factor is unable to recover by reason of a failure to have the debts vested in him owing to a defect in the factoring agreement itself. It seems reasonable that the management of the client should not be responsible for such a contingency and the professional adviser to the prospective client might well wish to have such eventuality specifically excluded from the document.

8.38 In the case of recourse factoring, bulk factoring or invoice discounting the management of the client company may be more reluctant to give such guarantees and indemnities. The excess recourse might arise from the insolvency of a debtor; and this may well be not only beyond the control of the management but also beyond their expectations. Factors normally consider themselves experts in the field of the assessment of trade credit; it would, therefore, be reasonable to expect the factor to be responsible for ensuring that his retention is sufficient to cover potential recourse for such bad debts. This reluctance to give personal backing in such a case may be overcome by restricting the guarantee and indemnity to losses occasioned by breach of warranty by the client company. Such a restricted form of personal undertaking would not apply to losses suffered by the factor by reason of insolvency of any debtor. It is in some cases arranged that the undertaking given by an individual member of the client company's management should relate only to functions over which he has control. For example, the financial director may give an undertaking restricted to the raising of invoices and exclude from it disputes or rejections by debtors arising from the quality of the goods delivered.

Charges on other assets

8.39   Another form of collateral security sometimes taken from corporate clients is in the form of a charge on other assets to secure the obligations of the client and recourse. Such charges are normally in the form of floating charges over the residual assets available after fixed charges on specific assets. If such specific assets are not already charged to secure other forms of finance the client may require to keep them free for this purpose. Furthermore, the main reason for the requirement for this form of collateral security is to enable the factor to appoint a receiver and manager to carry on the business and deal with disputes, rectification of defective products and other warranty claims by debtors relating to the goods supplied (see also 22.9–22.12). In taking this form of security the factor must bear in mind that it may be difficult to crystallise the charge until the level of recourse has in fact exceeded his retention so that he has become a creditor of the client. It certainly seems unlikely that the appointment of a receiver would be justified when the factor's concern would relate only to the level of potential recourse; and the actual level of recourse may be apparent only at a late stage in the insolvency of the client when the business had already ceased. Furthermore, a floating charge created within 12 months prior to the winding-up of a company is invalid save to the extent of cash paid to the company in consideration for and subsequent to the charge's creation, unless it can be proved that the company was solvent immediately after the creation of the charge. [*Companies Act 1948, s 322*]. (See also 'Tolley's Liquidation Manual', paragraphs 11.12–11.16.) It is doubtful if the payments against the purchase price of debts sold to the factor would qualify for this purpose. Therefore, the validity of such a charge would be in doubt for 12 months.

Termination of the agreement

Protection of the factor

8.40   Termination of a factoring agreement, in normal circumstances, may be effected by either party giving notice of an agreed period to the other. In the event of such notice being given the factoring agreement ceases on the expiry of the notice. In the case of a facultative agreement (see 7.18) no further offers are made after expiry; and no debts coming into existence after expiry of a whole turnover agreement vest in the factor. It is normal, however, to provide that the rights and obligations of the parties in relation to debts vesting in the factor at the termination date remain in full force and effect unaltered save, in the case of factoring with a financial facility, in one important respect. A factor would be reluctant to continue making payments of the balance of the purchase price of debts to the full extent provided for in the agreement after termination until they have recovered all their funds laid out by way of prepayments. He would also be reluctant to continue prepayments to the normal extent after notice. The level of retention has been fixed to provide for an expected level of recourse and, as the total of debts vested in the factor declines after termination (collections not being counterbalanced by new debts), the absolute value, though not the percentage, of retention declines. The level of potential recourse, however, does not decline in like proportion; for the debts liable to be recoursed are likely to be those that are slowest in collection. As a factoring executive once expressed it in an apt metaphor: 'it is the last of the food in the frying pan that sticks to the bottom of it'. It is sometimes stipulated, therefore, that after notice has been given no further prepayments (and in some cases payments of any sort) will be made until the factor has recovered all the funds he has provided by way of prepayments. If such a stipulation is combined with a long period of notice then the client may be placed in some difficulty if he wishes to cease factoring; he cannot refinance the debts by charging them until the agreement ceases and he cannot afford not to take prepayments until he has refinanced the debts.

8.41   Such provisions as described above have had the effect, in the past, of increasing the reluctance of professional advisors to recommend the use of a factor. It has frequently been alleged that it is easy enough to start a factoring arrangement but very difficult to terminate it when the client wishes to cease to use a factor. As a result most reputable factors will provide for prepayments and payments against the purchase price of debts to continue either on the normal agreed basis, or at least at a reasonable level, until the last debts have been collected or recoursed. Furthermore, many factors will be reluctant to bind a client, who wishes to terminate the agreement, longer than necessary. Often they will agree to forego the full period of notice provided that arrangements may be made by the client to repurchase the debts outstanding and refund to the factor all prepayments unrecovered. This may occur if the client can refinance by traditional means or transfer to another factor. It is normal for such releases to be agreed for such transfers and the leading factoring companies have made arrangements in order that such changes can be made with the minimum of aggravation to the client and no disruption of his business.

Change of mind by the client

8.42   It sometimes happens that a client changes his mind after having given notice of termination and wishes to continue. It seems that there is no problem in the revocation of notice *prior* to termination and a simple intimation to the factor of such revocation will keep the agreement alive. What is the position if the client changes his mind *after* the period of notice of termination has expired? It would seem then that the agreement has irrevocably terminated and that new agreements will be necessary.

Insolvency of client

8.43   Agreements also make provision for immediate termination on notice at the option of the factor in the event of bankruptcy, liquidation, receivership or material or persistent breach of the agreement by the client, or in other circumstances analogous to those in which a holder of a floating charge could effect crystallisation. It is often not considered advisable by the factor to terminate the agreement in such circumstances. If the business is continuing it may well be of help both to the business and the factor to continue the relationship. If the client has seriously or persistently breached the agreement he may be able to rectify matters (for example, by exchanging the right goods for faulty ones) and the factor may be in a position to adjust his retention to provide for the increased potential recourse. In a situation of insolvency the administrator may wish to continue the business for some time and adopt the contract; this aspect is dealt with more fully in Chapters 17 and 18. It is as well for the factor to provide in the agreement that, in the event of such immediate termination, the client must repay all previously made prepayments and that he will not be entitled to further payments on the maturity of debts. Alternatively, the agreement should provide for the immediate repurchase by the client of all outstanding debts (with the ownership remaining vested in the factor until the repurchase price has been paid). One or other of these provisions is important in the case of insolvency of the client when a guarantor is involved. The effect of either of these provisions may well be that the amount payable by the client to the factor will exceed the retention and the factor will thus become a creditor of the client. The factor may then make immediate demand on the guarantor and, if the guarantor is insolvent, prove in the estate at an early stage. The advantages of early proof are more fully dealt with in 18.16.

Chapter 9

The Factor's Charges and Accounting Procedures

9.1   This chapter considers how the factor accounts to his clients, pays for the debts purchased and calculates his charges. Typical arrangements for the following are explained:

— Administration or service charges (see 9.2–9.5 below);

— Other charges for special services (see 9.6–9.8 below);

— Finance charges (see 9.9–9.16 below);

— Accounting procedures (see 9.17–9.20 below);

— Time for payment of the purchase price of debts sold to the factor (see 9.21–9.23 below);

— Value added tax (see 9.24–9.25 below).

The administration charge

9.2   Almost invariably a factor provides for the payment to him of a fee by his client based on the total value of debts purchased. This fee is variously called a 'service charge', 'commission' or 'administration charge'; for the purposes of this chapter it will be referred to as the last named, the administration charge. The charge is levied either as a debit to the client's account with the factor and as a set-off against amounts payable to the client by the factor for the purchase price of debts sold to him or, more usually, as a deduction from the value of the debt (i.e. the amount payable by the debtor) in computing the purchase price. The administration charge is normally a small percentage, typically for the full service between 0.6% and 2.5%, of the gross value of each invoice representing a debt sold to the factor; such gross value normally includes value added tax without any deduction for settlement discounts.

9.3   The administration charge is to compensate the factor for the cost of his administering the sales ledger and collection functions and his acceptance of the credit risk. In the case of any form of factoring which includes protection against bad debts, the factor will bear the legal costs for proceedings to recover approved debts. In some invoice discounting or undisclosed factoring arrangements, the factor will absorb bank charges for the collection of customers' cheques and the premium payable for any insurance against the loss of accounting records. In the case of the full service these are the factor's responsibility in any case.

9.4   In addition, where finance is made available by way of prepayments, the administration charge is to some extent a commitment fee for the provision of funds. The rationale for the charging of a commitment fee is that the factor is making available to the client funds by way of prepayments on the client's demand without a formal overall limit. The availability of such funds is based entirely on the volume of the client's sales of acceptable goods to creditworthy customers. For this reason an administration charge will often be part of an arrangement for invoice discounting notwithstanding the absence of any substantial administration service or any relief from credit risks undertaken by the factor. In the case of invoice discounting, however, in many cases a monthly or annual charge of a specific sum may be levied instead of a percentage of the value of debts purchased. In some cases, there may be no administration charge at all; naturally, in those cases the finance charge (dealt with in 9.9–9.11 below) will be somewhat higher than in arrangements which include a charge based on the total value of debts sold. Similarly, in the case of bulk factoring in which the client is relieved of little, if any, of the administrative tasks, an administration charge is usually agreed and this should also be regarded by the client as a commitment fee for the provision of finance without formal limit.

9.5   The charge is usually levied on the gross value (including VAT) of each invoice notified to the factor or sent in with an offer and accepted by the factor and credit notes are rarely allowed as a deduction in computing the charge. In the case of any form of non-recourse factoring the factor is potentially on risk for the full amount of the invoice; if the client becomes insolvent before the issue of a credit note, that credit note may never be requested and issued even if it would have been justified had the business continued. In the case of all forms of factoring other than maturity factoring the factor has been liable to prepay, and may in fact have prepaid, on the basis of the invoice before a related credit note is issued. For these reasons the deduction of the value of credit notes, relating to returned or faulty goods or quantity discounts from the value of invoices, is not acceptable to the factor for the purpose of calculating these charges. However, there may be cases where a credit note is issued to correct an error and such a deduction may be justified. For example, an invoice for £1,000 may be raised in error as £10,000; the factor has purchased the debt of £1,000 and there never was a debt of a higher amount. In such a case, if the factor has not prepaid against the invoice, a refund of the administration charge on the excess would seem justified if the error was discovered promptly. The factor has never been, even potentially, on risk.

Other charges for services

9.6   The administration charge is to compensate the factor for providing the particular service offered. Therefore, if more is required from the factor additional charges for the extra service are sometimes stipulated. In particular many recourse factoring arrangements provide for recourse to be available to the factor a specific number of days after due date or after the end of the month in which the goods or services are invoiced. As a result, in some cases, where the client wishes the factor to continue to maintain a debt subject to recourse on his records, the agreement provides for a *refactoring charge* for each month during which the debt or any part of it is outstanding after the due date for recourse. It is also normal for additional charges to be made for sales analyses and other statistical information which may be produced as a by-product of the factor's computer based sales accounting. Charges are also sometimes made for the provision of additional copies of aged lists of debtors or other feedback of information where these might be required for a client's branches.

9.7   It has also been known for a non-recourse factor to charge a small fee for every application for a credit limit where the number of such applications is, or is likely to be, out of proportion to the sales volume of the client. However, such an arrangement would only be stipulated by a factor in extreme circumstances, because for a non-recourse factor the granting of credit limits is an accepted part of the service.

9.8   Normally, the main additional cost to the client is the requirement that he should bear all the costs and expenses, other than the factor's own administrative costs, relating to the collection of debts which are subject to recourse as regards the credit risk. In non-recourse arrangements these outside costs, mainly legal expenses, are borne by the factor in respect of approved debts and by the client on unapproved debts (see 8.24); where a debt is partly approved the costs are normally divided proportionately to the parties' interests in the debt. Naturally, in any recourse factoring, bulk factoring or invoice discounting arrangement, it is usual for all these costs to be for the client's account. This aspect is often not taken fully into account when a comparison of the cost of a recourse and a non-recourse arrangement is made by a prospective client or his adviser.

Finance charges: method of calculation

9.9   The purchase of a debt payable *in futuro* in consideration for immediate payment of all or part of the purchase price normally presupposes that the purchaser will be recompensed for the amount of finance provided by him for the period until recovery of the debt by a discount in the calculation of the purchase price. Such a discount would be the difference, or part of the difference, between the invoice value of the debt and the purchase price payable by the purchaser. The courts have distinguished discounts of this nature from the payment of interest. The discount is normally fixed and paid (in effect by the deduction in the calculation of the purchase price) in advance; interest accrues from day to day and is calculated and payable in arrears. (*Willingale v International Commercial Bank Ltd [1978] 1 AER 754; Chow Yoong Hong v Choong Fah Rubber Manufactory [1962] AC 209; and Lloyds & Scottish Finance Ltd v Cyril Lord Carpets Sales Ltd & Others (1979), an unreported judgment of the House of Lords*).

9.10   In factoring in the United Kingdom the calculation of the finance charge at the time of purchase of the debt, except in the case of very early providers of the service, has not been generally or widely adopted. Some factoring companies established in the early 1960's used this method of calculation taking their cue from the practice at that time in the United States and the practice of discounting bills of exchange. The method used was based on the calculation, at the start of a factoring contract, of the average period of credit taken by the client's debtors over the past one or two years. This period, which was referred to as a maturity period, was calculated for each batch of invoices submitted, either as an offer or a notification, by taking the average invoice date of the batch weighted by the amounts of the invoices. The discount for the batch, calculated for the maturity period, was deducted from the value of the batch for the purpose of crediting the client with the purchase price. The client was then allowed back interest at the same rate on a day to day basis for any undrawn part of the purchase price. The method has the advantage of certainty from the point of view of the client. It also creates an additional discipline on the factor to ensure that no extra latitude is given to the debtors and that the collections should be kept within the prescribed period. However, the method has been discarded and is not now generally used in the United Kingdom for the following reasons:

(*a*)   Whereas factors in the United States restricted their business to trades in which they were well experienced, covered a high proportion of the total sales of such trades and could to some extent dictate payment habits and trade usages, factors in the United Kingdom have been concerned with a wide range of trades and industries but with a very small proportion of each one. As a result it was not possible to determine with any accuracy future trends in debt turns merely by taking a past year or two.

(*b*)   The system allowed for no flexibility for the client to grant longer than normal terms in exceptional cases.

(*c*)   On the other hand the system did not allow for the shortening of the average if the client obtained business with large new customers who insisted on paying on short terms for substantial settlement discounts.

(*d*)   The desire of the client to allow extra indulgence to certain favoured customers in specific circumstances created difficulties.

(*e*)   Some clients became suspicious that the factors were pressing customers for payment with undue harshness in order to recover debts on average well within the maturity period and thus profit from the saving of their own finance charges.

As a result of these difficulties there were frequent negotiations for changes in the agreed maturity period. Such negotiations sometimes led to invidious differences of opinion between factor and client.

9.11   It is now generally considered that in the environment of British trade usages and habits of settling trade creditor's accounts it is not normally possible to make even a reasonably accurate forecast of the future movement of the maturity period. The factor does not need the extra discipline on his efforts to keep debt turns to a minimum because:

(*a*)   in the present competitive state of the market for factoring his reputation for efficiency in this sphere is of paramount importance; and

(*b*)   in the case of any non-recourse type of service the outstanding debts are at his risk; and

(*c*)   the factor wishes to invest his resources in as large a volume of factored sales as possible in order to obtain the maximum administration charges for any given amount of funds used.

Accordingly, the finance charge is now normally calculated on the day to day balances of unrecovered prepayments (or payments on a fixed maturity date), often referred to as the factor's 'funds in use', and charged at the end of each month. As has been mentioned earlier (see 2.7) the finance provided by the factor may be either:

(i)   by way of loan or advance to be set off against the purchase price when ultimately payable; *or*

(ii)   by way of a payment on account of the purchase price itself.

9.12   Whichever of the above methods (i) or (ii) is used the finance charge will normally be calculated on the same basis. The difference being that in the first case it will be referred to simply as interest and in the second as a 'discounting charge'. The latter is theoretically a discount deductible from the value of the debt in the calculation of the purchase price at the outset and, notwithstanding the provision in the factoring agreement to this effect, for simplicity it is normally calculated on the day to day basis referred to and charged at the end of each month.

9.13   There are variations in the method of arriving at the funds in use on a daily basis for the purpose of these calculations. The method used will depend on whether the ultimate date for payment of the purchase price is:

(*a*)   the collection date (the date when the debtor has paid the factor, or in the case of an approved debt in factoring without recourse, the date of the debtor's insolvency); or (*b*) the maturity date (the end of an agreed maturity period, as described above, after the invoice date – or, in some cases, after the date of purchase of the debt by the factor).

A typical method of recording the account of the client by the factor in each case is described in 9.17–9.23 below.

The memorandum account

9.14   For the purpose of calculating the finance charge (whether interest or discounting charges) a **memorandum account** will be maintained as follows:

(*a*) *Where payment is due on the collection date*:
The account, which may be referred to as 'discounting account' or 'funds in use', will be debited with payments to and charges to the client and repayments to debtors for credit balances, and credited with receipts from debtors. Broadly there should be recorded on it any entry that does not affect both a debtor account and the account with the client. The memorandum account should reflect, at any time, the difference between the total outstanding debtors (less any credit balances) relating to the particular client's business and unpaid balance of the aggregate purchase price of debts purchased as represented on the client's account with the factor. (See 'funds in use', Appendix VI.)

(*b*) *Where payment is due on a maturity date*:
The memorandum interest or discount account will comprise a combination of the daily balance shown on the three client accounts in the factor's books. An explanation of this system of accounting is set out in 9.21–9.23 below. The memorandum account, by a roundabout method, will represent the daily funds in use which is more simply provided for in the method described in (*a*) above.

Where payment of the purchase price is to be made ultimately on a maturity date it would naturally be possible to calculate the discount in advance, and provide for it in determining the purchase price of each debt. However, such a method would entail the crediting back to the client of interest, or a similar allowance, for the daily balance of the undrawn aggregate amount of the purchase price of debts sold to the factor and an adjustment for the effect of the average of payments by debtors received before or after the maturity date. Although the factoring agreement may provide for the finance charge, together with allowances and adjustments, to be calculated in this way, it is very often considered simpler to combine the calculations by merging the three items as described above in **memoranda accounts**.

'Value dating' of payments and collections

9.15   From the point of view of the client or his adviser, where calculations for finance charges are based broadly on amounts paid to the client and collections from debtors, care should be taken to find out in practice how the factor interprets the time of collection. It has not been uncommon for a factor to regard the despatch of a cheque to the client as the date from which the finance charge should be calculated. The rationale for this has been that if a cheque has been issued, particularly a cheque drawn on a town clearing branch, then it may be open to a client to obtain cleared funds on the same day. However, not all factors draw their cheques on City of London branches and few clients have bank accounts there. As a result of high interest rates and the additional burden placed on clients by having to pay finance charges for funds, for which their bankers have not yet given them credit, it is now not unusual for the factor to start his calculation of the finance charge, in respect of any cheque issued to the client, from the date on which the factor expects the cheque to be presented to his own bank. This, in present circumstances, is normally three working days after it has been despatched to the client by first class post. Naturally, if payments are to be made by automated transfer the finance charge must start to run from the date when the transfer is initiated; but unless the transfer is by Clearing House Automated Payments System (CHAPS) the charge will start to run before the client has the funds. Similarly, it is usual for the factor to allow a reasonable number of days for clearance of cheques received from debtors before applying them in a reduction of funds in use for these calculations. However, the prospective client or adviser should ensure that the average period is reasonable in the light of prevailing banking practices.

9.16 The question remains as to the factor's practice where the client's drawings from the factor lag behind the debtors' payments to the factor. Is a finance allowance to be made? Practices differ and the most usual are as follows:

(*a*) To make an allowance at rates approximating to rates for short term deposits with finance houses, calculated on a day to day basis on any negative balance of 'funds in use'.

(*b*) To calculate a similar allowance on any such negative balance but to allow it only as a set-off against future finance charges within an agreed period (e.g. three months). In such a case the allowance may well be at the same rate as the finance charge.

(*c*) Not to make any allowance but to pay ultimately strictly on the due date (i.e. maturity or collection date).

The rationale for the last practice is that it is not part of a factor's function to use his client's funds and that when his client has surplus funds he should place them with a deposit-taking institution. In such cases it is sometimes possible to make a special arrangement with the factor by which the client may take later payments in return for a specifically agreed allowance.

The client account: purchase price payable on collection

9.17 The normal method of accounting for payment of the purchase price on collection is the simplest form of client accounting by a factor both in conception and execution. A single account is maintained and rendered to the client at least once a month. It may be called 'the client balance account', 'the current account' or simply the 'client account', but in all cases it reflects all the transactions which affect the relationship between the factor and the client (see Appendix VI). The factor is buying debts for which he must pay subject to any countervailing rights so that, in essence, he is in no different position from that of a person buying goods from the client. The account represents mainly the credits for the purchase price of debts purchased by the factor (the invoice value less the factor's charges) and the debits for amounts paid by the factor to the client.

9.18   In view of the many and varied transactions between the parties other than the purchase of debts and payments there may be many other items debited to the account. The main items are:

(*a*) Payments made to or on behalf of the client.

(*b*) The amounts of credit notes issued by the client and notified to the factor.

(*c*) The full invoice value of debts which are the subject of recourse.

(*d*) Any items to be set off against amounts payable by the factor to the supplier (e.g. amounts owing for goods purchased by the client from another client of the factor).

(*e*) The amount of any settlement discount.

(*f*) The factor's charges. (Although these are usually expressed as a deduction to be made in arriving at the purchase price, for convenience the full amounts of the debts may be credited and the charges debited.)

The balance reflects at any time the amount payable at that time by the factor subject to his retention and the balance ultimately payable subject to further charges accrued and any recourse.

9.19   The advantages to the client of this method of payment and accounting are:

(*a*) simplicity;

(*b*) the immediate benefit of any improvement made by the factor in collections;

(*c*) the ability of the client to make special arrangements with customers for extended credit (with the factor's consent) without having to agree to an adjustment in the agreed maturity period;

(*d*) the immediate payment of the full purchase price (or unpaid balance of it) in respect of any approved debt in the event of the insolvency of the debtor before the end of the expected period of credit; and

(*e*) the immediate benefit of any change in the pattern of trade so that a higher proportion of sales are being made on shorter terms.

In this method of accounting, a sales ledger control or similar account showing the movements and total balances on debtor accounts is not usually supplied. However, frequent returns of invoices and credit notes processed, debtor payments received and deductions made are rendered by the factor to the client. In addition the factor will normally send an aged balance report at least once a month. In this way the client can keep in touch with the position on the debtor accounts and, if necessary, keep a memorandum debtor total account.

9.20   In order that he may know the availability of prepayment at any time it is usual for the client to apply to the factor for the figure either by telephone or telex. The current account balance is available to the client because his books will reflect the mirror image of his account in the client's records; but in order to know the availability, he will need to know the amount of the retention. He is able to determine it at every month end when he has the aged balance report and he can reconstruct it in between by using the reports of invoices and payments. However, the factor can normally determine the figure by on line access to his computer record, so that an application to him is the simpler way to ascertain the figure. In addition to the client account the factor will normally provide an account showing the entries arriving at the daily balance of funds in use so that the client will be able to check the finance charge made by the factor each month (see Appendix VI).

The client accounts: purchase price payable after a fixed maturity period

9.21   A typical system of accounting to the client for this method of payment of the purchase price comprises three accounts (see Appendix VII):

(1) *A sales ledger control account*:
This is strictly not a part of client accounting. The debts purchased vest in the factor and having been sold by the client they are not to be reflected in the client's accounting records. However, the account is of interest to the client so that he may be able to check on the efficiency of the factor in his collections and on the amounts of the finance charge levied on him. The account will be debited with the gross amount of invoices notified to or offered to and accepted by the factor, it will be credited with credit notes issued to debtors and notified to the factor and payments received from and discounts taken by the debtors. Any other entry on the debtor accounts will be reflected on this account, the balance of which represents the total balance of debtors outstanding on the factor's records, in respect of the business of the particular client less any credit balances which have emerged.

(2) *Debts purchased account*:
The gross value of each batch of invoices, when debited to the sales ledger control account, is credited to this account. When the end of the agreed maturity period in respect of any batch of invoices

notified or offered to the factor is reached the gross value of that batch is transferred to the client's current account (see (3) below) by debit to this account. The account, therefore, reflects the total value of debts purchased by the factor which have not matured whether such debts have been settled by the debtors or not.

(3) *The client current account*:
The value of debts purchased are credited to this account only when they have reached maturity. The account is debited with payments to the client, credit notes (which have been credited to the sales ledger control account) as soon as they have been notified and all the miscellaneous items debited to the client account under the payment on collection system (see 9.18(*a*) to (*f*) above). The balance on this account therefore represents the aggregate value of prepayments or advances before the maturity of debts purchased.

9.22   From the foregoing it will be apparent that:

(*a*) If the debtor control account balance exceeds the debts purchased account balance, then collections are being made on average after maturity;

(*b*) If the debtor control account balance is less than the debts purchased account balance, then collections are being made on average in advance of maturity.

Therefore, if at any time the resultant balance between these two accounts is added to (if (*a*) applies) or subtracted from (if (*b*) applies) any debit balance on the current account, the funds in use will be adjusted for the actual payment performance of the debtors. The result will be the same as the simple funds in use account of the other system (see 9.14 above). For the calculation of the finance charge therefore, all three accounts are combined.

For example:

		£
A	Client current account (prepayments outstanding)	20,000 DR
	Debtor control account (total unpaid debtors less Cr balances)	50,000 DR
	Debts purchased account (balance of unmatured debts)	45,000 CR
		£25,000

In this case the client has been paid £20,000 before maturity of the debts and is paying a finance charge of £5,000 for debts which have matured but have not been collected.

		£
B	Client current account	20,000 DR
	Debtor control account	40,000 DR
	Debts purchased account	45,000 CR
		£15,000

In this case total outstanding debts are less than those unmatured. On average they are being collected before maturity and the client is getting the benefit by a deduction in the calculation of the funds in use. It will be appreciated that if the current account is in credit, unless that credit is more than counterbalanced by a debit difference between the other two accounts, the funds in use will be negative.

9.23 The main advantage to the client of this system is that he is automatically entitled to the balance of the purchase price (or, if he has not been prepaid or received advances, the full purchase price) on a fixed date. However, in such arrangements the factor normally reserves the right to adjust the maturity period if payments are persistently later than the maturity on average over a long period. In most cases the client would be able to obtain a contrary adjustment if debtor payments were on average persistently in advance of maturity. Another benefit is that the client is usually in a position to assess the availability of funds, provided that (as is usual with such systems):

(*a*) the retention is a fixed percentage of all debts (i.e. not related to approvals); and

(*b*) the accounts are sent to him weekly.

Value added tax

9.24 Factoring agreements provide for the amount of any payment to be made by a customer to a supplier for goods and services, including the right to recover output value added tax relating to such goods or services to be transferred to the factor. The factor, in paying the purchase of a debt transferred to him, is in effect including in his payments to his client the amount of any such output tax. In factoring arrangements the invoice value and purchase price are, therefore, based on the gross invoiced amount including VAT.

9.25 The position as regards the factor's charges to his client has been as follows:

(1) value added tax at the standard rate has been applied to the administration or service charge as a charge for a taxable supply; and

(2) finance charges of the factor, interest or discounting charges, have been considered to be charges for exempt supplies.

The authorities take a view of the substance of factoring transactions, for the factor provides a service to his client by administering the sales ledger, collecting debts and taking responsibility for bad debt losses. In view of the fact that part of the factor's supplies, other than those of a factor providing maturity factoring only, are exempt, a factor is classified as partly exempt for the purposes of the regulations. (*Value Added Tax (General) Regulations 1980, SI 1980 No 1536, as amended by SIs 1983 Nos 295, 475; 1984 No 155*). As the right to recover input taxes is not available in respect of exempt supplies, the input tax is to be apportioned between the exempt and taxable supplies. The apportionment depends on the nature of the factor's business and, in particular, the proportion of his business which relates to the provision of finance (an exempt supply) as opposed to services. Some factors may benefit by Regulation 25 or Regulation 27 of the Value Added Tax (General) (Amendment) Regulations 1984 (*SI 1984 No 155*) whereby, in view of the pattern of their business, the exempt supply may be disregarded and they will recover all their input taxes against their taxable outputs. The tax applied to the administration or service charge is an input tax to the client and will be recoverable by him if his own supplies are taxable.

Chapter 10

The Factor's Assessment of a Prospective Client

10.1 It is usual for a factor, in giving consideration to the acceptance of a prospective client for the full service and the terms of the proposed arrangement, to make four distinct assessments:

(*a*) The risks arising from the service of protection against bad debts.

(*b*) The administrative burden to be borne by reason of the service element of the arrangement.

(*c*) The strength, profitability and prospects of the business of the prospective client and the use to which the factoring service will be put.

(*d*) The factor's security – the extent of the risk that the debts purchased may become irrecoverable otherwise than by reason of the insolvency of the debtors.

10.2 In order to make an assessment of all these features a factor should first make enquiries for basic credit information on the prospective client: this usually comprises the sight of audited accounts, a search at the Companies Registry (if a corporate body), a status report and, in particular in the case of a recently established business, enquiries regarding the previous business activities of the principals. In addition to these enquiries a full investigation of the activities of the business and its accounting records is usually made by members of the factor's staff. The investigation which is often referred to as a 'survey' is normally completed in a day by two people. The principal matters examined are described in the succeeding paragraphs.

The nature of the business

10.3 The ability of the factor to recover debts purchased depends very largely upon the product of the business, its acceptability by the customers and the usages and customs of the trade. The consideration of this aspect is important, not only as regards the factor's security, but also in relation to credit risks; the more attractive and important the product is to the customer, the nearer he will conform to the terms of payment. For example, a manufacturer will pay promptly for a special material which is not available elsewhere in order to keep continuity of supply. He may well delay payment of an individual item of printed advertising material which may be available next time through a number of other sources. In Chapter 5 a number of businesses were described which were likely to be unsuitable for factoring and the factor will need to consider each business individually in the light of the imagined attitude of the customers in the absence of the client to provide back up. No definite rules can be prescribed, because even within the same trade or industry the products vary considerably. It seems that the best guidelines are:

(i)   the nearer that a product is to being 'made, sold and forgotten', the better will be the factor's security; and

(ii)   the more competition there is in the trade or industry the greater will be the credit risks.

These are indeed very broad guidelines, for there are many exceptions. In particular in a very competitive industry the prospective client's product may be of such high quality that it is in demand by those of the highest standing. Naturally, the acceptability of the product and the type of business are germane to the prospects of success of the business.

The terms and conditions of sale

10.4   For his relationship with the debtors the factor must rely on the client's terms and conditions of sale. His right to recover the debts purchased is no better than provided for in the contractual relationship between the client and the debtors. The factor should examine carefully the provisions for payment, for the debtors' countervailing rights and for reservation of title where this is included. Where orders are taken by the prospective client for delivery of goods or the provision of services over a period of more than a month the question of a 'cut-off' clause (see Chapter 14) should be considered. The factor may have to require some changes in the standard terms before the start of factoring. The examination should also determine whether any quantity discounts, as described in 8.9, are given by the client. In some cases, in which the prospective client is selling to large and powerful customers, he may be obliged to sell on the basis of the customers' standard purchase contracts. In such a case the factor should examine the terms of the most important customers and in some cases may require the prospective client to seek waivers of certain provisions: for example, some set-off provisions wider than those arising in equity or by statute or prohibitions of the assignment of debts (see Chapter 13).

The financial position of the business

10.5   It is probable that before the survey the factor will already have examined audited accounts of the business for its last completed and previous two or three financial years (see 10.2 above). However, such accounts may not give an absolute indication of the up-to-date position and prospects of the business. There are some in the factoring industry who consider that a factor, in his consideration of a new client, should not be too concerned with this aspect; their view is that, if the factor's rights to collectable debts owing by creditworthy debtors are secure, the failure of the client will not be the cause of a loss. It is therefore sometimes considered that the detailed investigation of the viability of the business of a prospective client will cause them to miss a great deal of new business which will not be outweighed by the saving of the additional expense of a fast turnover of clients. The general view, however, is that:

(*a*)   the acceptance of businesses that are likely to fail increases the factor's expenses, by reason of the cost of setting up new sales ledgers and the recovery of the debts on old ones; and

(*b*)   such increases in costs may be reflected in the charges of the factor to all clients; and

(*c*)   such an attitude tends to lend credence to the allegations that a factor is a relatively expensive financier of last resort.

As a result most factors consider that an examination of the up-to-date financial position of the prospective client, his prospects, the viability of the business and the benefits which will accrue to it from the use of factoring is of the highest importance. For this purpose, apart from financial accounts, the examination will often include:

(i)   up-to-date management accounts; and

(ii)   an analysis of trade creditors by age; and

(iii)   the checking that amounts payable for PAYE, VAT and national insurance have been settled satisfactorily; and

(iv)   a consideration of cash flow forecasts.

Administration of sales records by client

Invoicing procedure

10.6   It is important for the factor to ensure that order/invoice cycle in the client's system is such that the invoices will represent only goods despatched in the United Kingdom to customers or services completed. It is also important for the factor to ensure that documents proving delivery or the completion of services, such as delivery notes or signed time sheets, will be readily available for him.

Sales ledger and source documents

10.7   An analysis of the ledger and invoices and credit notes over a period of one year should reveal the workload to be accepted by the factor. The following are normally extracted:

(*a*)   the average value of individual invoices issued;

(*b*)   the number of credit notes issued;

(*c*)   the proportion of credit notes issued by value to total gross sales;

(*d*)   the average number of remittances received each month and, in particular, the number that may be automatically appropriated to specific invoices;

(*e*)   the incidence of settlement discounts;

(*f*)   the number of active debtor accounts;

(*g*)   the number of new accounts opened or dormant accounts revived each month.

The percentage of credit notes, the incidence of discounts and the dispute ratio will also be most relevant to the factor's consideration of his security and the credit risk. Disputes and requests for credit notes very often serve to delay collection. For the purpose of determining the incidence of disputes and queries, customers' correspondence files should be scrutinised.

Assessment of credit risks

The quality and spread of debtors

10.8   Unless the number of debtors is unusually small, it is not normally possible or commercially acceptable to make a detailed investigation of all the debtors at the stage when a survey is conducted. To check the credit standing of several hundred debtors is expensive in staff time and in the cost of information. At this stage, therefore, the factor will obtain an indication of the general quality of the debtors by examining:

(*a*)   the quality of the largest 12 or 20 regular customers; and

(*b*)   the incidence of the placing of accounts for collection with a debt collection agency or solicitor; and

(*c*)   the average period of credit taken by the debtors (usually referred to by factors as the 'debt turn') over a period of at least one year and the comparison of this with the debt turn normally expected in the particular trade or industry.

The debt turn

10.9   The debt turn – the average period of credit taken by debtors – may also be an indication of acceptability or otherwise of the product. It may, however, be the result of the absence of good collection procedures by the prospective client – the very reason for his seeking the assistance of a factor. An allegation that a poor debt turn is the result of the lack of diligence should not be accepted by the factor at face value; a careful investigation may reveal some serious disputes, poor credit risks or even special arrangements such as consignment sales or long credit terms. The calculation of the debt turn may be carried out in a number of ways; but the most usual is to compare the average of month end totals of debts outstanding with the gross sales value:

$$\frac{AD \times 365}{S} = \text{Debt turn in days}$$

Where AD = average total debts at each month end over one year and S = gross sales value for the year.

The calculation can however, conceal distortions caused by the inclusion of:

(*a*) large disputed accounts;

(*b*) bad debts which have not been written off;

(*c*) accounts on which special terms have been agreed; or

(*d*) associated company current accounts.

If possible these distortions should be eliminated by excluding such accounts from the sales value and the totals of debts. The calculation may also be somewhat distorted by any delay in the issue of credit notes. In spite of the drawbacks of this method of calculation, it has the advantage of simplicity. It may not give a true absolute figure owing to the taking of the average of outstanding debts on the basis of end of month figures, as in many cases these are regularly the highest each month; if terms are monthly account, payments usually come in early in the second month after invoice date. It does, however, give a reasonable though crude indication of a trend and a comparison with others in the same type of business. By other methods the details are more difficult to extract and may also be distorted by special circumstances.

Encumbrances on the debts

10.10 A search of the Companies Registry in the case of a corporate prospective client will reveal any charge, that is subject to registration under Section 95 of the Companies Act 1948, unless it was created within 21 days prior to the search. However, as has been indicated in 8.5, there may be a number of encumbrances affecting book debts which would not be revealed on a search. *First*, as regards recent charges it is advisable for the factor to search again about four to six weeks after the start of factoring to see if a charge has been given just after the factoring agreement has been executed. It may then be a little late, but it is better that arrangements should then be made with the chargee for a waiver than some months later when the client may be relying more heavily on the finance provided.

Examination of statutory books

10.11 An examination of the register of charges and minute book at the company's registered office at the time of the survey should also be made. This may well reveal the existence of a recent charge or some other encumbrance, whether or not it is registerable. Enquiries should also be made regarding imports or other supplies on letter of credit terms for the possibility of provisions whereby proceeds of sale by the prospective client are to be held in trust for a bank or confirming house (see 16.11).

Suppliers' terms of business

10.12   A thorough examination of suppliers' terms of sale should reveal any rights of suppliers to the proceeds of the resale of their supplies by the prospective client (see 16.2–16.9). A comparison of the sales ledger with the purchase ledger may reveal the possible incidence of set-off available to debtors. Such encumbrances may be dealt with by waivers of their rights by the suppliers or the debtors concerned; but a high degree of incidence of such rights or availability of set-off may call for a constant monitoring of the business by the factor. In particular in some trades and industries sales to a concern's own suppliers may be endemic. In such a case many debtor accounts will need to be excluded, because the client cannot warrant that they are free from encumbrance. This and the degree of monitoring by the factor that is necessary may make the prospect unattractive.

10.13   Finally, an assessment should be made of the proportion of sales to government departments. The resulting debts are subject to possible set-off by the Crown not only for contractual debts owed by the concern to any department of the Crown but also to statutory indebtedness such as that for PAYE (see 11.44–11.47). Again unless a waiver of this right can be obtained, it may not, in the present state of the law, be possible safely to provide factoring with prepayments to a business which sells extensively to the government.

Special sales

10.14   The following debts are normally excluded from any factoring arrangement:

(*a*)   Debts owing by subsidiary, parent or fellow subsidiary companies or any business under common control with the client. It is not reasonable to expect a factor to relieve a client of the credit risk of his own associate and the provision of finance in respect of any such debt, in reality, provides no independent possibility of recovery.

(*b*)   Debts arising from consignment sales or sale or return transactions. If accepted at the delivery stage such a potential debt gives the factor no specific due date for recovery; and if the debt is to be transferred only when the goods have been accepted and a firm sale completed, monitoring of the arrangements by the factor is difficult.

(*c*)   Debts arising from sales to individuals. Factoring is not designed for the retail trade.

Invoices representing charges for moulds and tooling retained by the client for production purposes are sometimes excluded. They should certainly not be eligible for prepayments until there is evidence that production from their use is acceptable to the debtor. Moulds and tooling that have been paid for can also create difficulties in the collection of other invoices on the insolvency of the client if the administrator of the client's estate will not release them immediately upon request by the debtor. These difficulties may arise notwithstanding that, in insolvency, there is no set-off of a claim for the return of goods *in specie* against a claim for payment of money (see 'Williams and Muir Hunter on Bankruptcy', 19th Edition, p 190). Thus, the survey should reveal the extent of such special sales.

Special consideration of credit risks

10.15   Unlike a banker or other lender who seeks to reduce his risk to the minimum by taking security in addition to a thorough examination of the borrower's viability, a factor seeks the unsecured credit risks arising from trade sales. Like an insurance company, in respect of the credit protection service the factor can only find business where the risks exist; but he must ensure that the risks are reasonable and not unduly concentrated. He must also be sure that he is properly remunerated for taking the risks in that the credit protection element (CPE) in his administration charge is adequate. In accepting these risks in return for the receipt of a fraction of 1% of sales the factor expects the balance and pattern of the sales of the business to be such that the debtors run through the whole spectrum of quality, with the largest debtors being in the main well known companies of high credit-standing. For the factor will probably be expected to accept a number of smaller debtors whose credit-standing cannot easily be assessed; and the odds on failure of some of these smaller debtors may not be more than even money. If all the debtors are likely to be in the bottom end of the spectrum a proper assessment of the CPE may make the acceptance of the credit risk by the factor much too expensive for the prospective client. In such a case, where the gross profit margin of the business is likely to be high, it may be reasonable for the client to accept the credit risk himself. From the factor's point of view, provided that the retention were to be high enough to provide for the high level of potential recourse, it is probable that recourse factoring or invoice discounting might be provided.

10.16   As described in 10.8 above, some indication of the quality of the debts is available from a consideration, during the survey, of the largest debtors and an examination of the debt turn and of accounts put out of hand for collection. In addition, records of bad debts and their relationship to sales turnover should be obtained for at least three past years. If credit insurance has been used it must be noted that the accounts will show only the uninsured percentage written off. It is important that the records should also show the pattern of such losses. Many small losses may indicate that bad debts are endemic; a few larger losses may be due to special circumstances. Details should also be obtained of potential losses within the current outstanding debts and of accounts still in the hands of debt collectors or solicitors. Enquiry should be made as to whether credit insurance is or has been provided in the past and, if not, whether a proposal is being made as an alternative to factoring. The terms on which credit insurance has been provided or offered, if disclosed, will be helpful to the factor in his assessment of this element of the service. It should not be overlooked that the incidence of bad debts is also relevant to the administrative costs of the prospective factoring arrangement where the cost of legal proceedings on approved accounts is to be absorbed by the factor.

10.17   The foregoing matters are those usually examined by a factor where the full service is proposed. It may seem that for some of the variations of the service not all of these aspects require consideration. However, although there might be a differing emphasis for some of the variations it is considered that all aspects should be taken into account in relation to any form of the service. For example, it may be asked 'why consider the workload of the sales ledger where invoice discounting is proposed?'; in this case the answer is that the factor may have to take over administration of the sales ledger if the client fails to administer it efficiently. The credit risk is relevant to recourse factoring in considering the potential recourse element. In the case of maturity factoring encumbrances on the debts may hinder the provision of a good service and create a conflict in the collection of salvage after the factor has paid on maturity in respect of an uncollected debt.

10.18   In periodic visits to the client's place of business members of the factor's staff usually monitor the continuing efficiency of the client's administration – particularly in relation to the production of source documents and the continuing profitability of the business. The frequency of such visits and the items to which attention is paid depend upon the factor's assessment of the client from his experience of his own office. For example, this will depend to some extent on the incidence of disputes. Where the client continues to maintain the sales ledger, as in invoice discounting, such visits are made regularly by some factors and the items examined extend to the sales ledger and credit control (see 3.13). Note that a Checklist for the factor is provided in Appendix III.

Part C

The Relationship between the Factor and the Debtor

Chapter 11

Collection from the Debtor and the Debtor's Countervailing Rights

11.1 One of the principal functions of a factor is the collection of payments from debtors in the full service, maturity factoring and recourse factoring. In all forms of factoring considered in this book, as the ownership of the debts vests in the factor, it is his primary responsibility to collect them. However, in bulk factoring, agency factoring (in some forms) and all the forms in which notice to the debtor is waived, the factor allows the client to collect on his behalf. The procedures considered here are:

— The normal procedures of the factor's own staff (see 11.4–11.13 below);

— Legal remedies when these procedures fail (see 11.14–11.22 below);

— The debtor's defences, counterclaims and set-off (see 11.23–11.47 below).

Normal procedures of collection

Examination of client's terms of business

11.2 There is no contractual relationship between the factor and the debtor. In normal circumstances the factor is not a party to any contract with the debtor; his dealings with the debtor are as bare assignee of amounts payable by the debtor arising from a contract between his client and the debtor. It would be possible for him to be party to such a contract and to have full responsibility as a contracting party by means of a novation; this would mean the consent of all three parties. In the case of an assignment, unless it has been prohibited by the terms of the contract between the client and the debtor, as described in Chapter 13, the consent of the debtor is not necessary for the right of the factor to collect amounts payable under any such contract. However, as the factor's rights arise from the client's contracts with the debtors, the factor's rights to collect depend on the client's terms of payment. Therefore, before arranging his procedures to collect the debts sold to him under any arrangement for factoring whereby collection is to be the factor's responsibility, the factor must examine carefully the client's terms of business. In most cases the client will sell on standard terms; but in some cases the client's terms may vary according to the customer to be supplied. An example of the latter is the timber trade in which normal terms may vary from customer to customer between 30 days and 120 days and in which open credit may often be replaced by bills of exchange.

11.3   There are also many examples in which small suppliers to large and powerful retail concerns are unable to obtain orders otherwise than on the terms laid down by the debtor. At the outset the factor should therefore take careful note of terms of payment which apply to individual customers, where these are not standard. He should make provision for the client to notify him of the terms when application is made for the opening of a new debtor account or a request made for credit approval. The factor will have stipulated in the factoring agreement (see 8.3) the most liberal terms that he is prepared to accept in normal circumstances; but he may be prepared to consider more liberal terms in special circumstances if his approval is requested in advance.

The factor's collection procedures

11.4   Where the administration of debtor accounts and collection is to be carried out by the factor, the debtor will have been given notice on the invoice that payment must be made to the factor; the arrangement postulates that the client will have undertaken to do so. Efficient factors, having well in mind the importance of a good administration, keep the debtor accounts on an open item system (see 4.1–4.3). With accurate knowledge of the terms of each transaction the factor will be able to include the due date of each invoice with his input to his accounting records of the debts purchased by him. Thus, lists of invoices that are a specified number of days overdue can be produced for the factor's staff as a basis for their collection procedures. These procedures follow the normal commercial practices of credit controllers in commerce and industry. First, regular statements must be sent to debtors; such statements are usually prepared on an open item basis. The statements may well carry a reminder of the notice that the debts have been assigned. Although some large concerns disregard statements and pay only against invoices it seems that the majority of business concerns in the United Kingdom expect to receive a statement before making payment.

11.5   Two or three reminder letters for many debtors, often of increasing severity will usually be sent. These may be produced automatically by the factor's computer. For some debtors, particularly large purchasers of goods such as mail order houses or large retail chains, the factor may often be seeking payment for invoices raised by a number of his clients. In such cases routine letters have little effect and by frequent telephone calls a rapport may be built up between the factor's credit control staff and the accounts payable department of the debtor. As delays in such payment are often the result of queries relating to goods or invoices, such telephone rapport may help to dispose of the queries quickly and reduce the delay in payments Where it is known that the debtor is a subscriber to the telex, it is usually considered that telex messages produce a faster response than letters. Telex messages are, in many large concerns, seen by senior executives who, until the message has been received, may be unaware of an unresolved problem.

11.6   A few people in commerce and industry resent these letters or messages seeking payments for overdue debts. It may seem a little surprising that a person, who by failing to comply with a contract term, providing for payment on a due date, inflicts damage on his supplier by reason of increased finance charges, should evince such feelings. However, the fact that such feelings do exist must be carefully taken into account by a factor; for this reason the factor must be absolutely certain that he has recorded the correct due date of each transaction and has ensured that the client will consult with him in respect of variations from normal terms. If an unjustified demand for an alleged overdue account causes offence, it will probably be the factor's reputation that will suffer even if the fault was that of the client.

11.7   The timing of follow-up letters is considered, by some factors, to be a matter for the factor alone and set procedures are established. However, such set procedures may also be the cause of resentment on the part of debtors; in some trades and industries there are accepted periods of latitude sanctified by long usage and the factor would be well advised to take such practices into consideration. Most reputable factors now consult their clients carefully at the outset as to:

(*a*)   the type of letters or messages to be sent to debtors; and

(*b*)   the periods to be allowed to lapse between such letters; and

(*c*)   any debtors who expect special treatment (e.g. telephone calls).

Such procedures can be adjusted in the light of experience to ensure that the factor does not deviate too far from the narrow path between upsetting debtors and allowing the debt turn to lengthen.

Action when normal collection methods fail

11.8   When persuasion, cajolery or threats have failed to produce payment, then it is quite usual for the client to be consulted. For administrative convenience the client may waive consultation and, except in relation to certain specified debtors, leave it to the factor to take legal proceedings in such circumstances. However, in many cases consultation with the client may serve to avoid legal proceedings and the mark of a good collection system is the ability to obtain payment without resort to solicitors. The client may assist recovery at this stage by:

(*a*) holding up delivery of further supplies; and/or

(*b*) adding his own persuasion to that of the factor.

11.9   Where a debtor company of some substance wilfully refuses to pay or even to give any reason for failure to pay an overdue debt, it may in some circumstances be possible to avoid legal action by suggesting to the debtor that action may be considered by the factor, in consultation with his supplier, to petition the court for the debtor's winding-up. The courts frown on the use of the procedures for winding-up in order to effect debt collection. However, there appears to be no good reason why an aggrieved creditor should not remind his debtor that such a remedy is open to him if either:

(*a*) the debtor has neglected to settle a debt of more than £200 within 21 days of a written demand served at his registered office [*Companies Act 1948, s 223(a)*]; or

(*b*) it is proved to the satisfaction of the courts that the debtor is unable to pay his debts [*Companies Act 1948, s 223(d)*].

For the latter purpose the debtor's failure to respond to repeated demands for payments might well be evidence.

11.10   Finally, before recourse to legal remedies, it is advisable to request solicitors to send a letter of demand before proceedings are started. This is not a legal requirement but many such letters bring the response of payment, and the cost and trouble of proceedings are avoided. If proceedings are necessary the sending of letters of demand ensures recovery of scale costs in an undefended case.

Special circumstances

11.11   There are circumstances in which the collection procedures set out above cannot apply:

(1) *Transactions on bill of exchange terms*:
Where payment is to be by bill of exchange drawn either at the date of invoice or at the end of the month of invoice, one of three procedures may be adopted:

(*a*) The factor may draw the bill and send it to the debtor for acceptance.

(*b*) The client may draw the bill and send it to the debtor for acceptance and on its return endorse it in favour of, and send it to, the factor.

(c) The client may draw the bill, endorse it in favour of the factor and send it to the factor with the offer or notification and the copy invoice. The factor will then send the bill to the debtor for acceptance.

In the event that the client is the drawer it is not necessary that he himself should endorse the bill provided that the factor, as is usual, holds a power of attorney to do so on the client's behalf (see 8.14–8.19). From the point of view of the factor's security (b) and (c) are to be preferred; in both cases the factor will become a holder in due course. [*Bills of Exchange Act 1882, s 29(1)*]. As such the factor would be protected against the debtor's defences in respect of the underlying transaction or any counterclaims provided that he had no prior notice of them. However, as some clients expect that the factor should draw the bills as part of the service provided, method (a) is often adopted.

(2) *Transactions with debtors who practice 'self billing'*:
This practice has been adopted by some of the larger stores groups and mail order houses who often pay on short credit terms of 7, 14 or 30 days. The practice dispenses with the need for the client to raise invoices. The debtor raises his own internal document based on his order to the client and the goods actually received and accepted. If the client raises invoices for the purpose of notifying or offering debts to the factor, the invoice numbers will in all probability not be quoted on the debtor's remittance advices. As a result appropriation of payment becomes difficult particularly where goods have been rejected by the debtor or deductions made. The difficulties for the factor in this method of accounting can be overcome only by the adoption of some method by which the offers or notifications to the factor are based on reference numbers (e.g. of delivery notes) which will be quoted by the debtor. Furthermore, the factor will need to make arrangements with the client that the client will accept (or deal with) the debtor's debit notes or deductions promptly.

The benefits of an efficient collection service

11.12 An efficient collection procedure based on the actual terms of the transactions between the client and the debtors and on the practices of the particular trade is essential to an efficient factoring service. If automatic reminders or demands are to be produced by the factor's system they must be subject to the flexibility of the requirements of the client's business. An efficient service will:

(a) keep the debt turn to the minimum; and

(b) avoid invidious complaints from debtors; and

(c) flush out disputes and queries from the debtors at an early stage.

A precaution before legal proceedings

11.13   Before considering legal proceedings against a debtor company of substance, it is as well for the factor to bring the seriously overdue account to the attention of a senior executive of the debtor company by either a telephone call or telex. There have been many examples in which the staff of such debtor companies have disregarded or overlooked statements and reminder letters when:

(*a*)   the account has been considered as settled by a remittance to the client who has failed to pass it on to the factor; *or*

(*b*)   there is a prohibition on assignments in the purchase contract, which is not known to the factor and the debtor has purposely settled by payment to the client and disregarded the factor; *or*

(*c*)   there is a dispute of which the factor is unaware.

By such a notification of the position on the account to the company secretary or a director the position may be clarified. In the absence of a response it may be possible to bring matters to a head by a cancellation of the credit limit and a holding up of supplies by the client.

Legal remedies as final resort

11.14   If all other efforts to recover payment from a debtor have been exhausted and, in the absence of notification of a dispute or counterclaim, the factor (usually after consultation with his client) will have no alternative but to have recourse to legal proceedings. The factor will have either a legal assignment in accordance with the formalities laid down by statute [*Law of Property Act 1925, s 136*] or an equitable assignment, as described in 7.6. As was explained earlier, the difference is mainly procedural as regards the proceedings against the debtor for payment. In either event, naturally, notice must have been given to the debtor if the factor is to sue. In the case of a legal assignment the factor may sue in his own name alone; if the assignment is valid in equity only, the factor and the client should sue in their joint names.

Position where debts assigned in equity only

11.15   Accordingly, to save costs, delay and complications, it has been the practice for those factors, whose normal procedures of purchasing debts gave an equitable assignment only, to obtain a legal assignment before starting proceedings. The legal assignment would be executed by the factor himself on behalf of the client as assignor under the authority of a power of attorney held (see 8.14–8.19); this procedure saves time. However, such a legal assignment attracts stamp duty (see 7.8–7.11) and this will increase the costs which, in the case of an approved debt, may be borne by the factor in a non-recourse arrangement.

11.16   The purpose of the rule that requires the assignor and assignee both to be parties to an action for enforcement of an equitably assigned debt probably arose because *part only* of a debt may be assigned in equity, but not under the statute; and if that was the case it was reasonable that the court should require all interested parties to be before it. In factoring, however, it is normal that the whole debt is assigned and now, sometimes, factors will ask their solicitors to act in their own name alone as assignee even on an equitably assigned debt. It seems that, unless the debtor objects, the action should not fail only because a party has not been joined. This procedure normally saves expense and delay; but the factor runs the risk that the case may have to be put back so that the client may be joined. (*Rules of the Supreme Court, Order 15, Rule 6; County Court Rules, Order 5, Rule 6 and Order 15, Rule 1*).

Instructions to solicitors and pre-court steps

11.17   In instructing solicitors it is essential that the factor should be precise in the details given of:

(*a*)   The name and address of the debtor (registered office in the case of company);

(*b*)   The name and address of the client (registered office in the case of a company);

(*c*)   The amount of the debt;

(*d*)   The invoice dates and due dates.

As there are frequently arguments about dates of delivery of goods and terms agreed, it is advisable for the factor to check those again with his client before instructing solicitors. In particular he should enquire if the transactions were subject to any trade customs or course of dealing.

11.18   At this stage, having received a letter of demand from a solicitor and knowing that proceedings are contemplated, the debtor may well make an offer of payment by instalments. If such an offer is accepted it is important that the terms of the arrangement should be such that in the event of default on any one instalment the whole remaining outstanding debt becomes due immediately. Otherwise the factor may be left with the problem of having to sue on each instalment as it becomes due. It is also helpful for the factor to obtain post-dated cheques covering the instalments and personal guarantees of directors in the case of a debtor company.

11.19   If the debtor is a company and a winding-up petition has been threatened, consideration should be given as to whether to proceed with a petition (see 11.9 above). Furthermore, if another creditor's petition to wind the same debtor company up is advertised, it is advisable for the factor to instruct his solicitor to give notice of support; otherwise the debtor may settle with the petitioning creditor and the factor will then have to start proceedings anew. In the event of notice of support, the debtor would have to settle with the supporting creditor (the factor) in order that the petition might be dismissed; otherwise the factor would be substituted as petitioner.

Which court and enforcement of judgment

11.20 In the event that proceedings for judgment are to be taken, consideration must be given to the jurisdiction of the courts. County courts have jurisdiction for claims up to £5,000, but in the case of an assigned debt it is usual for the claim to be heard in the court of the area in which the debtor has his place of business. For this reason and because of the greater efficiency of the High Court and its procedures for execution of a judgment, it is usually considered advisable for the factor to sue in the High Court. However, it is unusual for a claim for under £600 to be pursued in the High Court; for no costs can be recovered there for such claims. If a dispute is envisaged then it may be advisable to start the case in the County Court in the name of the client. For in this way a 'Home Court' would be available to the client and a disputed case in the High Court might be put back for years. In any event such a disputed case would be the responsibility of the client; the factor would probably have already exercised his right of recourse. Only in the case of an insolvent client where the factor's retention is insufficient to cover all the recourse would the factor himself have an interest in such a disputed debt. If an acknowledgement of service indicating an intention to defend is entered in the High Court and it is expected that the defence will be spurious it may be advisable to proceed immediately for summary judgment. (*Rules of the Supreme Court, Order 14*).

11.21 When judgment has been obtained in the High Court the factor must consider the best way to enforce it. The choices include:

(*a*) Execution on the debtor's goods.

(*b*) A garnishee order on a debt owed to the debtor (e.g. a credit balance in a bank account).

(*c*) A charging order on property.

(*d*) A petition to wind up if the debtor is a company. The petition may then be based on the judgment.

(*e*) Proceedings for bankruptcy if the debtor is a sole trader or partnership.

The method used will depend upon the factor's assessment of the property of the debtor available to satisfy the judgment. In the case of bankruptcy proceedings the next step is to issue a Bankruptcy Notice; this is a notice to pay a judgment debt and failure to comply constitutes an act of bankruptcy upon which a petition may be founded. The issue of such a notice will sometimes bring forth payment. In considering which course of action to take the factor must consider the question of costs. Although in theory costs are awarded so that the loser pays all the costs of the case, the fixed costs awarded according to the scale do not cover all the costs of even the most straightforward case. If the proposals in the White Paper on Insolvency become law it will be possible for the factor to petition the court for the appointment of an administrator to a debtor company. This would have the effect of staying creditors' actions and rights to enforce payment whilst the business is carried on with a view to determining whether it may be saved.

Interest

11.22 Interest may be claimed if it is provided for in the terms of the contract giving rise to the debt. The rate is the rate stipulated in the terms. It is as well that the client should specify that interest is to run after as well as before judgment; otherwise contractual interest may be claimed up to judgment only and thereafter the factor will have to rely on statutory interest. In the absence of a provision for interest in the contract, discretionary interest may be claimed from the due date until judgment. The interest recovered by the factor must be credited to the client to compensate him for any delay in being credited with the payment. For it is the client, and not the factor, who will have borne the finance charges consequent upon the delay in payment.

The debtor's defences and counterclaims

11.23 In Chapter 8 the warranties normally given by the client were described. One of the most important of these is that by which the client undertakes that every debt sold by him to the factor shall be payable by the debtor as a valid collectable debt free from any defence or cross-claim. Accordingly, if the factor is unable to collect any debt that he has purchased, by reason of such a claim by the debtor, he will have the right to be indemnified by his client or to exercise his right of recourse. However, reimbursement from the client can normally only be obtained by set-off against the balance owing to the client in respect of other debts purchased. In a continuing agreement the level of the factor's retention, as a minimum balance, may well be sufficient to absorb any debts which are subject to recourse for this reason. It is in the situation of the insolvency of the client when the debtors are likely to look more closely at their rights that the level of these defences and claims for set-off increases. Such difficulties on the insolvency of clients have been the cause of many significant losses to factors since the service was introduced into this country. It is therefore important that a factor should be fully aware of the rights of the debtor in such a case. In the event of the insolvency of the client it may well be possible that a debtor may raise a defence or cross-claim that he may consider commercially justifiable but which, on examination, is not tenable in law.

11.24 The general rule is that the factor, as assignee, can be in no better position as regards his right to recover from the debtor than the client was at the time when the debtor had received notice of the assignment; as assignee, he takes the assignment subject to equities. Consider the words of James LJ in *Roxburghe v Cox (1881) 17 Ch D 520*:

'Now an assignee of a chose in action ... takes, subject to all rights of set-off and other defences which were available against the assignor, subject only to this exception, that after notice of an assignment of a chose in action the debtor cannot by payment or otherwise do anything to take away or diminish the rights of the assignee as they stood at the time of the notice'.

Accordingly, if a defence relating to defects or deficiencies in the very goods or service, that give rise to the debt in question, is raised by a debtor, the factor will be in no better position than the client (against whom, in the case of goods, a defence would be available to the debtor under *Sale of Goods Act 1979, s 53(1)(a)*). The defects or deficiencies must have been in existence at that time when the debt was assigned.

Equitable set-off by debtor against factor

11.25   As regards any counterclaims, the general view is that the debtor will be able to set off, in reduction or cancellation of the factor's claim for payment, any cross-claim arising out of the same contract as that which gave rise to the factored debt. In recent cases it has been held that the same rule should also apply to a cross-claim arising out of contract that is 'closely connected' with the contract which gave rise to the assignee's claim. (*Business Computers Limited v Anglo-African Leasing Limited [1977] 2 AER 741; 'The Nanfri' [1978] 2 Lloyds Rep 132; and 'The Raven' [1980] 2 Lloyds Rep 266, at p 272*). In respect of a counterclaim arising out of any other contract or on any other grounds the generally accepted rule is that the notice of the assignment fixes the rights of the parties. As a result after receipt of the notice the debtor cannot set off against the factor a debt which comes into existence subsequently even though it arose out of a liability that existed before the notice; but the debtor may set off against the factor a debt that accrued before the notice even if not payable until after it. (*Re Pinto Leite & Nephew [1929] 1 Ch 221*). For a thorough review of the law relating to the rights of a debtor in respect of set-off against an assigned debt the factor (and, indeed, the client and his adviser) can do no better than to refer to a transcript of the judgment of Templeman LJ (as Templeman J) in *Business Computers Limited v Anglo-African Leasing Limited [1977] 2 AER 741, at p 748*). After a detailed review of the authorities he summarised the position thus:

'The result of the relevant authorities is that a debt which accrues due before notice of an assignment is received, whether or not it is payable before that date, or a debt which arises out of the same contract as that which gives rise to the assigned debt, or is closely connected with that contract, may be set off against the assignee. But a debt which is neither accrued nor connected may not be set off even though it arises from a contract made before the assignment.'

11.26   It is apparent that, apart from the question of defences raised on account of defects in the goods or services supplied, the factor must be on his guard in relation to some ancillary transactions between the client and his debtors. The most common cause of such counterclaims are claims for set-off for goods supplied by the debtor to the client; if these goods were supplied before the assigned debt on which the factor is claiming arose, the debtor may well be able to set off notwithstanding that the two claims arose from entirely independent contracts. If the factor is providing his services in a trade where such transactions are endemic — for example the timber trade or steel stockholding — the factor may require the client to supply him with regular lists of purchase ledger balances. In these trades, and others, it is not uncommon for suppliers of goods to purchase certain sizes and qualities from other merchants who are normally their customers. If dealings are regular then the debtor account may have to be excluded. On the other hand if the factor was unaware of regular sales by the debtor to the client and the debtor had regularly paid the full amount to the factor, it might well be held that the debtor had waived his right to claim a set-off by a course of dealing.

11.27 The above considerations (see 11.25–11.26) relate to equitable set-off which strictly is a procedural matter; the debtor may claim the set-off as a shield to protect him against the factor's claim. However, the factor must also consider any set-off in insolvency [*Bankruptcy Act 1914, s 31 and its extension to liquidation by Companies Act 1948, s 317*] and contractual set-off.

Set-off in insolvency

11.28 The insolvency provisions, which are mandatory, will apply in all cases when:

(1) the claims of both parties are such as to result in a claim for payment of money (as opposed, for example, to a claim for the return of goods in specie); and

(2) the debts are owed to and by persons in the same right (as opposed, for example, to a claim by one party as a trustee); and

(3) both claims are provable in the insolvent estate.

Naturally, the set-off provisions in insolvency will not apply if the debtor's independent claim against the supplier did not arise before notice fixed the rights of the parties and the factor had become the creditor of the debtor. The same rules as those which apply to equitable set-off will determine the rights of the parties in this respect.

Contractual set-off

11.29 Contractual set-off may extend the right to set off almost without limit. Where a client had, before the start of factoring, made a contract with his client for all amounts owing both ways to be set off without limit, the factor might be held to be bound by the arrangement even if the cross-claim arose after notice of the assignment and out of entirely separate transactions. The factor would have purchased the debts subject to contract. If, before the set-off were to be claimed, no course of dealing had been established, the factor's rights to collect might well be subject to the contract for set-off. As a corollary, the client may be required by the factor to make contracts with his debtors (with whom such contra trading is usual) not to set off. Such a contract would be valid between the client and his debtor until insolvency of one or other occurred (when the insolvency provisions referred to above would apply), but would not bind the debtor as against the factor who was not party to the contract. If the debtor were to be given notice of the factor's interest and did not object it might be held that he had waived his right to set off as against the factor; but this is not certain. For this reason and, as the set-off provisions in insolvency cannot be waived or renounced by contract, it is better for the agreement not to set off to be made between the debtor and the factor himself. (*National Westminster Bank Limited v Halesowen Presswork & Assemblies Ltd [1972] 1 AER 641*). The factor is more concerned that the contract will not stand up in the insolvency of the client than in the insolvency of the debtor. In the latter case the most that he will lose by the set-off is any dividend from the insolvent estate; in the former case he may lose the whole debt.

The security afforded to the factor by notice to the debtor

11.30   It is apparent that the earlier the notice is given to the debtor the more secure will the factor be. Thus, the factor is in a more secure position with the full service, recourse factoring, some forms of agency factoring or bulk factoring, when notice is given on each invoice as soon as the debt is created than he is in an invoice discounting or undisclosed factoring arrangement. In addition to fixing the rights of the parties as regards certain defences and counterclaims, receipt by the debtor of notice also:

(*a*) prevents the discharge of the debtor by subsequent payments to the client;

(*b*) prevents changes in the terms of the contract of sale being enforceable against the factor;

(*c*) secures priority over other encumbrances (see Chapter 15);

(*d*) prevents a trustee in bankruptcy obtaining the benefits of the 'order and disposition clause' (see 7.31 and 18.10); and

(*e*) enables the factor to sue in his own name (see 11.14 above).

No positive liability of factor to the debtor

11.31   The questions of the factor's positive liability to the debtor and on credit notes apply only to factoring with notice to the debtor; they do not apply to invoice discounting or undisclosed factoring until notices have been given. Although a factor may have his own claim against a debtor reduced or extinguished by the debtor's countervailing rights, he incurs no positive liability to the debtor under the contract that gave rise to the assigned debt. As the bare assignee of the amount payable by the debtor he is not a party to the contract. Furthermore, it is also generally accepted that in most circumstances, once the debtor has paid the assigned debt to the factor, any claim by the debtor against the client, whether arising out of the contract that gave rise to the assigned debt or not, must be against the client. The factor is considered in most cases to have no liability to repay to the debtor; it has been said that although an assignee takes subject to equities he is not subjected to them. The burden of performance of the client's contract with the debtor can be shifted on to the shoulders of the factor only by a novation accepted by all three parties; but this has the effect of cancelling the old contract between the client and the debtor and creating a new one between the factor and the debtor. Such an arrangement is not part of the functions of a modern factor.

Position of the factor arising from total failure of consideration

11.32 In the paragraph above the absence of the factor's positive liability to the debtor was referred to as being generally accepted in most circumstances. A difficult and uncertain question of law arises when the debtor has paid to the factor in respect of a transaction in which there has been a total failure of consideration on the part of the client. This might occur if an invoice had been issued and either no goods or services had been supplied or the goods or services supplied had been lawfully rejected by the debtor for non-conformity with the contract. The avoidance of positive liability by the factor to the debtor arises from the absence of privity of contract between the factor and the debtor; but in such a case a claim by a debtor against a factor for repayment would be based not on the contract but on the quasi-contractual principle of restitution. There appear to be no reported cases nor any other authority in which recovery against an assignee in such circumstances has been claimed (see Goode 'Some Aspects of Factoring Law', 1982 JBL July, at p 339).

11.33 In practice the difficulty for the factor would arise only if:

(*a*) he had paid against the invoice representing the transaction in question; and

(*b*) his client was insolvent; and

(*c*) his retention was insufficient to cover his recourse.

In other circumstances it would be open to the factor to recover from his client, on the basis of the client's breach of warranty, and repay the debtor. Thus, there can be no question of the factor gaining by having been paid for nothing. In any case in which he might resist the debtor's claim he would have paid and been unable to recover from his client. Accordingly, as claims for restitution seem to rest mainly on the ancient principle of unjust enrichment, there seems to be some support for the view that the factor should not be liable to repay. On the other hand it seems possible that the debtor might claim restitution on the grounds of money paid by a mistake of fact. It is a well established principle of English law that money paid under a mistake of fact is recoverable (see 'Chitty on Contracts' 25th Edition, paragraphs 1949 et seq.). It seems possible that the debtor might claim that on receipt of the invoice he paid in the belief that the right goods had been despatched to him and that such a mistaken belief was induced by the legends on the very invoice.

11.34 In view of this uncertainty it is inadvisable for a factor to accept invoices purportedly representing debts for:

(*a*) deposits for goods to be supplied; *or*

(*b*) charges for service contracts where no service has been performed at invoice date.

Even if payment of the purchase price of such ostensible debts is to be made only when payment has been received from the debtor, the risk of repayment remains.

The factor's liability for credit balances

11.35 Not infrequently credit balances emerge on the accounts of debtors. The question of the responsibility of the factor for payment of any such credit balance to the debtor is the subject of much uncertainty and disagreement even between the factors themselves. Such uncertainty and disagreement arises because in most cases a credit balance is created by the issue by the client, and the acceptance by the factor, of a credit note representing a value exceeding the debit balance on the debtor's account. It is clear that a credit balance created by a debtor's payment, either duplicated or mistaken as to amount, is repayable as money paid by mistake.

11.36 The view that the factor has no responsibility for credit balances created by the issue of credit notes is based on the doctrines of the assignee's avoidance of any liabilities under the sale contract (see 11.31–11.34 above). Indeed, there has been a practice by which a factor may indicate to debtors the absence of responsibility for a credit balance created by the issue of a credit note. Such indication would take the form of a disclaimer in the assignment notices (see 8.8). However, apart from the position which may arise if the credit note has been issued in recognition of total failure of consideration, there are cogent arguments in favour of the factor's liability (see 11.32–11.34 above). First, if the credit note creates a credit balance it must surely be in recognition of an earlier overpayment because a defect or deficiency in the goods or services did not emerge until after payment. It is possible that the debtor could claim that the resulting balance represented his having paid too much in the first place by mistake of fact. His mistake was to assume that the goods or services were in order at the time when he paid; although the credit note was issued later it represented the facts in existence at the time of payment. Secondly, the debtor might claim that by a course of dealing the factor had given ostensible authority to the client to issue credit notes which adjusted the factor's account with the debtor.

11.37   A further uncertainty arises from the allegations of some suppliers of goods and services that credit notes do not create a liability to repay but may be dealt with by the debtor only as a set-off against amounts owing for further supplies. Such an argument may very well be acceptable in the case of a credit note for goods, which conformed to the sale contract, taken back voluntarily by the client. However, it can in no way be sustained in relation to a credit note which recognises a shortage or defect in the goods or services supplied when related to the contract.

11.38   In view of these uncertainties some factors have cut the Gordian Knot by making payment of all credit balances that agree with the debtor's records. In order to protect themselves in the uncertain state of the law regarding the obligation to pay in some circumstances, such factors take a specific authority from their clients to make all such payments howsoever arising. Such an authority would be by way of a clause in the factoring agreement itself. In effect the factor, in most cases, will be paying on behalf of the client because, as a corollary of the credit to the client of the value of debts purchased, the value of credit notes will have been debited to the client. The advantages of such a procedure are as follows:

(*a*)   It reduces administrative costs by reason of having to examine each credit balance, when claimed by a debtor, to determine where the responsibility lies.

(*b*)   It saves the factor the need to carry unclaimed credit balances in his records or the extra administration of transferring them back to the client. (The practice of keeping unclaimed credit balances in the records of a business for six years and of then taking them to the credit of revenue accounts is not considered to be valid. The statutes of limitation provide time limits for remedies; they do not cancel indebtedness.)

(*c*)   It improves the factor's reputation in the eyes of the debtors, and thus of the business world in general, by avoiding invidious arguments about relatively small sums.

(*d*)   It may serve to help debt collection. A debtor may be more cautious about making a payment if he has experienced difficulty in recovering a credit balance.

On the other hand, if unpaid credit balances can be transferred back to the client then the credit balance on the client's account will be increased. This may serve to give the factor a greater margin against which to debit items which are the subject of recourse. Such a benefit to the factor's security is only an advantage to the factor on the insolvency of his client and if the client's business has been correctly monitored by the factor this practice should not be necessary. (For the position in the United States where it appears to be a well established principle that a factor cannot be held responsible for a credit note issued by a client, see *McMullen Leavens & Co v L I Van Buskirk Co 275 App Div 701 affd 299 NY 784 (1949); and Crompton-Richmond Co v Raylon Fabrics Inc 33 App Div 2d 741, 305 NY Supp 2d 850 (1960).*)

Position of the factor on the insolvency of the client

11.39   Any difficulty or uncertainty in the factor's relations with a debtor during the currency of a continuing factoring arrangement will be governed to a large extent by the factor's relations with his client. Any disputes regarding goods or services, terms of payment or details on invoices are matters to be disposed of by the client under the warranties given in the factoring agreement. The repayment of credit balances will be governed by an authority in the factoring agreement itself or *ad hoc* arrangements between the client and the factor.

11.40   When the insolvency of the client occurs the agreement may cease and the factor, notwithstanding his continuing rights, may have no further practical way of enforcing them (see Part E). The factor may then need to adjust his collection and other procedures to ensure the recovery of all the funds in use. Whether and to what extent to make any adjustments will depend upon the circumstances and in particular on the following:

(1)   The type of factoring service provided.

(2)   Whether or not there are any guarantors (e.g. parent company or directors) to whom the factor may turn for practical assistance in order to avoid recourse under the guarantees.

(3)   The factor's experience of the running of the factoring arrangements and, in particular, the incidence of disputes and of the issue of credit notes.

(4)   Whether or not there are any provisions in the factoring agreement for changes in the rights and obligations of the factor.

11.41   In the case of a maturity agreement the factor will not need to make any substantial changes in his procedures. His funds in use will be nil under an agreement by which he pays the client as he collects, and no more than small in proportion to the debts outstanding where he pays on a fixed maturity date. The factor may have the right to transfer the debts back to the client and so come off risk as regards the insolvency of any debtor; but in such a case it would be usual to make arrangements to continue to collect (see Part E). In such an event his collection procedures should be unchanged.

11.42   In the case of invoice discounting and undisclosed factoring, if notices have not already been given to the debtors, they should be given forthwith and arrangements made to collect direct from the debtors. The relationship between the factor and the debtors will be the same as in the case of full or recourse factoring save that the factor should in no case have any responsibility for credit balances. Any of the client's customers who were creditors at the date of insolvency, would not have been aware of the factor's interest nor would they have made any payments direct to the factor. In such circumstances there should be no requirement to notify them of the factor's interest.

11.43 If the factoring arrangements have included prepayments and full notice and collection from the debtors the factor should consider the following adjustments to his normal arrangements:

(1) All original credit notes should be passed to the factor for approval before onward transmission to debtors. In this way the factor may ensure that the administrator is not agreeing to unjustified diminution of amounts owed to the factor.

(2) Even if authority has been taken in the factoring agreement to pay credit balances, any large balances should be investigated. The origin of the balance should be determined to ensure that repayment is likely to be the responsibility of the factor. If this is not so, then it may be necessary for the balance to be transferred back to the client so that the holder of the balance may only have the right of proof in the insolvent estate.

(3) In some cases it may be necessary to inform the debtors that any goods to be returned must be returned direct for the factor's account in accordance with his instructions. It is usual for the factor to have rights to returned goods to which the assigned debts relate.

(4) The question of the transfer back to the client of debts outstanding, where this is provided for in the factoring agreement, will be considered only when all funds in use have been recovered. In the meantime the factor may have the right to specify that all debts previously approved become subject to full recourse on the insolvency of the client.

(5) It is normal for the factor to take the right to compromise with debtors over disputes, once the client has become insolvent. However, it may well be advisable, even if not legally necessary, for the factor to consult with the administrator of the insolvent estate and any guarantors before making any such arrangement relating to a substantial debt. In any event the administrator might be entitled to expect that the factor would exercise due skill and care in the collections and disposing of disputes.

(6) The factor might consider some delay in transferring back to the client any debts subject to recourse. If there is doubt about a full recovery of funds in use, it is better for the factor to retain a doubtful or disputed debt than to have no debt at all.

(7) It is advisable, also, for the factor to arrange that all cheques and

11.44 *Collection from the Debtor and Debtor's Rights*

other negotiable instruments made payable to the client and received by the factor after the client's insolvency are actually endorsed in favour of the factor when arrangements have previously been made for such cheques to be paid into the factor's account without endorsement (see 8.16). Such endorsement will normally be made by the factor himself by the authority of a power of attorney. The purpose of endorsing is to ensure that the factor then becomes a holder in due course and may be able to overcome any late defences or counterclaims or a countermand of payment by the debtor to his banker.

Crown set-off

11.44 The rights of set-off between the Crown acting through government departments and a solvent person are governed by Section 35(2) of the Crown Proceedings Act 1947 and the Rules of the Supreme Court (*RSC Ord 77, r 6*). The general effect of these *inter alia* has been that set-off is not available to the Crown without leave of the court:

(*a*) if the claim is against a government department and the counterclaim relates to another department; or

(*b*) if the Crown is sued in the name of the Attorney General.

Until 1979, the position in Bankruptcy and Liquidation was uncertain (see 'Williams & Muir Hunter on Bankruptcy', 19th Edition, p 203). In that year, in *Re Cushla Limited [1979] STC 615* set-off between a claim by the liquidator of the company for repayment from the Customs and Excise and a claim from the Inland Revenue against the company was considered. It was held that the statutory provisions for set-off should apply and that they were mandatory. [*Bankruptcy Act 1914, s 31, as applied to companies by Companies Act 1948, s 317*]. Although both debts arose from statutory provisions, as opposed to rights under contracts, it is now generally accepted that in the insolvency of a person, whether natural or incorporated, claims against and by separate government departments may be set off.

11.45 It is further accepted that the set-off will apply even if one of them arises out of a contract and the other is statutory. An attempt was made in Scotland by the liquidator of Upper Clyde Shipbuilders Limited to obtain payment of a sum due from the Ministry of Defence arising out of a contract free from the set-off of amounts due by the company to other departments including the Department of Trade and Industry and the Inland Revenue. (*Smith v Lord Advocate 1981 SLT 19*). That attempt failed and the court applied the common law rules of set-off in bankruptcy which were said to have long provided in Scotland remedies similar to those provided for in England by Section 31 of the Bankruptcy Act 1914. In the judgment the Crown was referred to as being regarded in the common law of Scotland as an 'indivisible entity'.

11.46 The result of these cases seems to be that there remains little doubt of the ability of departments of the government, by whom contract debts are owed to insolvent businesses, to set off claims by any government department, whether contractual or statutory, against that business. The Cork report has recommended that there should be no set-off allowed between claims by and against different departments and that contractual and statutory claims by and against the same department should not be subject to set-off. (Report of the Review Committee on Insolvency Law and Practice 1982, Cmnd 8558, paragraphs 1342 to 1347 and 1362). However, until such time as the law is changed, factors will have to take these developments in the law carefully into account. A debt owing by a client to the government cannot be set off against an independent debt owing by a government department already vested in the factor, in respect of which notice of the assignment has already been given when the former debt arose. However, as most clients will owe substantial sums for PAYE and other taxes and for VAT at most times, it is apparent that the assignment to the factor of debts owing under contracts with ministries will usually be encumbered with potential set-off for earlier amounts owing.

11.47   The position is aggravated by the practice of government departments in forbidding assignments of amounts due under their purchase contract. In consequence, in the absence of special permission for the assignment, the factor will not obtain a valid assignment of the debts purchased by him, as regards his rights against the debtor (see Chapter 13) and, therefore, even subsequent liabilities of his client to the government may be set off. Accordingly, it is difficult for a factor safely to provide any variant of the service that includes a prepayment facility to a business which sells a substantial part of its output to the government.

Chapter 12

Insolvency of the Debtor

12.1   This chapter starts by considering the position of the factor when a receiver is appointed to a debtor company by a secured creditor, out of court, by virtue of the provisions of the creditor's charge. This is the most common situation met in the receivership of a trading company. Thereafter the chapter considers the factor's procedures on the liquidation or bankruptcy of an unincorporated debtor (12.5–12.10 below), his recourse for unapproved debts (12.11–12.14 below), procedures for the recovery of VAT (12.15–12.18 below), and the problems arising from reservation of title by the client (see 12.19–12.21 below).

Receivership

12.2   In these days it is usual for most of the property of the debtor to be charged to the creditor by way of fixed charge, but there will be residual assets the subject of a floating charge and the instrument of charge will normally provide for the receiver to be the agent of the company and to have powers of management in addition to the power to take possession and sell the property. In the White Paper on Insolvency it is proposed that his position as agent should be regularised by statute. The effect of the appointment of the receiver and his taking possession in such a case will be to crystallise the floating element of the charge (if it has not already crystallised). Where all the property of the company is the subject of the charge the directors' ability to manage the company's property will be suspended as the property will be in the possession of the receiver. (However, unlike the position in a liquidation, the directors' powers to manage are not affected to the extent of any property not in the possession of a receiver: see *Newhart Developments Ltd v Co-operative Commercial Bank Ltd [1978] 2 AER 896.*) As a result, any proceeding to recover an unsecured debt such as that vesting in the factor under a factoring agreement will be nugatory.

12.3   The only remedy reasonably open to the factor in such circumstances will be to petition for the winding-up of the debtor company. This may be desirable for either or both of two reasons:

   (*a*)   in order to obtain a recovery of value added tax included in the debt purchased by the factor (see 12.15–12.18 below); or (*b*) when the receivership is close to completion and the directors have refrained from taking steps to put the company into voluntary liquidation, notwithstanding that it is insolvent, and there are assets surplus to the claims of the debenture holder and preferential creditors.

Before taking such action it is advisable to make an attempt to ascertain the position of the business. Receivers have at present no legal responsibility to unsecured creditors (apart from their statutory duty to preferential creditors: *Companies Act 1948, s 94*—see also 'Tolley's Receivership Manual', paragraph 3.22). There is, however, a developing doctrine analogous to a duty of care and in recent years it has been the practice of receivers, carrying on the business of a company, to consult major creditors, often by means of contact with an informal committee. The White Paper proposes statutory obligations on receivers for the provision of information to unsecured creditors. It may well be that the best prospects for unsecured creditors will be obtained by the sale of the business as a going concern. The power of the receiver to carry on the business may well be prejudiced by a winding-up order which has the effect of terminating the ability of the receiver to bind the company as agent (*Gosling v Gaskell and Grocott [1895–9] AER Rep 300*), though not his power to realise the property of which he is in possession. In view of this prejudice to the ability of a receiver to continue a business, there are proposals in the White Paper for application to the court for the appointment of an administrator (as described in 17.17) in such circumstances.

12.4   While a receiver and manager is carrying on the business of a company it is often necessary for him to purchase from suppliers with which the company has done business in the past. A factor will, therefore, often be asked to approve debts, to be offered or notified to him by a client, which have arisen from sales to a receiver. In such circumstances a receiver is personally responsible for orders placed by him except insofar as he has excluded such personal liability in the purchase contract. [*Companies Act 1948, s 369(2)*]. Therefore, if the factor is to give an approval on the standing of the receiver only (for example, on the grounds that he is a member of an established professional body and is experienced in receivership) he must ensure that his approval is given strictly on condition that:

(*a*) the order does not include a condition excluding the receiver's responsibility; and

(*b*) the order is signed personally by the receiver or some other person authorised by him in writing.

In the event that the receiver's personal responsibility is to be excluded (and the partners of some major accountancy firms specialising in receivership now adopt such an exclusion as normal practice) the decision as to approval of the proposed credit becomes an almost impossible one for the factor. He cannot know sufficient of the conduct of the receivership to decide if the trading will be successful and whether there will be assets in the business available to settle the proposed debt. For, if the receiver's personal responsibility is excluded, debts for current trading will be paid only to the extent that the property of the company possessed by the receiver allows.

The factor's procedures in liquidation or bankruptcy of the debtor

12.5   On the making of a receiving order in respect of the property of an unincorporated debtor, unsecured creditors are no longer able to exercise their rights and remedies for the recovery of amounts owing to them by that debtor and, in general, no legal proceedings may then be started. [*Bankruptcy Act 1914, s 7(1)*]. Similar rules apply in the case of an order for the winding-up of a debtor company [*Companies Act 1948, s 231*], and in the case of its voluntary winding-up (either members' or creditors') the property of the company is to be distributed *pari passu* in the satisfaction of its unsecured debts after payment of preferential creditors. [*Companies Act 1948, s 302*].

12.6   As a result, except in rare cases where proceedings against the debtor and the remedies available thereby have reached an advanced stage (as described below), once the factor has been notified of an impending winding-up or bankruptcy of a debtor further proceedings will be fruitless. The factor should therefore normally ensure that proceedings against the debtor are stopped to avoid further costs when:

(*a*) he is aware of an act of bankruptcy or a receiving order in respect of an unincorporated debtor; or

(*b*) he receives a notice of a meeting of the creditors of a debtor (whether incorporated or not); or

(*c*) he is aware of a petition to wind up a debtor company.

In order to be aware of (*c*), the factor should ensure that each publication of the London Gazette is checked against his records. In the White Paper there are proposals for procedural changes which will affect the commencement of bankruptcy and winding-up by the court. The concept of 'acts of bankruptcy' is to be abolished if the proposals are implemented; the general effect will be that the commencement of winding-up and bankruptcy will be the court orders. Petitions for winding-up will not be advertised.

Conflicts between execution creditors and administrator of insolvent estate

12.7   A difficult question arises as to the disposition of:

(*a*) the goods the subject of an execution by an unsecured creditor; or

(*b*) the proceeds of a garnishee order; or

(*c*) the security given by a charging order,

when bankruptcy or winding-up commences and the execution or attachment has reached on advanced stage. (See 'Williams and Muir Hunter on Bankruptcy', 19th Edition, pp 315–329.) In bankruptcy the general rule is that the creditor cannot retain the benefit of the execution or attachment unless it is completed before the receiving order, or notice of an act of bankruptcy or of a petition. [*Bankruptcy Act 1914, s 40(1)*]. There are further rules for the sheriff:

(i) to deliver goods taken in execution (but before sale) to the official receiver upon notice of a receiving order against the debtor; and

(ii) to hold any moneys received on sale of the debtor's goods, or paid by the debtor to avoid execution, for 14 days and to pay such moneys to the official receiver or trustee if a receiving order is made founded on a petition presented within that fourteen days.

[*Bankruptcy Act 1914, s 41*].

The latter rule applies only to judgments of over £250. Similar rules apply in the case of an impending winding-up of a debtor company. [*Companies Act 1948, ss 325, 326*]. For the purposes of these rules relating to companies, a petition to wind up and the notice of a meeting at which a resolution is proposed for the winding-up of the debtor company are respectively substituted for a petition for bankruptcy and an act of bankruptcy.

12.8   These rules have created many questions of interpretation in practice and also, because the courts have discretion to grant relief in favour of the judgment creditor, they have been considered by the courts on many occasions. The courts have weighed the balance between the principle that as far as possible unsecured creditors should be treated on a *pari passu* basis and sympathy for an alert creditor who takes efficient action to recover his debt. The tendency now seems to be towards the parity of treatment. The latest in this line of cases relates to a creditor whose charging order *nisi* on his debtor's property was made absolute by the District Registrar two days after a resolution was passed for the winding-up of the debtor company. The House of Lords in that case decided that the parity of treatment of unsecured creditors should prevail and the creditor was unable to retain the benefit of his charge. (*Roberts Petroleum Ltd v Bernard Kenny Ltd (in liquidation)* [*1983*] *1 AER 564*).

12.9   When proceedings have reached an advanced stage and liquidation or bankruptcy has intervened, the factor should take careful legal advice as to the chances of success in taking further action. In the absence of success in his action, the factor will be left with his right to prove.

12.10   Proof of debt should be completed and submitted at the earliest possible stage because:

(*a*) the factor may wish to attend the meeting of creditors and use his experience to influence the conduct of the winding-up for the benefit of creditors; and

(*b*) if he holds a guarantee (e.g. from a parent company or director of a debtor company) he may claim the full amount of his debt and, at the same time, make a claim on the guarantor.

Payments made by a guarantor *after* the receiving order or commencement of winding-up (whether before or after proof) are not to be deducted from the amount claimed in the proof. (See 'Williams and Muir Hunter on Bankruptcy', 19th Edition, p 183 and 'Tolley's Liquidation Manual', paragraphs 17.35 to 17.51.) Naturally, the creditor is not to be allowed to obtain more than the full amount by the aggregation of payment from both parties and once the full debt has been paid by the guarantor, the right of proof passes to him. However, the guarantor has no right of subrogation to the creditor's right to prove until the whole debt has been paid either by the guarantor or the aggregation of the guarantor's payments with dividends from the debtor's estate. For this reason it is important that, if a debt is to be guaranteed subject to a limitation, the guarantee should relate to the whole debt subject to a limitation on the guarantor's liability. If the guarantee is for part only of the debt the guarantor may be subrogated on settling that part which is guaranteed. (*Re Sass [1896] 2 QB 12*). Formerly, proofs of debt in bankruptcy and liquidation were submitted to and admitted by the trustee or liquidator in the name of the factor. This was valid even if the assignment was equitable and not legal. In these days however, proof of debt is normally submitted by the factor in the name of the client but at the address of the factor. The factor is able to do this by reason of his power of attorney normally given in a factoring agreement (see 8.14–8.19). The reason for this change is to be found in 12.15–12.18 below. After proof has been accepted by the administrator of the estate of the debtor, the factor should make arrangements to enquire periodically as to the conduct of the liquidation or bankruptcy and to ensure that dividends are received by him. The importance of the latter is demonstrated by the fact that it has been known for a dividend to be sent to the client who later became insolvent. Although the dividend should have been held in trust for the factor by the client it was not kept separately and, as a result, was lost.

Factor's recourse for unapproved debts

12.11 In arrangements for factoring which do not include any protection for the client against bad debts, recourse of debts unpaid otherwise than by reason of a breach of warranty by the client (e.g. because the debtor disputes liability) is often available to the factor a specific number of days after due date or after the month of invoice. In such arrangements, which are not uncommon in recourse factoring, bulk factoring and invoice discounting, the insolvency of the debtor may very often occur after the relevant debt has revested in the client. The factor may therefore be unaffected by the insolvency of the debtor. It may also be provided that recourse should also be available to the factor on any earlier insolvency of the debtor and in such cases the factor may not need to attend to the formalities such as covering meetings of creditors and submitting proof of debt to the administrator of the debtor's estate.

12.12 In arrangements which include protection against bad debts (the full service, maturity factoring, agency factoring, in its second sense, or undisclosed factoring), the factor will, to the extent of his approvals, be unable to effect recourse solely for the reason that the debtor fails to pay by reason of bankruptcy or liquidation. Accordingly the factor will need to attend to the formalities referred to in 12.11 above for his own account in respect of approved debts. It is not unusual for the amount of a proof to relate to indebtedness that is partly approved and partly unapproved. In such circumstances it is normal practice for the factor to submit proof for the *whole* debt and to receive and account to the client for the client's share of any dividends or other recoveries. This is regarded as part of the factor's service and some factors will even deal with these matters on behalf of the client for wholly unapproved debts.

12.13 In all cases, the recourse will be effected in such a way that the factor is repaid the full invoice value of the unapproved part of the debt either at the date of the commencement of the insolvency or on a fixed maturity date. The unapproved part of the debt, or the whole of it if wholly unapproved, will then vest again in the client. If the client then so requires it, or if the factor does not provide collection of salvage as part of the service, arrangements must be made with the liquidator or trustee to pay dividends on the indebtedness, which has revested in the client, direct to the client.

12.14 The recourse arrangements in the factoring agreement may be framed either:

(*a*) as the obligations of the client to repurchase an unapproved debt (or part of a debt) at due date or maturity date or on insolvency; or

(*a*) as a guarantee by the client to the factor of due payment by the debtor.

The framing of the recourse arrangements as a guarantee is to be preferred: in the case of an insolvent client and an insufficient retention to absorb the claim by the factor under the guarantee for recourse, the factor may claim the full amount of the debt from debtor and client. The client will not be able to be subrogated to rights against the debtors until he has, in effect, paid for the full recourse. The factor will not then be obliged to reduce his claim in either estate until he has received 100% of the debt in aggregate (see 12.10 above and *Re Sass* [*1896*] *2QB 12*). It is doubtful if a similar arrangement could be made in selling the debt back to the client.

Recovery of value added tax

12.15   VAT relief is now available in respect of the tax element in debts owed by individuals or firms in bankruptcy and companies in creditors' voluntary or compulsory winding-up. However, the relief is available only to the supplier of goods and services and not to an assignee of the debt. (*Finance Act 1978, s 12; the Value Added Tax (Bad Debt Relief) Regulations 1978 SI 1978 No 1129; and see VAT leaflet No 8/78/VAC, issued by HM Customs & Excise*).

12.16   Where a debt is assigned in equity only and no notice of the assignment has been given, there can be no doubt that the client, as supplier, is the only person able to sue to recover the debt and consequently to prove in the insolvent estate. As a result the client will be able to recover the VAT on receipt of a certificate of admission of his proof from the liquidator or trustee. The position will be the same if the factor releases his equitable interest in the debt back to the client and so notifies the debtor.

12.17   Where the arrangements for factoring are entirely with recourse, there is no problem: the debt will be reassigned to the client who will be entitled to the relief. Arrangements should be made by the factor in a *non-recourse* factoring agreement, under which debts are normally assigned equitably, for any debt owed by the debtor the subject of bankruptcy or winding-up (otherwise than purely for reconstruction) to be repurchased by the client. If the debt is approved the repurchase price will be nil because the factor has agreed to bear the credit loss. The factor may then arrange for the proof to be admitted in the name of the client, as supplier, who is the sole owner of the debt and entitled to the bad debt relief from VAT on the admission of the proof. For administrative purposes the factor may make the arrangements with the administrator of the insolvent estate to issue a certificate which will enable the client to recover the VAT element in the debt. The arrangements will include a provision for the amount payable by the factor for the debt to be reduced *pro tanto*; the full value of the debt including VAT will have been the basis of the calculation of the purchase price, so that the factor may then charge back to the client the amount of VAT recovered.

12.18   Relief is not available otherwise than on the official insolvency of the debtor and for the purposes of the regulations neither receivership nor a members' voluntary winding-up are considered to be insolvency.

Reservation of title in the client's terms of sale

12.19   The widespread practice of the reservation of the ownership of goods to a supplier until the purchaser has paid for them has been looked upon equivocally by factors. The subject is more fully dealt with in Chapter 16 from which it will be apparent that difficulties can be created for the factor where his client purchases goods on such terms. However, the factor has no need to dissuade his client from including such terms in his own conditions of sale. The effectiveness of the terms are questionable if:

(a) the terms are unclear and may be interpreted as a charge (*Re Bond Worth Ltd [1979] 3 AER 919*); or

(b) the goods have been mixed with or incorporated into other goods (*Borden (UK) Ltd v Scottish Timber Products Ltd [1979] 3 AER 961; Re Peachdart Ltd [1983] 3 AER 204*).

12.20 If the goods are clearly traceable and identifiable the terms may enable the supplier to recover his goods and resell them (*Hendy Lennox (Industrial Engines) Ltd v Grahame Puttick Ltd [1984] 1 WLR 485*); the proceeds of resale may well be more than the amount of any prospective dividend on an unsecured claim in the debtor's estate. Although in many cases the resale value of the goods and the trouble of tracing and recovering them will influence the supplier to abandon the goods and rely on his proof, there seems at present to be no clear disadvantage to the supplier in incorporating such terms. He has the benefit of being able to make an election either to recover the goods or to prove.

12.21 At present there appears to be no disadvantage in recovering goods under those terms from the point of view of VAT recovery if the debtor is bankrupt or in creditors' or compulsory liquidation. In the case of a receivership of the debtor when no bad debt relief is available, there is a positive advantage in recovering the goods. Liquidators and trustees normally expect that on such a recovery the invoice should be cancelled in full by a credit note for the return of the goods; the credit note would automatically reduce the supplier's output VAT. However, the issue of a credit note in such circumstances will preclude the supplier from availing himself of his right to prove in the debtor's estate for any loss and expenses on resale. It would seem that otherwise such a claim for damages on the exercising of the right of resale should be admitted. [*Sale of Goods Act 1979, s 48(4)*].

12.22 If the debt arising from a sale on these terms has been purchased by the factor with recourse to the client, then the decision as to whether or not to rely on the terms and recover the goods will rest entirely with the client. The factor will have exercised his right of recourse and recovered the amount of the debt from the client most usually by a debit to the client's account and a reduction *pro tanto* in the next payment to the client. If, however, the debt is an approved debt it must be the factor's decision. In the event that he wishes to recover the goods and resell, then he will normally have the right to do so independently of his client; a typical factoring agreement will provide for the assignment to him, along with a debt, of all the client's rights under the sale contract giving rise to the debt (see 8.28–8.29). However, the factor will doubtless need the client's help and assistance in disposing of the goods; in the event of non-payment owing to the debtor's insolvency, as the debt is approved and not subject to recourse, he cannot expect the client to buy the goods back for their full invoice value in all circumstances.

Chapter 13

Contract Terms Prohibiting Assignments

The pre-1978 view of the effect of terms prohibiting assignments

13.1   The contracts entered into by a factor's client with his 'debtors' may contain terms prohibiting the assignment of the client's rights. Until the judgment in *Helstan Securities Limited v Hertfordshire County Council* in 1978, the general view of the law was that the effectiveness of a term in a purchase contract or a contract for services which purported to make inalienable the bare right to receive payment was to be distinguished from a term which prohibited the assignment of the general rights of either party. It used to be considered before this decision:

(a) that an assignment of the general rights in contravention of such a contract term would be effective neither between the debtor and the assignee nor between assignor and assignee; but

(b) that an assignment of the bare right to receive payment would be fully effective to vest the right in the assignee provided that

(i) the assignee took the assignment in good faith without notice of the contract term; and

(ii) the assignee gave value.

Although doubts had been raised regarding this concept, the general view of factors was that they had little to fear from the introduction of such terms into the purchase contracts of their client's debtors. An authority for this general view was found in the words of Darling J in *Shaw & Co v Moss Empires and Bastow (1908) 25 TLR 190* (at p 191) that such a term seeking to prohibit the assignment of a debt 'could no more operate to invalidate the assignment than it could interfere with the laws of gravitation'. If a client assigned a debt to a factor in breach of his contract with his debtor, which contained a term prohibiting the assignment, then naturally the debtor must have a remedy. It was considered that the debtor would have no right to disregard the notice of the assignment provided that the factor took in good faith and gave value; the debtor's remedy would be a claim against the client for damages for breach of contract. In most cases the debtor would have suffered no damage: he would be required to pay the factor no more than he would have to pay the client in the absence of an assignment. Only if the client became insolvent and the debtor had a claim against the client, which had arisen out of a separate contract after receipt of the assignment notice, would the debtor's position have been detrimentally affected by the client's breach of the contract term.

The position since the 'Helstan' case

13.2   The general view held by factors up to 1978 was upset by the *Helstan* case. (*Helstan Securities Ltd v Hertfordshire County Council* [*1978*] *3 AER 262*: for a review of this case see Goode 'Inalienable Rights?' (1979) 42 MLR 553). In that case a roadwork contractor had provided services to a local authority under a contract which included a term by which the contractor should not assign the contract or any part thereof or any benefit or interest therein without the written consent of the local authority. The contractor assigned to a finance company the right to receive payment from the local authority. The local authority declined to recognise the assignment. The assignment was held to be invalid by the court. That such a term in a purchase contract should give the debtor the right to ignore a notice of assignment and obtain a good discharge of the debt by paying the debtor may cause some difficulties to a factor. The widespread use of such terms by the client's debtors will detract from the factor's security. However, even greater difficulties can be caused to a factor if the words of the judgment are to be interpreted to mean that the assignment was completely invalid; that is to say, even as between the assignor and assignee. The decision in the case depended only on the narrower question of whether or not the debtor was obliged to pay the assignee, but the words of the judgment might well be interpreted in the wider sense. If the latter interpretation is to be accepted then factors are subjected to even more serious risks. There is now a possibility that debts assigned to a factor in contravention of such contract terms may not vest in the factor; such debts, if unpaid at the commencement of client's insolvency, may well be claimed by the administrator of the estate. Furthermore, if the wider view is accepted, the provisions in a factoring agreement, by which remittances received by a client in payment for a factored debt are to be held in trust for the factor (see 8.18–8.19), may be of doubtful validity where the debt arises from a contract which includes such a term. However, it seems very doubtful if such a contract could extend the prohibition to the alienation of the proceeds of the debt after they had come into the hands of the client.

The use of 'ban on assignment' terms

Use by large purchasers of goods and services

13.3   Terms whereby suppliers may not assign their claims are to be found almost invariably in government and local authority purchase contracts. They are sometimes used by large and powerful purchasers of goods and services such as retail stores groups and mail order houses. In the *Helstan* case, the view was expressed that a prospective assignee can protect himself by making proper enquiries regarding the terms of the contract out of which the debt to be assigned arises. Such a procedure may be possible in the case of the proposal to purchase a single large debt; and, certainly, a factor should arrange to be consulted by his clients before they accept exceptionally large orders so that the factor may examine the contract terms in advance. However, in the normal continuing relations between a factor and his client whereby a large number of relatively small debts are purchased by the factor such investigation of the contract terms is clearly impracticable.

13.4   Representations have been made on behalf of factors to government departments, local authorities and other large purchasers of goods and services. These representations have been based on the grounds that the difficulties caused to factors affect their ability to provide an efficient and economical service to small businesses with the ultimate benefit to the purchaser of a more efficient supply. These representations have been only partly successful. Most big purchasers agree that they would in most cases consent to the assignment to a reputable factor if such consent were requested; they appear to wish to avoid assignments to unknown, and perhaps 'objectionable', assignees. The reasons advanced for avoiding such assignees are described in 13.8 below. The difficulty remains that, owing to the number of transactions, it is difficult for the factor to know when and to whom to apply for consent; nor is it an administrative task that may economically be undertaken. It also seems surprising, in view of its policy of encouraging small businesses, that notwithstanding representations the government has not seen fit to outlaw the practice. It is the long credit taken by large purchasers of goods and services that is one of the greatest difficulties encountered by small businesses; and it is the help to overcome these difficulties, to be given by factors, that is being hindered by the practice.

United States practice compared

13.5   As it is large purchasers who normally insist on such terms, it might be considered that the practice is brought about by inequality of bargaining power. The attitude of the UK government is in contrast with the philosophy in the United States. In the US the practice is outlawed and the Uniform Commercial Code S9–318(4) provides:

'(4) A term in any contract between an account debtor and an assignor is ineffective if it prohibits assignment of an account or prohibits creation of a security interest in a general intangible for money due or to become due or requires the account debtor's consent to such assignment or security interest.'

The official comment on this sub-clause includes the following:

'This gradual and largely unacknowledged shift in legal doctrine has taken place in response to economic need: as accounts and other rights under contracts have become the collateral which secures an ever increasing number of financing transactions, it has been necessary to reshape the law so that these intangibles, like negotiable instruments and negotiable documents of title, can be freely assigned.'

With the increasing use of factoring in all its forms to assist the growth of small businesses so that the economy may be regenerated, the economic need for a similar statutory provision appears to be just as pressing in the UK.

The risk for the factor

13.6 There seems little doubt that once a debtor, in whose purchase contracts such a term was included, had established a pattern of paying the factor in respect of invoices bearing the assignment notice, the debtor would be held to have waived the prohibition. The factor should, therefore, be vigilant in the investigation of contract terms between his client and any debtor who either:

(*a*) persistently makes payment to the client; or

(*b*) sends remittances to the factor by way of cheques made payable to the client.

In the event that a debtor refuses to consent to the assignment it may well be possible to persuade him to make his cheques payable to the client but to send them to the factor. In such an event the factor's right to collect will be by authority of the power of attorney given in the factoring agreement (see 8.14–8.17).

13.7 The risk to the factor created by such contract terms is obviously greater in invoice discounting and undisclosed factoring in which payments are in normal circumstances made by debtors to the client in the absence of assignment notices. In such cases, there can be no course of dealing established and the factor should ensure that contracts with the more important debtors are examined on periodic audits by the factor's staff.

The rationale for inclusion of terms prohibiting assignment

13.8 The reasons for the inclusion of terms prohibiting the assignment of amounts payable in purchase contracts are not hard to find. Such reasons are also well known in several Continental countries. The practice is well known in Germany in particular where the ban on assignments ('Abtretungsverbot') is recognised in the German Civil Code and creates difficulties for factoring companies there (BGB paragraphs 398–413). The reasons for the use of such terms include:

(*a*) The debtor wishes to avoid the danger of having to pay a second time if his staff overlook the notice of assignment and pay the client in the first place.

(*b*) The notice of an assignment can restrict the debtor's rights of set-off in relation to claims subsequently arising (see 11.30).

(*c*) The debtor may wish to avoid having a vigilant and efficient collector of debts as his creditor instead of one who is inefficient or will give greater latitude.

There would seem little in the rationale for the use of the practice to outweigh the telling arguments in favour of its abolition, however, especially as a second payment is rarely demanded when the first payment has been made to the client by a genuine error.

Methods by which a factor may overcome the problem

The mischief

13.9   There seems to be no cure, from the point of view of the factor, for the position whereby a debtor, using a ban on assignments in his purchase contract, gets a good discharge by paying to the client. This, however, is not the main mischief in the use of these terms: provided that a factor may trust his client or can monitor the factoring arrangements closely, he may be sure while the arrangements are continuing that all remittances sent to his client are passed on to him. It also seems unlikely that a debtor can, in any contract with the client, require that the client shall be unable to make an agreement to make over the proceeds of a debt when received (see *Goode op.cit.*). In invoice discounting or undisclosed factoring all payments go to the client and whether the debt arises from a contract including such a term or not the debtor will get a good discharge; the debtor will have received no notice. The mischief arises from the uncertainty, following the *Helstan* case, as regards the validity of an assignment, in contravention of such a term, as between the client and the factor. If the debts are not assigned they do not vest in the factor and in receivership, liquidation or bankruptcy may be claimed by the administrator of the estate. Naturally, if there has been a course of dealing by which the debtor has paid the factor in the past it is likely that the assignments of new debts may be valid. However, this is not certain and the position in relation to debtors who had no previous dealing must be considered.

13.10   However, in view of the uncertainty, two methods of overcoming the difficulty have been established:

(*a*) A provision in the factoring agreement itself by which any debt that fails to vest in the factor by assignment shall be held by the client in trust for the factor. This provision is similar to that used by some factors in Scotland (see 7.33–7.39).

(*b*) A fixed charge on any debt that fails to vest in the factor to secure all the client's obligations to the factor. Such a charge would be evidenced by a separate document and registered in the usual way at the Companies Registry. The charge would not need to provide for the appointment of a receiver but would have to give an irrevocable power of attorney to the factor by which he would be able to collect the debts in the client's name.

13.11 The charge would seem to give the factor greater security than the trust provision. If the debtor's purchase contract terms have the effect of making a transfer of the ownership of the debt impossible by assignment, then it would appear that not even the beneficial ownership can be transferred in equity. It is doubtful therefore, if that is indeed the correct interpretation of the law, whether the trust would be created. On the other hand, a charge, unlike a mortgage, does not require any transfer of ownership: it is an encumbrance that attaches to an asset and gives the chargee the right to have the liabilities to him of the chargor discharged out of the proceeds of that asset (see Goode 'Commercial Law', Penguin Education/Allen Lane, p 714). Accordingly, if on the insolvency of the client the funds in use will not be fully recovered by the collection of debts that are impeccably assigned, the factor would then become creditor for the balance of the funds. He would be able to recover the indebtedness by collecting the debts charged to him in the name of the client.

Limitations of the solution

13.12 Where such a charge is to be taken and at the outset of factoring there is another charge outstanding affecting the client's debts, the factor should make sure that the waiver from the holder of the other charge (see 15.10–15.13) should refer to debts 'charged to' as well as 'purchased by' the factor. Unfortunately, this solution is not available to a factor in relation to a client that is not an incorporated company. There appears to be no way of taking a security over the debts of a partnership or sole trader without an assignment. For a similar reason a fixed charge on existing and future debts is not possible in Scotland. Naturally, the taking of such a charge does not preclude the need for the factor to be especially vigilant to ensure that remittances received by the client are passed on to him in their original form. The factor will not be able to obtain a second payment by claiming that payment to the client does not discharge the debtor's indebtedness if the debtor has banned assignments in his purchase contracts.

Chapter 14

Other Terms in Contracts of Sale Affecting the Factor

14.1   Chapter 5 described the results of factoring for a client who sells on terms and in accordance with trade usages that do not provide a collectable debt at invoice date free from potential countervailing rights of the debtor. In Chapter 10 it was recommended that the factor, on assessing the suitability of a prospective client, should pay particular attention to the terms on which the client sells. As was said, in many cases because of the debtor's greater bargaining power, these terms may be the debtor's standard terms of purchase. In either case the rights of the factor can be no better than those given to him by the contract out of which a purchased debt arose. The difficulties created by prohibitions of assignments have been dealt with in Chapter 13. The other common cause of difficulty for the factor is the acceptance by the client of a contract either:

(*a*) to provide services over a period of more than one month under which each month's work performed is to be invoiced; or

(*b*) to make several separate deliveries of goods each one of which is to be invoiced separately.

The possible consequences of the purchase by the factor of debts represented by such invoices and the prepayment of part of the purchase price of such debts are described in the following paragraphs. Such contracts may be of fairly short duration and often do not exceed a few months, but for practical purposes they are often referred to by factors as 'long term' contracts. It would be administratively impractical for a factor to examine every order for goods or services taken by a client; but he should be aware, from his initial examination of the prospective client's business when such a contract is likely and ensure that the client is fully aware of his responsibility to consult the factor before his acceptance of it.

Long term contracts

Contracts for service

14.2   Lawyers divide long term contracts into two categories: 'entire contracts' and 'divisible contracts'. Under an **entire contract** the debtor has no liability for payment until performance of the whole contract has been completed (see 'Chitty on Contracts' 25th Edition, paragraphs 1399 et.seq.). A **divisible contract** will provide for payment for part performance. Whether a contract is divisible or entire depends on the terms of the contract itself and, if provision is made for the invoices to be issued by the supplier of services periodically, then in the absence of any specific provision in the contract the presumption may be that the contract is divisible. However, unless the terms of the contract are examined carefully by the factor, he will not know to which type of contract the debts notified or offered to him are related.

14.3   The consequences of the failure by the client to complete a contract for services, in respect of which the factor has already prepaid against an invoice raised for part of the work done, may be as follows:

(1)   If the contract is entire the debtor will not be obliged to pay any part of the invoice already issued unless the whole contract is substantially completed. (*Bolton v Mahadeva [1972] 2 AER 1322; Hoenig v Isaac [1952] 2 AER 176*). Even if the contract is substantially completed the debtor will be able to set off, as against the factor's claim for payment, a counterclaim for breach of contract because the claim and counterclaim arose from the same contract. (*Government of Newfoundland v Newfoundland Railway Co (1888) 13 AC 199; Roxburghe v Cox (1881) 17 Ch D 520; Business Computers Ltd v Anglo-African Leasing Ltd [1977] 2 AER 741; and 'The Nanfri' [1978] 2 Lloyds Rep 132*).

(2)   If the contract is divisible the debtor will be obliged to pay the invoice for part performance provided that the invoice relates to a separable part of the contract; but the debtor will be able to set off his counterclaim for breach of contract.

The debt which is not payable by the debtor because it relates to part (but not substantially the whole) performance of an entire contract will be subject to recourse to the client who will be in breach of warranties given in the factoring agreement. For the same reason such a debt arising under a divisible contract or relating to the substantial completion of work under an entire contract, which is subject to a counterclaim for damages, may be recoursed to the client. In the one case the debt is not a legally binding obligation of the debtor and in the other is subject to a counterclaim; in both cases the client will have warranted otherwise (see 8.2). Naturally, in a continuing arrangement an occasional experience of such an uncompleted contract is unlikely to be a problem; the recourse may be effected by the factor against the retention or further debts sold to him by the client. The difficulty will be acute if the bulk of the client's business relates to long term contracts and the client becomes insolvent.

Contracts for the supply of goods

14.4   Where there is a contract for the sale of goods to be delivered by instalments, which are to be invoiced and paid separately, it is a question to be determined by a construction of the contract whether any defect or default in any one or more of the deliveries may give the debtor the right to repudiate the whole contract or only the right to a claim for compensation. [*Sale of Goods Act 1979, s 31(2)*]. However, the normal presumption, in the absence of anything to the contrary in the contract, is that each delivery according to the contract is to be invoiced and paid for separately. In this respect the factor may be somewhat better off in relation to a debt arising from a contract for the sale of goods than in relation to one arising from a contract for services. However, the factor will, in relation to a contract of sale, be subject to a counterclaim by the debtor if the client wrongfully fails to deliver a further instalment. [*Sale of Goods Act 1979, s 51(1)*]. The position will be exactly as described in 14.3 above in respect of an incomplete divisible service contract. Furthermore, if the debtor has accepted one or more of the instalments of goods and not the whole quantity contracted for, the factor may well be able to rely on the Sale of Goods Act 1979 and to claim payment of the price of the goods as a part delivery accepted by the debtor. [*Sale of Goods Act 1979, s 30(1)*].

14.5   An uncertainty that very often affects the factor's consideration of a long term contractual arrangement between a client as supplier of goods and a debtor is the practice of some purchasers by which the goods to be purchased are specified but the exact quantity (or even the price) is subject to periodic call off. Such arrangements are common among large retail chains. The specification of the product, and often its price, are agreed with the manufacturer, but the quantities to be supplied are called for direct to the manufacturer by branches as required. Whether such an arrangement constitutes a binding contract, so that failure to deliver any goods called off would give the debtor the right to set up a counterclaim against amounts payable for deliveries duly made, depends upon the degree of the uncertainty in the contract. It would seem that if the price and the quantity to be delivered were both to be agreed from time to time the arrangement could be held to be a letter of intent (see 'Chitty on Contracts', 25th Edition, paragraph 111). In such a case it would appear that the individual calls for supply of a specific quantity at a specific price might be regarded as separate contracts; and the factor would be able to accept the debts arising from such deliveries without any anxiety.

Cut-off clauses

14.6   In view of these difficulties arising from the client's long term contracts with his debtors, where such contracts are a normal part of the client's business or where an individual contract of such a nature constitutes a large part of the client's business, it is advisable for the factor to stipulate that the debts arising from such a contract will be approved and eligible for prepayment only if a 'cut-off clause' is included in the contract.

14.7   The purpose of such a clause is to divide the contract so that each delivery may be deemed to constitute a separate contract. An example of such a clause in a contract for services would be:

'This contract is divisible. The work performed in each month during the currency of the contract shall be invoiced separately. Each invoice for work performed in any month shall be payable by the customer in full, in accordance with the terms of payment provided for herein, without reference to and notwithstanding any defect or default in the work performed or to be performed in any other month.'

Or, in a contract for the sale of goods:

'This contract is divisible. Each delivery made hereunder:

(i) shall be deemed to arise from a separate contract, and

(ii) shall be invoiced separately and any invoice for a delivery shall be payable in full in accordance with the terms of payment provided for herein without reference to and notwithstanding any defect or default in the delivery of any other instalment.'

Undertaking from the debtor direct

14.8   Alternatively, it may be possible for the factor to obtain from a debtor who is anxious to maintain continuity of supply from the client an undertaking on the following lines:

Re: XYZ Limited ('the Company').
'In consideration of your continuing your factoring services for the company we hereby undertake to pay in full the amount of any invoice for goods sold to us (services completed for us) by the company and accepted by us without any deduction or set-off in relation to any claim we may have or expect to have against the company in respect of any goods (services) provided or to be provided by the company which are not the subject of the said invoice.'

Contracts for 'sale or return' or 'sale on approval'

14.9   In the description of the factor's assessment of the suitability of a prospective client in Chapter 10, it was indicated that the factor should be on his guard for sales (or purported sales) effected on the basis of sale or return or sale on approval. In fact, goods delivered on these terms are by no means *sold*. In effect the client has sent goods to the debtor and made him an offer to buy:

(*a*) under 'sale on approval' if the goods are on inspection, considered to be suitable; and

(*b*) under 'sale or return' if they can be made the subject of a sub-sale by the debtor.

Rule 4 of Section 18 of the Sale of Goods Act 1979 provides that the property in goods sent on these terms passes when the debtor signifies his approval or acceptance of the goods, or does any act which adopts the transaction, or retains them for more than a reasonable time. In these circumstances, as the client warrants that all invoices notified or offered to the factor relate to valid collectable debts in relation to goods sold and delivered, no copy invoices relating to such sales should be sent to the factor on delivery. The factor cannot accept as representing valid debts invoices that may be cancelled by the return of the goods at the option of the debtor. Furthermore, in view of the uncertain period during which the debtor has the option to purchase and the difficulty of monitoring such transactions it is doubtful if the factor should accept debts arising from such a sale even when an event has occurred to make the sale firm.

14.10   Difficulties have been met by factors on the insolvency of clients in trades in which such terms are usual. There will be allegations by debtors in possession of slow moving lines that the goods were sent on 'sale or return'. A similar situation may arise when the client sells on terms that are loosely referred to as 'sale or exchange'. For example if the client is selling books or records, he may agree to send certain titles on the basis that, if the debtor cannot sell them, he may exchange them for others for which the debtor has received a demand. The difficulty arises on the client's insolvency; there are no goods to send in exchange and the debtor will allege that he is entitled to return what he has in stock for credit. A factor would be well advised to avoid such arrangements.

Part D

Conflicts with Third Parties

Chapter 15

The Factor's Conflicts with Other Assignees and Chargees

The factor's position vis à vis other assignees and chargees

15.1   This chapter and Chapter 16 deal with the factor's position when claims are made by third parties to the ownership of, or security rights over, debts purchased by him. In this chapter the factor's position in relation to claims by other assignees and chargees is considered; in the next his position in relation to other third parties. Questions of priorities in relation to security rights over personal property are some of the most difficult in English law; and some of these relating to the ownership or charging of *choses in action*, such as trade debts in which a factor deals, are the subject of marked uncertainty. (For a full review of these problems see Goode 'Legal Problems of Credit and Security', 1982, Sweet & Maxwell.) Ownership has been mentioned, as well as charging, in this connection because often the borderline in substance between one and the other can be very narrow, although the difference may in form be distinguishable. (For example, for the distinction between block discounting agreements for financing by purchase with recourse instalment credit agreements and the lending on security of such agreements, see 7.14–7.17 and *Olds Discount Co Ltd v John Playfair Ltd* [*1938*] *3 AER 275 and Lloyds & Scottish Finance Ltd v Cyril Lord Carpets Sales Ltd (1979) House of Lords (unreported).*) The difficulties appear to arise from the history of the development of English law from the original concept, that a consensual security could be implemented only by possession, to certain non-possessory forms of security. This took place in the absence of a statute to regulate these matters and to provide for a comprehensive code of registration such as is found in the United States. (Uniform Commercial Code Section 9—adopted by every state in the US except Louisiana).

15.2   *The Factor's Conflicts with Other Assignees*

Circumstances in which other charges may be created

15.2   The absence of any arrangements for registration of the discounting or factoring of debts, save for the registration of an arrangement with an unincorporated firm in accordance with Section 43 of the Bankruptcy Act 1914, can create problems for a factor. He may have difficulty in determining whether his prospective client has already sold his trade debts elsewhere.

15.3   If the arrangements for such sale were already in effect he would be likely to discover it on his survey; most factors arrange for payments from debtors to be paid direct to their own bank accounts, even if the arrangements are undisclosed. Furthermore, most factors provide for their clients to note confidential arrangements on their sales ledger records. If the prospective client has entered into an agreement with another factor, but it has not started, there may be no means of finding out unless the prospective client is a company and a resolution authorising the agreement was properly recorded in the minute book. Naturally, in the case of full factoring the original agreement would be rapidly discovered at the start of the new arrangements, when the second factor failed to receive receipts from debtors, either direct or by onward transmission. However, such situations have arisen and it is as well for the factor to understand, as far as the uncertainty of the present law allows, what the priority rights of the parties may be. More usual is the entry into an agreement for factoring, in one form or another, by a company combined with the giving of a charge on book debts to a bank at about the same time.

15.4   The double assignment or the charging of debts assigned or agreed to be assigned to a factor may arise otherwise than by fraud. It may possibly occur by negligence or a misunderstanding of the legal significance of the arrangements, or the documents giving effect to them, by the proprietor of a small business. On a number of occasions a general charge including a fixed or floating charge on all book debts has been executed by a company during the currency of an agreement for factoring by which all such book debts have been or are to be sold to the factor. It is understandable that the directors of a small company may not understand the significance of the charge; but it seems that to request the execution of such a document in such circumstances, without excluding the debts which are subject to the factoring agreement or at least consulting with the factor, is a matter of negligence on the part of the official of the bank or finance company. In many such cases the bank would be fully aware of the factoring arrangements, seeing most, if not all, the company's cash inflow coming from the factor. In any event, as factoring is not uncommon these days among small businesses, it would seem that an enquiry should be made about the disposition of the book debts. Provided that the conflict of interest is discovered while the business is solvent, then normally the difficulty is overcome by an agreement between the bank or finance company and the factor and the completion of a waiver or priority agreement. However, as some of these conflicts do not emerge until insolvency intervenes it is necessary to consider the priority rules, considered below.

The rule in Dearle v Hall: priority of charges

15.5   The general rule based on the case of *Dearle v Hall (1823) 3 Russ 1*, which has stood the test of time for 160 years, is as follows: as between two assignees, *the first to give notice to the debtor has the prior right* provided that he was not aware of an earlier assignment at the time of the assignment to him. The fact that the assignee claiming priority under this rule became aware of an earlier assignment after his own assignment does not preclude his giving notice first and obtaining priority. The case itself related to equitable assignments of equitable interests in a trust. (In 1823 statute had not yet recognised assignments of *choses in action*.) As regards equitable interests, the rule appears to have statutory recognition as there is a reference to it in this respect in Section 137 of the Law of Property Act 1925. The material date would appear to be that on which the notice is received by the debtor rather than that on which it is despatched. (This view is based on the analogy with the date of the completion of a legal assignment by notice. See 7.5 and *Holt v Heatherfield Trust Ltd [1942] 1 AER 404*.)

15.6   As regards a conflict between an assignee under an equitable assignment and a subsequent assignee whose assignment is in statutory form, where the later assignment was taken for value and without notice of the prior equitable interest, there is no precise authority. It is, however, generally accepted that, in such a conflict, the prior equitable assignee would prevail provided that he gave value and first notice to the debtor. This is the consequence of the statutory provisions for the requisites of an assignment whereby the rights of the assignee are 'subject to the equities having priority over the assignee'. [*Law of Property Act 1925, s 136(1)*]. This rule is generally accepted notwithstanding that it is contrary to the usual rule that, as between an equitable interest and a later legal interest acquired for value and without notice of a prior encumbrance, the legal interest supplants the equitable interest.

15.7   Where the conflict is between two assignees who both have valid assignments in statutory form there can be little doubt that the first to complete his assignment must prevail. By the first completed assignment both legal and beneficial interest in the debt has been transferred and the assignor has nothing more to assign. As the receipt of notice by the debtor completes the statutory formalities, in such a conflict also the first to give notice will prevail; and for the same reason he will prevail if he is in conflict with a prior equitable assignee of which he has no knowledge and whose assignment has not been notified.

15.8   Thus, in all cases the result is the same: *the first to give notice has the prior right to collect*. The logic of the rule is unassailable: if it were not so, the debtor would never know, on receipt of notice, that he was paying the person who had the prior right and, thus, properly discharging his indebtedness.

The importance of early notice by the factor

15.9   In 11.30 the advantages were set out of the factor's giving notice to the debtor at an early stage. One of these was the securing of priority over other encumbrances. The foregoing description of the effect of *Dearle v Hall* emphasises the importance to the factor of getting out his notice as early as possible after the assignment of each debt has been effected. In the case of a factor who uses the 'whole turnover' type of agreement, whereby debts vest in him immediately upon their coming into existence, for the full service or any other form of disclosed factoring the notice may be sent by the usual legend on the invoice as soon as the debt comes into existence and even before the factor has been notified by the submission of copies. Where the factor uses a 'facultative' type of agreement, the assignment takes effect only when the offer has been made and accepted, or deemed to be accepted, by the factor. Unless, therefore, the factor arranges for originals of the invoices to be sent to him for onward transmission he cannot be certain that the notice on the invoice has not been sent before the assignment has been made. In such an event it is doubtful if the notice would be valid for the purposes mentioned in this chapter; it seems unlikely that a notice specifying the assignment of a particular debt can validly be given until the assignment has been made. No doubt the subsequent statements would bear a further legend reminding the debtor of the assignment and such a legend would be a valid notice; but it would in fact be a great deal later than is desirable. Naturally, where invoice discounting or other undisclosed arrangements are used, the factor is in more danger from competing assignments. This aspect is taken into account in assessing the suitability of the client (see Chapter 10).

Waivers from the third party: a safeguard

15.10   In view of the difficulties and uncertainties in the law, whenever a factor finds that a client or a prospective client has agreed to give a right to purchase debts or a security right over them to a third party, or is under an obligation to do so, the factor should obtain a waiver from that third party. It may be that the factor has been advised that in the event of a conflict his rights will prevail; but, in view of the uncertainty of the law in many circumstances, it is as well to obtain agreement in advance as to the priorities. Even the 'winner' of such a conflict may well have found it worrying and most invidious. The waiver will normally specify that the third party who holds or expects to hold an interest in the debts to be sold to the factor:

(*a*)   acknowledges that he is aware of and consents to the factoring agreement;

(*b*) agrees that the debts sold to the factor under the agreement shall be free from any security right in his (the third party's) favour;

(*c*) stipulates that the waiver does not preclude his taking security rights over any amount that may become payable by the factor to the client for debts purchased under the factoring agreement; and

(*d*) reserves the right to terminate the waiver in certain circumstances (e.g. crystallisation of the charge in favour of the third party or on notice to the factor) but without prejudice to the factor's rights to the debt already vested in him.

Whether or not this last reservation can be insisted upon by the giver of the waiver will depend upon the nature of his security rights and his probable rights to priority over the factor in the absence of the waiver.

Form of waiver

15.11 Waivers are sometimes in the form of agreements between the parties. Their effectiveness will depend upon the presence or otherwise of consideration flowing from the factor. It would, of course, be possible for a waiver to be valid if given under seal where there was no consideration, but, certainly in the case of a bank waiver, the factor would be unlikely to obtain it under seal. The usual consideration would be based on the fact that the factor had entered into the factoring agreement at the request of the third party and had thereby improved the fortunes of the client and consequently the security of the third party. Alternatively, the factoring agreement may have enabled the third party to reduce his exposure to risk.

15.12 More often, however, a waiver is drafted not as an agreement but as a letter informing the factor of a fact. The fact is the consent given to the client by the third party for the client to enter into the factoring arrangements by which debts are to be sold to the factor free from the encumbrances in favour of the third party. If the factor were to make the arrangements to his detriment and be approached by the third party with a demand that the factor give up his rights to the debt, it would seem that the third party would be estopped from denying the consent.

15.13 A question has arisen as to whether or not an assignee of the third party's security right would be bound by a waiver given by the third party. For example, a finance company holding a charge on book debts to secure a fixed sum debenture might, after having given a waiver to a factor, assign the debenture together with the security for value. Would an assignee who had taken the security in ignorance of the waiver be bound by it? There is no authority for such a question, but the view of a leading academic is that the assignee would be bound. (*Goode, op. cit., at p 53*).

Types of conflicting charges

Prior floating charge

15.14 The precise nature of a floating charge on the assets of a company is difficult to define and the judiciary have found it necessary to describe it by such metaphorical expressions as 'hovering' and 'ambulatory'. However, the concept that it does not attach to any asset over which it is effected until crystallisation is well understood; until that time the company over whose assets it has been created may deal with them in the normal course of business and dispose of them free from the charge. The most usual criteria by which a charge is considered to be floating are:

'(1) if it is a charge on a class of assets present and future;

(2) if that class is one which, in the ordinary course of the business of the company, would be changing from time to time; and

(3) if you find that by the charge it is contemplated that, until some future step is taken by or on behalf of those interested in the charge, the company may carry on its business in the ordinary way as far as concerns the particular class of asset . . . '

(*Yorkshire Woolcombers Association Ltd [1903] 2 Ch 284*).

Therefore, the charge does not by itself prevent a company, over whose assets (including book debts) it has been created, from selling its book debts in the normal course of business. It seems likely that in these days to sell book debts by way of factoring or discounting would be considered to be 'in the normal course of business'.

15.15 However, most floating charges over book debts include a covenant from the chargee that he will not dispose of any book debt by way of factoring or discounting whilst the security remains effective. Although it would be normal for a factor to make a search at the Companies Registry before offering an arrangement for factoring to a company (see 10.2) and although a charge on book debts is to be registered [*Companies Act 1948, s 95(2)(e)*], two possible situations must be considered:

(1) What would be the position as between the factor and the chargee if the charge included such a restriction, the restriction was noted on the registration details and the factor failed to search? The factor is invested with constructive notice of the existence of the charge by its registration. It is usually considered, though, that the constructive notice extends only to the particulars that are required to be filed: its date, the amount secured, the property charged and the chargee. It remains uncertain whether the factor could be held to have notice of the restriction. One academic view is that such restrictions are so usual now that the factor could be said to have inferred knowledge of it. (Farrar 'Floating Charges and Priorities' (1974) 38 'The Conveyancer' (NS)315; but for a contrary opinion, see *Goode op.cit., at pp 25 & 26*).

(2) A similar uncertainty remains as to whether the factor could be held to have inferred knowledge of such a restriction if the registration particulars made no mention of it.

15.16 It is clear that, if the factor has notice, whether constructive or actual, or knowledge, whether inferred or actual, of such a restrictive covenant in a floating charge on the assets of a prospective client company, he would not, without a waiver, obtain priority as regards his purchase of book debts under a subsequent factoring agreement. His agreement takes effect subject to the prior equities of which he has knowledge or notice. The rule in *Dearle v Hall* (see 15.5 above) will assist only one who takes an assignment in good faith without knowledge of prior rights to the debt. In this connection the words of Browne-Wilkinson J in *Swiss Bank Corporation v Lloyds Bank Limited and others* [1979] 2 AER 853 may be relevant:

'. . . the court will restrain a person from enforcing his contractual rights so as to cause a breach of another contract of which he had full knowledge when he entered into his own contract.'

(The judge was referring to *Manchester Ship Canal Co v Manchester Racecourse Co (1901) 2 Ch 37*.)

Subsequent floating charge

15.17 It is usual for factors to know about existing charges on the assets of a prospective client company when considering a factoring arrangement; and it would be usual for the factor to make arrangements with a chargee either by way of clarification of the effect of the charge or by means of a waiver before the start of factoring. However, it may happen that a client company should execute a new charge affecting book debts to a bank or finance company during the currency of a factoring agreement. As pointed out in 15.4 above, the execution of a charge in most circumstances arises from a misunderstanding on the part of the directors of the company of the legal effects of the charge and the factoring agreement. If a charge taken in such circumstances is a floating charge and includes a covenant by which factoring or discounting of debts is not to be effected by the client, the effect upon the existing factoring agreement must depend upon the type of agreement used, as follows:

(1) **Whole turnover agreement.** Provided that the agreement itself gave effect to the assignment of the debts immediately upon their coming into existence, then it would seem that the creation of the floating charge would not affect it in any way. The charge, including any restriction (both of which take effect in equity), must be subject to the prior equitable rights of the factor and would not prevent the vesting of further debts in the factor. Thus, there would never be any debts (save for any excluded from the factoring agreement) to which the charge could attach.

(2) **Facultative type of agreement.** Less certain is the position as regards an agreement under which the debts remain vested in the client until

accepted by the factor. The factor would have constructive knowledge of the charge as soon as it had been registered. It seems possible that, unless it could be shown that the chargee was aware of the factoring arrangement at the time when the charge was created, the factor would be bound by any restriction in the charge.

If the chargee was clearly aware of the factoring arrangements before he took the charge, on the basis of the dicta of Browne-Wilkinson J quoted in 15.16 above, it is likely that he would be unable to enforce the restriction as against the factor. In these circumstances the factor with a facultative type of agreement might well prevail and *a fortiori* a whole turnover type of agreement would certainly take priority over the charge.

15.18   As such charges are normally taken by the client's bankers and in order to strengthen the factor's case for priority, the factor should ensure that any banker of the client is fully aware of the factoring arrangements from the outset. This may be done by a simple exchange of letters by which the banker acknowledges the existence of the arrangements or by referring to the agreement on every occasion on which a payment is sent to the client's banker for the account of the client. It is also usual for a factor to make periodic searches, but such searches, even if conducted at frequent intervals, will serve only to inform the factor of a *fait accompli*. In a perfect world such searches should not be necessary as the factoring agreement will include a warranty by the client not to create charges affecting book debts. However, as it has often occurred that clients execute such documents in ignorance and as a charge may be given in favour of a bank or finance company that is not the client's main bank such searches should be made. It is better that the factor should be aware of the charge at an early stage so that the factoring arrangement may then be brought to the attention of the chargee and the priority position acknowledged.

15.19   It is apparent that as regards debts purchased by a factor after registration of a floating charge, the priority rule in *Dearle v Hall* will not assist the factor, although he will be likely (except in the case of invoice discounting or undisclosed factoring) to have given notice to the debtors first. This is because he will have constructive knowledge of the prior equitable rights of the chargee. Accordingly one must look to the aspects enunciated above in order to determine the priorities between the factor and the holder of a floating charge. In the absence of the knowledge on either side it seems that the rule in *Dearle v Hall* would operate to determine the prior right to debts purchased by the factor after execution of the charge but before registration. It is difficult to imagine such a conflict arising because it would postulate a crystallisation of the charge before the debts purchased by the factor, prior to registration of the charge, had been settled. As the charge must be registered within 21 days of creation such a situation seems most unlikely.

Prior fixed charge

15.20 It has for some years been generally accepted that it is possible to effect a fixed charge on the book debts of a company, present and future, so that the charge shall attach to each such debt as a specific charge as soon as the debt is created. The concept has gained recognition by the court. (*Siebe Gorman & Co Ltd v Barclays Bank Ltd [1979] 2 Lloyds Rep 142*). Such a charge will also take effect in equity. As in the case of a floating charge, the rule in *Dearle v Hall* will not assist the factor in relation to a fixed charge existing and registered at the date when the factoring agreement commences; for the factor will have constructive notice of the prior equitable rights of the chargee as soon as the charge is registered. Furthermore, unlike the position relating to floating charges, by its very nature a fixed charge does not allow the chargor to dispose of the charged assets or to deal with them in any way free from the charge. Of the three characteristics (referred to in the *Yorkshire Woolcombers* case—see 15.14 above) which must necessarily be present for a charge to be floating, book debts will of their nature have two. Therefore, the third characteristic, that is to say that the chargee is at liberty to deal with the asset in the normal course of business until crystallisation, must be absent. The chargor must not be able to dispose of the debts but must pay the proceeds as directed by the chargee or the charge will be considered to be floating. It follows that the factor, with constructive knowledge of a fixed charge, cannot in good faith purchase the chargor's book debts.

15.21 Such charges also normally include a restrictive covenant by which the chargor undertakes not to purport to assign or charge the charged debts. Curiously, in *Siebe Gorman & Co Ltd v Barclays Bank Ltd* (*[1979] 2 Lloyds Rep 142*), the registration of a fixed charge on all book debts did not prevent the plaintiff from taking assignments of debts from the chargor subject to the bank's prior charge. However, the bank's charge on the assigned debts was held to secure only amounts of indebtedness to the bank incurred before the assignments and remaining outstanding. As the bank had not ruled off the account and started a new one, credits to the account since the assignment up to the insolvency of the chargor/assignor had almost extinguished the pre-assignment indebtedness. The question of the restrictive covenants in the charge document were considered and the judge found that the assignee had no knowledge of them—either actual or constructive. Presumably the restrictions had not been noted with the registration details on the file. As with the case of a floating charge, it is not certain if the filing of such details invests a person, who does not actually look at the file, with constructive knowledge of the restrictions. What the outcome would have been if the details had been on the file it is difficult to determine. It would seem that if the assignee was shown to have actual knowledge of the restrictions he might not have succeeded; in such a case the dicta of Browne-Wilkinson J in *Swiss Bank Corporation v Lloyds Bank Limited and Others* mentioned at the end of 15.16 above might well apply.

15.22 On the basis of the facts in this case, in the absence of any knowledge of restrictive covenants in the charge document a factor might be able to purchase debts already the subject of a registered fixed charge. His rights would then extend only to the equity remaining in the debts after the charges had been satisfied out of the proceeds to the extent of the chargor/assignor's liability incurred prior to each assignment. The factor's position in the case of a conflict with the holder of a fixed charge is unlike his position *vis à vis* a floating charge. In the case of an existing fixed charge a waiver or priority agreement is essential.

Subsequent fixed charge

15.23 In the event of the factor's client creating a fixed charge on book debts after the start of factoring, the position seems to be little different from that described above in relation to floating charges. The question of priority will depend upon the type of factoring agreement and whether or not the chargee was aware of the factoring arrangement at the date of the charge's creation. If he were *not* so aware, the position would be:

(1) **Whole turnover agreement.** The agreement provides that the debts vest in the factor immediately upon creation and it is generally considered that there is no *scintilla temporis* after creation of each debt before it vests in the factor. As a result the factor's prior equitable rights should prevail. The charge will not find any book debts on which to fasten, save those excluded from the factoring agreement and amounts payable by the factor to the client.

(2) **Facultative agreement.** In this case the factor would be in some difficulty. The charge would attach to each debt as it is created and the offer to the factor would be of debts subject to a charge.

15.24 In both cases, however, if it could be shown that the chargee had actual knowledge of the factoring arrangements, the factor might be assisted by the dicta of Browne-Wilkinson J mentioned in 15.16 above. This might be of help to the factor whose arrangements are facultative and would, in the case of a whole turnover agreement, provide assistance where none might be needed. However, the factor's procedures for notifying banks and periodic searches apply no less to fixed charges than to floating charges. These procedures should be as described in 15.18 above.

Chapter 16

The Factor's Conflicts with Other Claimants to Debts

16.1　In Chapter 10 it was emphasised that, in reviewing the suitability of a prospective client for factoring, the factor must ensure as far as he can that the nature and pattern of the business is such that there will be no encumbrances in favour of third parties on the debts to be sold to him. In this chapter the conflicts that may arise with third parties having rights in relation to the client's trade debts (other than registerable charges) are described more fully. A realisation of the difficulties that may arise from such conflicts may serve to ensure that both the factor and the client, and possibly the client's adviser, operate the business of the client and the arrangement for factoring in such a way as to minimise the incidence of the encumbrances. For example, the client should as far as possible refuse to purchase from suppliers whose terms of payment include reservation of title to goods sold which extends to rights over the proceeds of the sub-sale of such goods. Reservation of title is considered next and then the position of parties claiming rights to the debts. The most important of these are pledgees of imported goods, carriers and mercantile agents.

'Romalpa' clauses

Background

16.2　The expression 'Romalpa', which has been generally applied for some years in commerce and industry to conditions in sale contracts which reserve to the seller rights to goods sold until payment has been made by the buyer, arose from the case which gave publicity to the practice, *Aluminium Industrie Vaassen BV v Romalpa Aluminium Ltd [1976] 2 AER 552.* The practice, which is more properly to be referred to as 'conditional sale' or (to avoid confusion with the definition in Section 25(2) of the Sale of Goods Act 1979) 'reservation of title', has for many years been employed in Germany almost without exception and is recognised in the Civil Code. (BGB paragraph 455). In its most comprehensive form it not only gives the supplier the right to recover from his insolvent customer goods supplied and actually still in the possession of the customer but not paid for, but also gives an unpaid supplier rights to the following:

(*a*) any goods (even those for which payment has been made) originating from the supplier for satisfaction of indebtedness for all goods supplied and not paid for; and

(*b*) any work in progress or finished products in which goods originating from the supplier are comprised; and

(*c*) any indebtedness owing to the customer and arising from sub-sales of goods mentioned in (*a*) and (*b*).

(*a*) and (*b*) are usually referred to by factors internationally as 'extended reservation of title' and (*c*) as 'prolonged reservation of title'.

16.3   The practice of reserving title had also in various forms been long established in some other European countries, notably the Netherlands. In its simple form it had long been established in the United Kingdom; several important companies in engineering and textiles had incorporated such reservation in their conditions of sale. However, the practice did not, until the mid 1970's, come to the general notice of grantors of credit–nor to the accountancy and legal professions as a whole–and was discussed mainly between experts and practitioners in insolvency. The reason for this is not well understood and may have arisen from the failure of insolvency practitioners to bring it to the notice of other professional men and of industry for fear that the practice should become more widespread. The attention of the banks, commerce and industry was drawn to the practice by the wide publicity given to the *Romalpa* case. This case broke new ground, not for its confirmation that such conditions were effective against goods still retained in their original state by the buyer (which had never seriously been disputed), but for its upholding the right of the supplier to trace his rights through to the proceeds obtained by his customer for the sub-sale of goods for which the customer had not paid to the supplier (prolonged reservation of title). Until the report of the *Romalpa* case, the practice had not been of concern to factors, for the question of prolonged reservation of title had not been considered as a possibility in the United Kingdom; the other forms which related to goods only would not affect the factor's rights to debts purchased.

The effect of 'Romalpa' on factors

16.4   Once the *Romalpa* case had brought the practice in its various forms to the notice of factors, a number of questions had to be answered.

(1) Would a client who had not paid his supplier for goods sold to him under these conditions be able to give his own customer a good title in respect of any sub-sale? If he was not able to do so then any debt purchased by a factor might be valueless; the debtor would in no way pay for goods claimed from him by the original supplier. However, the debtor would in normal circumstances obtain a good title. The position in all but exceptional cases will be covered by the

statutory exception to the ordinary rule that *nemo dat quod non habet*. [*Sale of Goods Act 1979, s 25(1); Factors Act 1889, ss 2(1), 9*]. This provides *inter alia* that, where a buyer in possession of goods with the consent of the true owner delivers them, in accordance with a contract of sale, to another who receives them in good faith and without knowledge of the rights of the original seller, that other person obtains a good title.

(2)   In the case of reservation of title in its simple form, without any stated term, by which it is provided that the supplier is to have the proceeds held for his account by his buyer (the factor's client), may the supplier nevertheless attach any proceeds of the sub-sale? Such a possibility has been considered either by way of an equitable tracing right or a common law right to follow proceeds (see Goode 'The Right to Trace and its Impact on Commercial Transactions', (1976) LQR Vol 92, especially pp 547 to 560). In a recent case, *Hendy Lennox (Industrial Engines) Ltd v Grahame Puttick Ltd [1984] 1 WLR 485*, unlike the position in *Romalpa*, the express terms referred only to the goods and not to the proceeds of the sub-sale of such goods and there was no provision by which the 'buyer' was a fiduciary agent. In that case the original supplier's claim in respect of such proceeds failed.

Although the case related to the sub-sale by the buyer of equipment to which the goods originally supplied had been attached and the claim was to a proportion, and not the whole, of the proceeds, it seems unlikely that the courts will consider a term relating to the proceeds to be implied; it seems that the courts will not import a term which the parties would have included had they thought it appropriate. Furthermore, in practice, it is normally considered by suppliers whose terms include merely simple reservation of title that their rights extend only to goods remaining in the possession of the buyer.

(3)   To what extent will such terms, and particularly the right to proceeds arising from prolonged reservation of title, validly apply where goods have been the subject of a sub-sale otherwise than in their original form? In most cases the supplier has been unable to establish his rights to the unsold goods remaining on the buyer's premises and *a fortiori* to the proceeds of any resale. (*Re Bond Worth Ltd [1979] 3 AER 919; Borden (UK) Ltd v Scottish Timber Products Ltd [1979] 3 AER 961*, and (more recently) *Re Peachdart Ltd [1983] 2 AER 204*). But where the goods supplied to the client, although incorporated into other goods, were still clearly identifiable through not having been changed in form and being marked with a serial number, it may well be that the supplier's claim might be upheld. (*Hendy Lennox (Industrial Engines) Ltd v Grahame Puttick Ltd [1984] 1 WLR 485*).

The problem of priority of claims

16.5   The main question to be answered is: if the supplier to the factor's client can establish his right to the proceeds of sub-sales by the client, is it the supplier or the factor that has the prior right to the proceeds of the debts, arising from the sub-sales, assigned to the factor? This question is unresolved. A widely accepted opinion is that the prior right must go to the claimant, the notice of whose claim has been given first to the debtor, provided that, in the case of the factor whose right would arise after that of the supplier, he had no knowledge of the supplier's terms. This is based on the rule in *Dearle v Hall* (see 15.5). If notice of the assignment to the factor is on the invoice this notice is likely to be first in time so that, by this argument, the factor should prevail. (See Goode op.cit. and 'Commercial Law', Penguin Education/Allen Lane, p 872; for a contrary opinion see D M McLaughlan 'Priorities–Equitable Tracing Rights and Assignments of Book Debts', (1980) LQR Vol 96, at pp 90 to 100).

16.6   A more compelling argument in favour of the factor's case under arrangements in which he is responsible for collections, and where he purchased the debts in good faith and for value without any knowledge of the supplier's alleged rights, is as follows:

(*a*)   The supplier must have envisaged that his transaction with the client would have resulted in a sub-sale (whether or not this was explicitly stated in the contract term), by which the client would have given his debtor a good title to the goods (see 16.4(1) above);

(*b*)   As between the client and the debtor the client had the right to receive payment;

(*c*)   That right to receive payment could be transferred to a factor in return for settlement of the debt by way of payment of the purchase price by the factor to the client. Such an arrangement for collection of debts is now considered to be in the normal course of business.

If such an argument were to be accepted then the proceeds vesting in the supplier under his prolonged reservation of title would be the payments made or to be made by the factor to the client.

Position in Germany may be relevant

16.7   It is interesting to note that in Germany, where the practice of reserving title has been generally used for far longer than in the United Kingdom, a conflict between a factor and a supplier to the factor's client was resolved in favour of the factor on the basis of this argument. (BGH decisions of 7.6.78 and 12.10.78; see Klaus Bette 'Factoring and Prolonged Retention of Property Title'—Factoring Handbuch, edited by Prof Dr K F Hagenmuller and Herr H J Sommer, published by Fritz Knapp Verlag). It is interesting also to note that this decision relates solely to factoring without recourse; in Germany factoring with recourse is considered not to constitute an outright sale of the debts to the factor but to be an arrangement for financing on the security of debts.

Question of inferred knowledge

16.8   A further question remains if the latter argument expressed in 16.6 above is not tenable; in what circumstances can the factor be considered to have knowledge of the supplier's terms? This is important if the factor wishes to rely on the principle of *Dearle v Hall*—he must have clean hands. It seems unlikely that a factor purchasing a myriad of small debts on a continuing basis could be expected to have investigated every one of his client's purchase contracts. Even if he may have noted the terms of some of the most important suppliers at the time of his survey, he is not to know from whom and on what terms his client will purchase subsequently.

Position of factor summarised

16.9   As a result of the foregoing it seems that, in relation to the danger of such a conflict and in order to ensure, as far as possible, his rights to debts purchased by him are not encumbered by claims of suppliers to his client, the factor might reasonably take the following view:

(*a*) he has little to fear in the case of a manufacturer unless the original goods remain clearly identifiable and have not changed their form; and

(*b*) he should not be unduly concerned if the supplier's terms are of simple reservation of title and do not relate to the whole of the proceeds and place the client in a fiduciary capacity.

However, if the client's business is such that goods are passed through to the debtors in identifiable and unchanged form, it would be advisable for the factor to examine the client's terms of purchase with any major supplier *at the outset*. If any such supplier includes terms that may appear to give him rights to proceeds, then the client should be advised either (i) to obtain a waiver for the factor recognising the factor's prior rights, or (ii) if this is refused to purchase elsewhere. Furthermore, the client should ensure that, during the currency of factoring, he purchases only from those that do not insist on prolonged reservation of title. The client is likely to succeed, for in such relationships the purchaser usually has superior bargaining power. Such arrangements are a precaution to avoid conflict, but the better opinion is that, if there were to be a conflict, the factor's rights would prevail on the basis of the arguments stated above.

16.10   It seems that the courts in Scotland are even less likely than those in England to uphold a supplier's rights to the proceeds of sub-sales by his buyer. (*Clark Taylor & Co Ltd v Quality Site Development (Edinburgh) Ltd 1981 SLT 308*).

Goods released on trust receipt

16.11   A conflicting claim to debts sold to a factor, similar to that which arises when a client purchases on 'Romalpa' terms, might well occur where the factor's client, having obtained the physical release of goods pledged to a bank or finance company against the execution of a trust receipt or letter of hypothecation, sells those goods in the normal course of business and offers or notifies the resulting debts to the factor. The trust receipt or letter would normally provide, not only that the goods remain pledged to the bank or finance company until paid for, but also that any proceeds of sale were to be held in trust for it. The factor may well have purchased the debts in good faith and for value and without any knowledge, not only of the release of goods, but also of the arrangement for the pledge in general. As a security right by means of physical possession the pledge would not require registration; and this physical possession is deemed to continue in spite of the release of the goods on trust. (*North Western Bank Ltd v John Poynter Son & MacDonalds (1895) AC 56*). The uncertainty of such a situation, which may too easily occur, is compounded by the fact that it has not even been the subject matter of any published comment nor any reference in any standard textbook. In view of the uncertainty a factor should make frequent enquiries of any client who is likely to import on these terms and ensure that any likely conflict is avoided by the issue of a letter of waiver by the bank or finance company concerned. In the absence of such a waiver, the resulting debts would have to be excluded because the client cannot give the usual warranty that the debts notified or offered are free from any encumbrance.

The liens of a carrier

16.12   The question of a carrier's lien on goods, despatched by a client to a debtor, is not strictly a question of a conflict between the factor and the carrier relating to rights to debts purchased by the factor. On the insolvency of the client there may well be an unpaid carrier who has a general lien on such goods in respect of which the client had responsibility for delivery to the debtor's premises. Such a claim to the goods will obviously impair the factor's right to recover any related debt. As previously described (see 8.30) factors normally accept notifications or offers submitted as soon as goods have been placed in transit in the United Kingdom to debtors. If the carrier seized the goods, the debtors would not pay and the client would be in breach of his warranty that the debts were *bona fide* obligations of the debtors.

16.13   This aspect may not be too serious a problem in the case of domestic sales in relation to which delivery may take only two or three days. Even if the carrier's charges for all his sales are the client's responsibility, the aggregate of unpaid debts may well be fully absorbed by any retention made. Indeed in many cases in the event of insolvency and an insufficient retention it may sometimes be worthwhile for the factor to settle with the carrier in order to release the goods to the debtors and recover the indebtedness. However, in the case of export sales in circumstances in which the client is responsible for carriage and freight charges, the amounts payable may be considerable and, in view of the longer transit time, the aggregate of the outstanding invoices represented by goods which have not reached the debtors may be a large proportion of the whole.

16.14   It is therefore important, particularly in the case of exports, that the factor should monitor the client's account with carriers and forwarding agents whenever the business of the client is such that he is likely to be responsible for these charges. Furthermore, this aspect needs to be considered carefully in the case of an importing client whose business is such that the goods are despatched from his overseas supplier direct to the customers. In such a case the factor should accept responsibility for the debts only when the underlying goods have been placed in transit to the debtors in the United Kingdom.

The rights of a mercantile agent

16.15   A mercantile agent (or factor in the original sense) has a prescriptive right, born of long usage in the law merchant, to a lien on his principal's goods in his possession and on the proceeds of the sale of those goods effected through his agency. As a result, if a client sells to the debtors through a mercantile agent it is likely that the agent's lien would attach to the proceeds (i.e. the debts) in priority to the factor's rights to debts resulting from the agent's sales on behalf of the client. The factor's rights to any such debt under the assignment to him cannot be better than the client's rights at the time of the assignment. This question does not appear to have been decided in the courts in the United Kingdom and it would not appear to be a serious matter for factors in their domestic businesses because few businesses employ mercantile agents in this country. To be a mercantile agent, for this purpose, the agent must sell in his own name without disclosing that of his principal (per Lord Denning in *Rolls Razor Ltd v Cox [1967] 1 AER 397*). However, the priority of a mercantile agent in these circumstances has been accepted in international trade in Europe; this would be particularly relevant if, as is often the case, the agent invoiced in his own name and the principal (the factor's client) were to be undisclosed to the debtor. A factor should be on his guard if his client factors his exports and is likely to use a mercantile agent. Agreement between the factor and the agent should be reached at the outset. Obviously, if the agent is adamant about retaining his rights and the client persists in using him, then the client will be unable to warrant that these debts are free of encumbrances and they will have to be excluded from factoring.

Part E

Insolvency of the Client

Chapter 17

Receivership

Relations between the receiver and the factor

17.1   This Part of the book considers the situation of the factor when his client becomes insolvent. First it looks at the position on the appointment of a receiver for a client company (this chapter), then on a winding-up or bankruptcy (Chapter 18) and finally on miscellaneous matters associated with factoring and the insolvent client (Chapter 19). It may happen that the holder of a charge on all the assets and the undertaking of a client company appoints a receiver, with powers of management, in accordance with the provisions of the instrument of charge. The relations between factor and such a receiver have sometimes been a matter of misunderstanding and they are therefore, considered here. The situation in which a receiver is appointed by the court or in accordance with the Law of Property Act 1925 is unlikely to arise.

Effect of the appointment of the receiver

17.2   In these days the charge will in most circumstances be fixed on real property and debts and floating on other assets such as stock and work-in-progress. The effect of the appointment will include the following:

(*a*)   The floating element of the charge will *crystallise*, if crystallisation has not occurred beforehand on some other event giving rise to it according to the instrument of charge (e.g. execution by a creditor on an asset of the company). The charge will thus become fixed on all assets and attach thereto.

(*b*)   In the absence of a resolution for the winding-up of the company or of a court order to that effect, the receiver will usually become the

158

agent of the company in accordance with the terms of the instrument of charge. (See 'Tolley's Receivership Manual', paragraph 3.17.)

(*c*) His appointment does not discharge or terminate the company's normal commercial contracts. (*Re Newdigate Colliery Ltd [1912] 1 Ch 468*). However, the other parties have no means of enforcing them against the company itself as the receiver is in possession of all the property of the company. He is not liable on them nor can they be enforced against him. (*Airlines Airspares Ltd v Handley Page Ltd [1970] 1 AER 29*).

(*d*) He has no responsibility towards unsecured creditors, other than his statutory responsibility to pay preferential creditors such amounts as are payable to them in priority to the secured creditor in respect of the floating element of the charge. [*Companies Act 1948, s 94*]. There is, however, a developing concept of a duty of care in the realisation of assets.

(*e*) Unlike the position in a winding-up (see 18.1), the directors' powers do not cease and they may continue to exercise them in relation to any property or rights of which the receiver has not taken possession to the extent that they do not interfere with the receiver's rights. (*Newhart Developments Ltd v Co-operative Commercial Bank Ltd [1978] 2 AER 896*).

Factor's rights on the appointment: general

17.3   The factor's rights on the appointment of a receiver to take possession of the property of a client company will depend upon the terms of the factoring agreement. Most usually the agreement will provide for one or more of the following options by the factor:

(*a*) To terminate the agreement forthwith by notice; *or*

(*b*) With or without termination of the agreement:

(i) to refrain from making any further prepayments or other payments to the client until all funds in use have been recovered; or

(ii) to require that all prepayments should be repaid; *or*

(iii) to have all debts vested in the factor repurchased for their full invoice value on the basis that they shall not vest in the client until the full amount of the repurchase consideration has been received by the factor.

17.4   In the usual situation in which the receiver is in possession of all the assets of the company neither (*b*)(ii) nor (*b*)(iii) above will be of much immediate help to the factor. In both those cases the factor will, if he has prepaid on the debts purchased to the full, become a *creditor* ; in the former case (*b*)(ii), to the extent that his unrecovered prepayments exceed the retention (unpaid balances owed to the client see 2.7 and 2.8) and in the latter (*b*)(iii), to the extent that the total invoice value of the debts exceed the retention. The receiver will not be responsible to him and the directors will have no rights in respect of assets with which to deal with the factor's demand for repayment. In both cases, however, the factor will be in a position to make a demand on any guarantors without waiting for the final outcome–whether or not the funds in use will be fully recovered from payments by debtors.

17.5   Whichever of the options in 17.3 above is available to and exercised by the factor, it is usual for the factor to be able to refrain from making further payments to the client until all funds in use have been recovered. The balance on the factor's account in favour of the client will normally be an asset subject to the charge and in the possession of the receiver; accordingly, the amount ultimately payable to the client, after taking into account all recourse and any other set-off, will be payable to the receiver unless by that time he has obtained his discharge. In the case of the receiver's discharge before payment is to be made by the factor, then such payment will fall into the hands of any liquidator subsequently appointed or, in the unlikely event of a solvent company, it will be payable to the company itself.

17.6   In all cases the factor's rights *in relation to the debts vesting in him* remain unaltered on the appointment of the receiver. In particular:

(*a*)   The factor's powers to execute legal assignments and to endorse the client's name on negotiable instruments will be unaffected, provided that the power of attorney given to him in the factoring agreement is stated to be irrevocable (see 8.14 to 8.17); and

(*b*)   Any trust provisions in the factoring agreement (see 8.18), by which remittances for debtors received by the client are to be held for the account of and sent to the factor, remain in effect.

17.7   It is advisable for the factor's staff to make early contact with the receiver in order to explain the effects of the factoring agreement in this respect and particularly to ensure that remittances paid by debtors to the receiver in error are passed on promptly. This will be in the interests of both parties; for otherwise further demands for payment may be made by the factor and this will detract from the goodwill of the business and may impair the factor's collection procedures. Although the receiver is not obliged to carry on the factoring agreement and would be most unlikely to do so in its existing form, the agreement remains in force unless terminated either by the receiver, as agent for the client, or by the factor. The receiver being responsible neither for the client company's contracts nor for unsecured claims will *not* be responsible for any recourse or other amount chargeable by the factor to the client, save to the extent that the factor may be able to set such claims off against a balance owing to the client. On the discharge of the receiver the question of termination of the factoring agreement, if the factor has not or does not take steps to terminate, will be for any liquidator appointed or, in the rare event of no liquidation (see Chapter 18), the directors.

Factor's position as regards existing debts

17.8   The factor may have available to him and may exercise, the option of terminating the agreement and assigning back to the client all outstanding debts. The assignment back may arise from the nature of the factoring contract; if the contract is for recourse or bulk factoring or invoice discounting, all the debts will have been purchased by the factor with full recourse. On the other hand the reassignment may arise from special provisions in the agreement which come into effect on insolvency as described in 17.3 above.

17.9   Where prepayments have been made and have not been fully recovered on appointment of a receiver, the factor will still be interested in collecting the outstanding debts in order to recover his funds in use. However, the advantage to the factor of having the right to sell the debts back to the client is that he will no longer be responsible for any credit risk. The term in the agreement will provide that the client should re-purchase the debts at their full invoice value and this would apply notwithstanding the recovery of a lesser amount; the debts will however, *remain the factor's property until the repurchase price has been paid*. As the client has no funds with which to pay, the payment must come from the factor's collections. So, in this way, or by a direct provision in the agreement cancelling the factor's responsibility for collection or credit risk on the occurrence of insolvency (including receivership) of his client, the factor may continue to collect for his own account until he has recovered the funds he has laid out by way of prepayments. At that stage he may have no further responsibility. In the absence of provisions in the factoring agreement as described in 17.3 above, in the case of the full service or maturity factoring, the factor will be responsible for the ultimate collection and the credit risk on all approved accounts even after his recovery of the funds in use.

17.10 Where the arrangements for factoring have included the administration of the debtor accounts and collections and the factor has the right, as described above, to have the outstanding debts reassigned, it may well be worthwhile for the receiver to make arrangements with the factor to continue to collect and record the debts. Such an arrangement will save the receiver from the administrative burden of taking on the sales ledger accounts and effecting collection. Such arrangements may often be made with a factor for little, if anything, in the way of an additional charge in return for efficient co-operation from the receiver's staff in providing some important administrative back-up from the client's records. Examples of this back-up are:

(*a*) the provision of proof of delivery of goods where this is required by a debtor; and (*b*) help in dealing with disputes or warranty claims relating to the goods.

No doubt the receiver will in any case appreciate that such co-operation is in his interest; the factor's recoveries are ultimately for the benefit of the estate of the client.

17.11   The appointment of a receiver and the crystallisation of the charge will not affect the factor's rights to the debts vesting in him at the date of appointment. The factor's rights to such debts in relation to a holder of a charge will normally have been regularised by a waiver. If there is no waiver then his rights will be determined as described in Chapter 15.

Position as regards debts coming into existence after the appointment

17.12   If the factor or the receiver takes steps to terminate the agreement, no debts coming into existence after such termination will be offered to or notified to the factor and the factor will have no rights in relation to such debts. In the absence of such termination the factoring agreement will remain in effect, but the receiver will not be obliged to carry out its provisions and would be unlikely to wish to do so otherwise than described as in 17.14 to 17.15 below. The factor's only remedy on the receiver's refusal to honour the provisions of the agreement would be against the company for breach of contract and as such he would be unsecured. Certainly, in the case of a facultative type of factoring agreement under which the factor has no rights in relation to any debt until it has been offered to and accepted by him, the factor would have no rights to any debt not offered to him before the receiver's appointment. Thus, in such a case, there may be debts which have come into existence before the receiver's appointment and which have not been offered, or perhaps not even invoiced, which will not vest in the factor unless the receiver agrees, as agent of the company, to offer them. In the case of a whole turnover type of agreement under which the debts vest in the factor as they come into existence, any debts not notified but in existence before the receiver's appointment may be claimed by the factor as his property.

17.13   In the case of either type of agreement there is no doubt that, in the absence of any agreement by the receiver to continue, no debts created after the receiver's appointment will vest in the factor. All the assets are in the possession of the receiver and, although the receiver is the agent of the company, any further sales made by him are for the benefit of the chargee. For this reason, where a charge on a company's assets is in existence before the factoring agreement, it is not unusual for any waiver letter or agreement for priorities, to specify that the waiver shall not apply to any debts coming into existence after the crystallisation of any floating element in the charge.

Continuation of the arrangement for factoring by the receiver

17.14　On many occasions a receiver carrying on the business of a client company will wish to use the factor's administrative and collection services. He may wish to avoid having to set up a sales ledger and may benefit from protection against bad debts. Thus, where the factoring agreement was for the full service, recourse factoring or maturity factoring it is often arranged for factoring to continue. In particular collections from debtors will benefit by an absence of disruption arising from a change. In many cases, also, a receiver may need finance to carry on the business to an extent greater than is to be provided by the chargee.

17.15　The receiver will not accept responsibility for the client company's liability to the factor, existing at the date of his appointment, for recourse and other items chargeable under the agreement. The continuation may be effected in either of the following ways:

(*a*)　by a novation (i.e. a tripartite agreement rescinding the two party contract in consideration of a new contract on the same terms between one of the parties and the third party); *or*

(*b*)　a completely new agreement.

In the case of a novation, the agreement must specify that a new account will be opened and that debit or credit entries arising from transactions relating to debts which were offered to or vested in the factor before the appointment should be on the old account. Whether the arrangements are continued by a new agreement or a novation, the factor will normally expect that the receiver should not exclude his personal responsibility for his obligations under the agreement (responsibility for contracts made by a receiver appointed out of court in accordance with Section 369(2) of the Companies Act 1948: see also 'Tolley's Receivership Manual', paragraph 3.17).

The position of the receiver subsequent to a winding-up order

17.16　A difficult conceptual question of law arises as regards the impact of winding-up, whether by the court or voluntary, on the position of a receiver. There is no doubt that he ceases to be the agent of the company and his power to bind the company ceases. (*Gosling v Gaskell and Grocott [1895–9] AER Rep 300; Thomas v Todd [1926]2 KB 511*). He does not then become the agent of the debenture holders and, although there is some uncertainty regarding his position, it is generally considered that he continues to act in relation to the property of the company as a principal. It is generally considered also that on a winding-up his authority to carry on the business, save as is necessary for the beneficial realisation of the property in his possession, is revoked. However, his power to deal with the company's property in the name of the company is unaffected. (*Sowman v David Samuel Trust Ltd [1978] 1 WLR 22*: see also 'Tolley's Receivership Manual', paragraph 3.17). In view of the foregoing it seems likely that, if a receiver has made arrangements to continue factoring either by a novation or a new agreement, he will be able to continue to factor debts only so long as it is necessary for him to carry on the business to effect realisation of the property in his possession. In order to avoid this uncertainty it is often arranged by a receiver who sees a benefit in carrying on the business for an indeterminate period that the business of the company should be 'hived down' into a new subsidiary company. This will also facilitate the sale of the business as a going concern. Where factoring has included sales accounting and collections, it is often arranged for the factor to enter into a factoring agreement with the new subsidiary and this should be a simple matter for the factor who will already have the debtor accounts on his records. If prepayments are required for the new subsidiary then it might be advisable for the factor to obtain the receiver's guarantee and indemnity in respect of the obligations of the subsidiary under the new agreement up to the date of its disposal. Furthermore, the agreement with the subsidiary should give both parties the right to terminate upon such disposal.

Appointment of administrator proposed in White Paper

17.17 In order to facilitate rehabilitation of companies in financial difficulties, the White Paper on Insolvency proposes a new statutory procedure for the appointment of an administrator by the court on the application of a creditor or the company itself. The order will be made at the discretion of the court on the basis of jeopardy to the general body of creditors or insolvency of the company and the prospects for rehabilitation or the interests of interested parties. It is proposed that an administrator may be appointed *whether or not* a floating charge exists. In view of the difficult position of a receiver wishing to carry on the company's business in the event of the commencement of the company's winding-up, it is suggested that the appointment of an administrator in such circumstances may be of benefit to all those interested.

17.18 The effect of the appointment of an administrator would be to stay all proceedings against the company and creditors' rights to enforce security or payment. The White Paper also proposes a stay on the right of a creditor to levy execution, except where proceedings have already been started, and to petition for winding-up. The powers of the directors would be curtailed. The administrator's powers would be similar to those of a receiver and manager appointed under a floating charge including the power to carry on the business. It is proposed that he should be the agent of the company and should be personally liable for any obligations which he may incur. The administrator will have the duty to prepare plans for saving the company, to hold a meeting of creditors and report back to the court with the views of the meeting within three months. The court may confirm his appointment and he will then be required to report periodically to a committee of creditors.

17.19 Until the proposals become law it is not possible to determine what the position of an administrator will be in relation to factoring arrangements which may already be in effect with the company when he is appointed. One may surmise, however, that the position will be similar to that which obtains on the appointment of a receiver and manager under a floating charge: it seems likely that all debts vested in the factor on the date of the administrator's appointment will be unaffected, but that the administrator will not be obliged to carry on the factoring agreement. It is expected that in most cases the administrator would in fact wish to carry on any form of factoring arrangement, in effect on his appointment, which included the administration of the sales ledger. There seems little doubt that the rehabilitation of the company would not be assisted by the distraction of having to set up a sales ledger and credit control administration. In such an event it also appears likely that the agreement will have to be varied to provide that the administrator takes no responsibility for recourse for pre-administration debts or that a new agreement will be completed.

Chapter 18

Winding-up and Bankruptcy

The effect of a winding-up by the court

18.1 The previous chapter considered the effect of receivership on a factoring agreement. A winding-up of, or bankruptcy proceedings against, the factor's client will, of course, affect the arrangements for factoring and the effects of these proceedings are considered separately in this chapter. The factoring agreement is not terminated automatically by a winding-up order on a client company, but the factor has no means of enforcing its continuation as all actions against the company are stayed except by leave of the court. [*Companies Act 1948, s 231*]. On the making of the order the director's powers cease and the liquidator takes possession of the assets of the company for the purpose of their realisation and the distribution to creditors and contributories. Before a meeting of creditors is held to appoint a liquidator, the official receiver becomes provisional liquidator. Furthermore, the liquidator may disclaim the factoring agreement as an onerous contract with leave of court. [*Companies Act 1948, s 323*]. As a result the factoring agreement will, almost invariably, terminate as at the date of the order. However, as regards debts already vested in the factor at the commencement of the winding-up (see 18.2 below) the rights of the factor remain unaffected. The extent to which those rights may be exercised is described later in this chapter (see 18.14–18.19 below).

18.2 The position as regards the debts which come into existence after the commencement of the winding-up may create some difficulty for the factor. Any disposition of the property of the company, including 'things in action', made after the commencement of the winding-up is *void* save as ordered by the court. [*Companies Act 1948, s 227*]. The commencement of the winding-up is the date of the presentation of the petition on the basis of which the order was made or any earlier resolution to wind up. [*Companies Act 1948, s 229*]. The position of the factor in relation to debts offered and accepted or notified after the commencement of winding-up appears to be as follows:

(a) Where the factoring agreement is on a **facultative basis**, it seems clear that any debts accepted by the factor after the commencement of winding-up will not vest in the factor unless the court orders otherwise. This will apply notwithstanding any payment by the factor on account of the purchase price of such debts and it is doubtful if the factor would be other than an unsecured creditor in respect of recovery of such prepayments. As a petition, on which a winding-up order is grounded, does not have to be advertised until seven days before the hearing the factor may be paying on account of debts which will not vest in him for some weeks (or in the long vacation — months) before he is aware of the petition.

(b) In the case of a **whole turnover agreement** by which the debts vest in the factor without further formality as they come into existence, it would seem that the factor's rights to all debts, not only those notified but all that come into existence before the appointment of the liquidator, will be unaffected. The disposition of the debts, although then not in existence, takes place in equity at the time of the execution of the factoring agreement. Although property, which is not in existence but to be acquired at a future time, is not assignable in law, it is *assignable* in equity. However, this view is based on analogy only and there is no precedent on this aspect in relation to a factoring agreement. (*Holroyd v Marshall (1862) 10 HLC 191; Tailby v Official Receiver (1888) 13 App Cas 523; Re Lind, Industrials Finance Syndicate Ltd v Lind [1914–15] AER Rep 527*).

18.3   In the case of a facultative type of agreement (and probably also in the case of a whole turnover agreement) when the factor hears of a petition to wind up he should:

(a) suspend payment to the client, as his factoring agreement should give him the right so to do; and

(b) advise his client to make application to the court under Section 227 of the Companies Act 1948 for an order validating the assignments made under the factoring agreement since the date of the petition (or any earlier resolution to wind up).

The court will decide the issue on the basis of benefit to the client company. If it can be shown that the continuation of factoring will assist the business, then a validating order may be made. If such an order is made, it will be necessary for the factor to make an assessment of the advisability of making further prepayments on:

(i) the quality of the client's business (i.e. degree of potential recourse); and

(ii) the probability of a dismissal of the petition.

18.4   In view of the relation back of the commencement of compulsory winding-up, factors should be vigilant to watch for petitions in relation to their clients. In the White Paper on Insolvency it is proposed that petitions for winding-up should not be advertised, but that the commencement of winding-up should be the court order. Therefore, if these provisions become law *bona fide* transactions up to the date of the winding-up order will be valid as long as there is no element of an undue advantage.

The effect of voluntary winding-up

18.5   The commencement of voluntary winding-up, whether preceded by the filing of a declaration of solvency under Section 283 of the Companies Act 1948 (members' voluntary winding-up) or not (creditors' voluntary winding-up), is the date of the resolution by the shareholders to wind up. [*Companies Act 1948, s 280*]. The liquidator is appointed at the meeting at which the resolution to wind up is passed. [*Companies Act 1948, s 285*]. (See also 'Tolley's Liquidation Manual', paragraphs 4.12 et seq.) If no declaration of solvency has been filed, a meeting of creditors must be held either on the same day or the next following day and at the meeting the liquidator should be confirmed in office or another person appointed in his place. [*Companies Act 1948, s 293(1), as amended by Companies Act 1981, s 106*]. (See also 'Tolley's Liquidation Manual', paragraphs 4.54 et seq.)

18.6   The effect of the commencement of voluntary winding-up on the factoring agreement is exactly the same as the effect of winding-up by the court (see 18.1–18.4 above). This effect is the same whether the winding-up is a members' or a creditors'. In particular the powers of the directors in relation to the business of the company cease on the appointment of a liquidator. [*Companies Act 1948, s 285(2)*]. (See also 'Tolley's Liquidation Manual', paragraphs 6.5 and 6.6.) As a result, for the reasons described in relation to winding-up by the court, the factoring agreement will not continue; the liquidator will be able to carry on the business only as far as is necessary for beneficial realisation of the property of the company. He will probably be unwilling to carry on the factoring and there will be no way to enforce it.

18.7   As regards debts in existence at the commencement date the position will be the same as in the case of winding-up by the court. However, the difficulties which may be created, especially for a factor with a facultative type of agreement, by the relation back to an earlier date do not exist. Admittedly, as he is neither a member nor a creditor, he will not be entitled to notice of either a members' or a creditors' meeting. However, if he is monitoring the client's business adequately, he should be aware of the calling of the meetings which must be by at least seven days notice. [*Companies Act 1948, s 293(1); Companies Act 1981, s 106(1)*].

18.8   There is, however, one danger for which the factor should watch. This is a practice which has grown up in recent years by which:

(*a*)   a meeting of members of a private company is assembled without notice, the notice being waived; and

(*b*)   a resolution passed for the winding-up of the company and the appointment of a liquidator; and

(*c*)   the creditors' meeting called for some days later.

This is contrary to the provisions of the Companies Acts, but the resolutions are not thereby invalid. [*Re Centrebind Ltd [1966] 3 AER 889;*

Companies Act 1981, s 106(2)]. (See also 'Tolley's Liquidation Manual', paragraph 4.27.) Even if such an immediate start of liquidation may catch the factor unaware, he is unlikely to have further debts offered or notified to him. If they are so offered or notified, it will be with the authority of the liquidator and, as the agreement will not have been terminated, such debts will vest in the factor. In such a case he will not run the risk, as in the case of winding-up by the court, by which he may have purported to purchase debts which in the event may not vest in him. As in the case of other forms of insolvency, the factor with a whole turnover type of agreement has the advantage that all debts created up to the date of the appointment of the liquidator will vest in him even if not notified. In the White Paper the practice is recognised but, in order to prevent abuse, it is proposed that any liquidator appointed before a creditors' meeting should be a provisional liquidator with power only to protect the assets of the company.

Bankruptcy of the client

18.9 In order to determine the rights of the parties in relation to the factoring agreement on the bankruptcy of the client the following rules must be borne in mind:

(*a*) The commencement of bankruptcy is the earlier of:

(i) the act of bankruptcy on which the receiving order is made; and

(ii) the first of any earlier acts of bankruptcy committed by the bankrupt within three months before presentation of the petition;

and the trustee's title to the property of the bankrupt relates back to that time. [*Bankruptcy Act 1914, s 37*]. Note that if the provisions proposed in the White Paper become law, the commencement of bankruptcy will be the court order.

(*b*) The bankruptcy does not determine the bankrupt's contracts, but the trustee may disclaim any that are unprofitable to him. [*Bankruptcy Act 1914, s 54*].

(*c*) Payments to the bankrupt and assignments by and transactions with the bankrupt for valuable consideration, which take place before the receiving order, shall in general not be invalidated, provided that the other party had not, at the time, notice of an available act of bankruptcy. [*Bankruptcy Act 1914, s 45*].

18.10 In applying these rules to the position of the factor on the bankruptcy of his client the following provisions, more fully described in Chapter 7 (see 7.29–7.32), in relation to factoring with sole traders and partnerships must also be taken into account:

(*a*) the invalidation of a general assignment of book debts unless registered as if it were a bill of sale (see 7.29 to 7.30) [*Bankruptcy Act 1914, s 43(1)*]; and (*b*)   the 'order and disposition' or 'reputed ownership' clause (see 7.31). [*Bankruptcy Act 1914, s 38(2)(c)*]. If the proposals in the White Paper come into effect, however, this provision will be repealed and the following paragraphs should be read with this in mind.

18.11   The type of arrangement for factoring and the type of agreement (whether facultative or whole turnover) are also relevant, so that giving effect to the above rules it appears that the effect of bankruptcy on the relations between the factor and the client are as follows:

(1)   Whole turnover agreement, whether for factoring with notices to debtors or without—not registered as if it were a bill of sale:

The agreement will be totally void as against the trustee who will be able to claim all debts outstanding at the date of his appointment and all debts that have come into existence with effect from the commencement of bankruptcy as described above. If the debts have been settled, the factor will have to pay over the equivalent value realised to the trustee.

(2)   Whole turnover agreement for factoring without notices to debtors (i.e. undisclosed or invoice discounting)—duly registered:

As more fully discussed in 7.31, it is not certain that registration would serve to take the debts out of the 'order and disposition clause'. If not the position would be as in (1) above owing to the relation back of the trustee's title to the commencement of bankruptcy. The better view is that registration would give effect to the position that the debts were no longer in the client's apparent ownership; if this is so, the position would be as for factoring with notices to debtors as described in (3) below.

(3)   Whole turnover agreement for factoring with notices to debtors— duly registered:

It is a well established principle that *choses in action* not yet in existence may be assigned so that the transfer of ownership will take effect immediately upon their coming into existence. (*Tailby v Official Receiver (1888) 13 App Cas 523*: see also Goode 'Commercial Law', Penguin Educational/Allen Lane, at p 744). In the case of a whole turnover agreement, that clearly defines the debts to which it relates, all debts up to the date of the receiving order, or any earlier appointment of the Official Receiver under the Bankruptcy Rules [*Bankruptcy Act, s 8*], will vest in the factor, provided that it was executed before notice of an available act of bankruptcy. This is irrespective of any such subsequent notice to the factor; relation back and the provisions of Section 45 do not apply if the assignment, effected by the agreement itself, was executed before such notice. On the receiving order the official receiver becomes receiver of the property of the bankrupt client until a trustee is appointed. Thus, the client will have no means of creating any further debts. Although the official receiver (through the appointment of a special manager under Section 10 of the Bankruptcy Act 1914) or the trustee (with the consent of the committee of inspection: *Bankruptcy Act 1914, s 56*) may carry on the business, neither will be bound by the agreement and the trustee may disclaim it.

(4) Facultative agreement for factoring without notices (i.e. undisclosed or invoice discounting):

As the agreement provides for individual debts to be assigned specifically Section 43 does not apply so that registration is most unlikely to have been effected. In such a case the assigned debts will be claimed by the trustee in accordance with the 'order and disposition' clause. [*Bankruptcy Act 1914, s 38(2)(c)*]. The trustee will be entitled to all debts in existence at the commencement of bankruptcy or which have come into existence thereafter or the realised value of any such debt as has been settled by the debtor.

(5) Facultative agreement for factoring with notices to the debtors:

The debts specifically offered to and accepted by the factor vest in the factor. Further debts offered by the client and accepted by the factor, without notice of an available act of bankruptcy, up to the time of the receiving order will vest in the factor providing that he has given value for the assignments. [*Bankruptcy Act 1914, s 45*]. With effect from the date of the receiving order the position will be the same as in the case of a whole turnover agreement as in (3) above.

18.12 It should be noted that unless notice to terminate is given either by the factor or the trustee in accordance with the provisions for termination, the agreement remains in effect. Thus, should the debtor not be adjudicated bankrupt or on the client's discharge from bankruptcy, the arrangements may continue under the original agreement.

18.13 Should the official receiver or trustee continue the business it is likely that they will not use the factoring services under the agreement. The trustee would probably disclaim the agreement as an unprofitable contract. If the trustee wishes to operate the factoring arrangements, he will not be willing to accept responsibility for any recourse of debts sold to the factor by the client. It will therefore be usual for him to seek a new agreement.

Factor's rights on winding-up or bankruptcy of client

18.14 The rules for determining which debts vest in the factor following the commencement of winding-up or bankruptcy of the client have been described in 18.1 to 18.13 above. It is important that the factoring agreement should provide that, *notwithstanding termination of the agreement*, following such insolvency the factor's rights in relation to those debts which undoubtedly vest in him should remain in full force and effect. In particular it is important that the factor should retain:

(*a*) the power of attorney by which he may execute legal assignments and endorse negotiable instruments in the name of the client; and

(*b*) the right to have remittances, received by the client in respect of assigned debts, passed to him immediately upon receipt and, pending such passing on, held in trust for him.

Co-operation of the administrator of the client's insolvent estate

18.15 It is as well for the factor to make contact with the trustee or liquidator at the earliest possible time after his appointment in order to ensure that these rights are fully understood. In particular it is important that any remittances relating to assigned debts received by the trustee or liquidator are passed on quickly to the factor; a delay in receipt of such remittances by the factor may cause uncertainty as to the position on debtor accounts and thus impair collection procedures. Co-operation of the trustee or liquidator should be sought by the factor. As in the case of receivership the administrator of the estate may be in a position to help resolve disputes. It is in the interests of the estate of the insolvent client that the factor's collections should be as effective as is possible; in this way the factor may recover all his funds in use and be able to remit as much as possible of the balance of the purchase price unpaid at the commencement of the insolvency.

Exercise of rights to terminate or have debts repurchased

18.16 Apart from the special procedures to be taken on the insolvency of the client as described in Chapter 11 (11.39–11.43), the factor must consider which of the rights given to him in the factoring agreement, described in 17.3 to 17.7, he should exercise. Alternatively, the agreement may provide that on the insolvency of the client all previously approved debts become unapproved; these rights should be available to the factor on:

(*a*) in the case of a company, a petition to wind up, or a resolution to wind up; and

(*b*) in the case of an unincorporated firm, an act of bankruptcy; and

(*c*) in either case, the calling of a meeting of creditors.

The exercise of any of the rights referred to above is unlikely to bring any payment to the factor, as, even if a demand is made before a resolution to wind up, a winding-up order or a receiving order, the insolvent client will be unable to pay. The procedure will, however, enable the factor to crystallise a claim against the client's estate at an early date. This is particularly important when there are guarantors of the obligations of the client to the factor. If proof is submitted for the full sum owing by the client, it does not have to be adjusted downwards for payments for guarantors (subsequent to the receiving order or commencement of winding-up) until 100% of the amount, for which proof has been submitted, has been received in aggregate from all sources including dividends from the client's estate. (*Re Sass [1896] 2 QB 12*). Naturally, the proof will have to be adjusted for the payments from debtors which go to reduce the factor's deficiency. These payments are not analogous to payments from guarantors or the principal debtor–the client. The exercise of such rights will also give the factor the opportunity to make early claims on any guarantors. If any such guarantor is insolvent it will give him the benefit of early proof described above.

18.17 The exercise of the right to have all the debts repurchased at their then invoice value as recorded in the factor's books will also have the effect of relieving the factor from any credit risk undertaken (e.g. in the case of the full service or undisclosed), provided that the collections made in aggregate from solvent debtors are sufficient to cover the funds in use.

18.18 When the equivalent of the factor's funds in use has been recovered from the debtors, the repurchase price of the remaining debts may be set off against the credit balance on the client's account in the factor's records. At that stage the ownership of the debts will pass to the administrator of the insolvent client's estate. The factor may then be prepared to make arrangements with the administrator whereby the factor will continue to collect. As described in relation to receivership (see 17.10), the consideration for this may be a small fee or, indeed, such a fee may be waived if the administrator has been co-operative in helping to solve disputes and queries on debtors accounts. Where a maturity type of agreement contains such a provision, the factor will be able to exercise his choice as to whether or not to continue collections as soon as the insolvency occurs. There will be no, or little, funds in use to recover so that the re-purchase price of the debts sold back to the client's estate may be set off immediately against the credit balance in favour of the client in the factor's records.

18.19 In order to be in a position to deal promptly with debtors' queries and disputes, it is as well for the factor to obtain from the client the originals of all delivery notes and other means of proving delivery as soon as insolvency is thought to be impending. If possible, files of the client's correspondence with debtors should also be obtained. The factoring agreement should give the factor the right of access to all such material.

Chapter 19

Miscellaneous Problems on the Insolvency of the Client

19.1   Apart from the particular problems stemming directly from the appointment of a receiver, or from liquidation or bankruptcy, other miscellaneous problems can arise on the insolvency of a client. This chapter first examines the factor's position as regards credit balances on the debtor's account (see 19.2–19.4 below), and then his position on the attachment of a balance owing by a factor to his client by a creditor of the client (see 19.5–19.8 below).

Credit balances on the debtor's account

19.2   The question of the factor's liability for credit balances emerging on a debtor's account was included in Part C (see 11.35–11.38) because it is naturally part of the relationship between the factor and the debtors. The problem only arises from factoring arrangements that include notices to debtors. Although the position is clear in the case of a credit balance arising from a straightforward overpayment or duplicate payment by the debtor owing to an error, the uncertainty regarding the liability or otherwise on the part of the factor for credit balances arising from the issue of credit notes becomes acute when the client has become insolvent. In the former case there can be no doubt at all that the factor is responsible; the overpayment is money paid to the factor by a mistake of fact and he is bound to refund it.

19.3   Where the credit balance relates to the issue of a credit note by the client before the appointment of a receiver or the commencement of bankruptcy or winding-up, the position is not clear. There is also a conflict between the administrator of the estate and the 'debtor' (who is now a creditor). The debtor naturally wishes to be repaid by the solvent factor rather than prove in the client's estate. Administrators of the estates of insolvent clients often contend, with support from their legal advisers, that the credit balance should be removed from the factor's records by a credit to the account of the client in the factor's records. This would have the effect of:

(*a*)   increasing the balance owed by the factor to the client's estate (or reducing the factor's claim on the estate); and

(b) allowing the claimant of the credit balance the only remedy of proof as an unsecured creditor in the insolvent estate of the client.

This seems to be based on the view that the assumption of liability for the credit balance by the factor involves a transfer of liability from the client to the factor. Obviously one cannot assign a liability; only by a novation may it be transferred from the client to the factor. However, those who accept this line of reasoning overlook the more compelling arguments that support the view set out in Chapter 11 (see 11.36) that the liability was the factor's in the first place. There is a further argument in favour of the factor's responsibility for such a credit balance in the case of the client's insolvency. The credit note will have been notified to the factor in accordance with the terms of the factoring agreement by which the factor will have been authorised to debit the amount to the client's account and reduce the balance owing to the client. The administrator of the estate on taking possession of the client's estate would not appear to have the authority to reverse a transaction that has already taken place. The fact that the factor has not paid the claimant does not appear to be relevant; the claimant has received the credit note and his account has been credited in the factor's records. If the view that the factor must transfer such balances back were to be sustained, why not balances that had already been settled? The date on which the factor pays seems to be irrelevant to the issue.

19.4   Certainly, debtors on factor's records have become concerned when, after years of having dealt with the factor on their purchases ledger account they are suddenly faced with the loss of their claim on a credit note. Such a situation may detract from the image of factoring. For this reason reputable factors have been known to refute the claims of administrators for the transfer of such balances, in spite of the fact that such a transfer might well be to the financial advantage of the factor.

Attachment of balance owing by the factor to the client by creditor of client

19.5   The fact that a business is using a factor for any form of disclosed factoring is usually well known in the particular trade or industry; certainly all his debtors will know and most trades have a well developed 'grape-vine'. As a result it sometimes occurs to a client's creditor, who has encountered some difficulty in obtaining payment, to obtain judgment and then attach the amount owing by the factor to the client by means of a garnishee order.

19.6   However, experience has shown that most of these efforts at self-help by unpaid creditors fail. The reasons for this are not hard to find:

(a) The garnishee order *nisi* restrains the garnishee (the factor) from parting with moneys 'due and accruing due' to the judgment debtor (the client). It is generally considered that this phrase means moneys actually payable on the day when the order is served. If a client is in

175

such an illiquid position that a creditor must go to these lengths to obtain payment, it is unlikely that the client's account with the factor will contain a credit balance in excess of the factor's retention; and that is not then due to the client.

(*b*)   Most such businesses, if carried on by incorporated companies, have charged their assets to a bank and most bank's forms of charge include fixed charges on book debts. The amount owed by the factor to the client is undoubtedly to be classified as a book debt and the fixed charge attaches to it as soon as it comes into existence.

(*c*)   Even if the client's charge to a bank is floating as regards book debts, it is likely that the charge would crystallise either automatically or by some action on the part of the bank when the garnishee order is issued. The charge, if crystallised before the garnishee order is made absolute, has priority.

(*d*)   Where there is no charge in favour of a bank it is likely that, by the time a creditor takes such extreme action, the client company will be in serious financial difficulties and proceedings for liquidation, either voluntary or compulsory, may be taken before the order is made absolute. The order will fail if a petition for winding-up has been presented [*Companies Act 1948, s 325(1)*], and is likely to fail if a meeting of creditors has been called, before the order has been made absolute (see 12.7).

(*e*)   In the case of an unincorporated client the order will fail if the creditor has notice of a petition for bankruptcy or a receiving order is made before the attachment has been completed. [*Bankruptcy Act 1914, s 40*].

19.7   The garnishee order will specify a date for a hearing at which the court will decide whether or not to make the order absolute, taking into account:

(*a*)   whether or not it can be shown that the sum in question was in fact due to the client on the day of the service of the order; and

(*b*)   whether there are any other claims on the sum in question; and

(*c*)   whether proceedings for liquidation or bankruptcy have been started.

The factor should arrange to be represented at the hearing by a solicitor and if cause is to be shown why the order is not to be made absolute (e.g. the sum was not due or there is a charge on it) it may be convenient for the client to be represented by the same person provided that there is no conflict of interest.

19.8   In the meantime if the sum in question was, in fact, payable at the time, the factor should retain it in addition to his normal retention; but it is usually considered that he may continue to make payments to the client against the purchase of further debts notified or offered to him. Even if no amount was payable to the client on the day of the service of the garnishee order, in view of the absence of absolute certainty (there has been no reported case relating to a factoring account), it would be advisable for the factor to make an additional retention of the amount in the order, plus a margin for costs, against further amounts becoming payable to the client.

Part F
International Factoring

Chapter 20

Systems for International Factoring

The 'two factor' system

20.1   When a factor's client requires a form of factoring that includes notices to and collection from the debtors in respect of sales outside the United Kingdom, the factor may use the 'two factor' system by employing the services of a correspondent factor in each of the countries to which his client may sell. Under this system the factor whose client is the exporter is referred to as the 'export factor' (EF) and the correspondent in the debtor's country the 'import factor' (IF).

20.2   The EF remains responsible to his client for all aspects of the service and the client has no contractual relationship with the IF. However, the IF will be responsible to the EF for the credit risk on the debtor accounts in his country and for collection. The IF, with the knowledge of the law and trade usages of the debtor's country, is in a far better position to assess the credit standing of the debtor and to collect from him. Furthermore, he is obviously able to communicate with the debtor in his own language and thus avoid irritations, which may arise from demands for payment in a foreign tongue, or delays in the notification of disputes.

Characteristics of two factor systems

20.3   A typical two factor system works like this:

(1) At the outset, the EF obtains from the client the normal information obtainable on a survey of the client's business (see Chapter 10).

(2) The EF passes to each IF the following information relating to the client's business in the IF's country:

(*a*) Nature of goods or services provided;

(*b*) Estimated sales volume;

(*c*) Terms of payment;

(*d*) Number and type of debtors;

(*e*) Expected number of invoices and credit notes for the stated volume of sales.

(3) Each IF considers the information and indicates his terms (administration charge for his part of the service).

(4) On receipt of all quotations from IF's the EF will be able to determine his own terms.

(5) When the arrangement starts, the procedure for the client is exactly the same as for sales within the UK (see Chapters 2 and 3) except that:

(*a*) the notice of assignment on his original invoices directs the debtors to pay to the appropriate IF; and

(*b*) he needs to supply an extra copy of each invoice to the EF for onward transmission to the IF.

(6) On notification or acceptance of each debt the EF transfers it to the appropriate IF who is supplied with a copy invoice.

(7) The IF is then responsible for collections, accounts to the EF who, in turn, accounts to the client.

(8) Where the arrangements are for factoring without recourse, details of the debtors, together with required approvals, are submitted by EF to IF. The IF gives his approvals either by credit limits or approval of specific orders according to the arrangements in force between the factors. The EF gives the equivalent approval to the client. In such a case it is often arranged that the IF will pay at the latest 90 days after due date for any approved debt unpaid otherwise than by reason of a dispute.

(9) The IF will take no responsibility for disputes, but will assist in their settlement if required.

The arrangement in diagrammatic form is shown in Appendix VIII. Naturally, on a reciprocal basis factors in the United Kingdom act as import factors for overseas factors in respect of sales by their clients to customers in the UK.

International factoring chains

20.4 The operation of the two factor system is normally carried out by members of groups of factors – commonly referred to as 'chains'. Each chain will endeavour to have a member in every major trading country; otherwise it may be difficult for members of the chain to offer a comprehensive export service to their clients. At present the two factor system is available to cover exports to almost every country in Western Europe, North America and Australasia and to Malaysia, Singapore, Hong Kong, Japan, Israel and South Africa; the facilities are being developed in other markets. Some chains restrict membership to one company in each country; such a chain is known as a 'Closed Chain'. In a closed chain the members would be likely to be associated through holdings in their shares. In the case of an 'Open Chain', with no formal restriction on the number of members in each country, no linking shareholdings are necessary.

20.5   The members of the chain agree to abide by the regulations laid down by a central secretariat on behalf of the governing body. These regulations cover the relations between the factors in their factoring operations and are likely to include:

(1)   The information to be given to the IF in order to enable him to form a judgment on the prospective business and the required credit approvals.

(2)   Regulations for entering into factoring arrangements.

(3)   Regulations covering approvals and cancellations of approvals.

(4)   Methods of dealing with notification of and settlement of disputes between the client and the debtor and the effect of any such dispute on any credit approval.

(5)   The EF's undertaking that debts transferred are valid, payable debts free from encumbrance, and that they vest in him so that he is able to transfer them to the IF.

(6)   Responsibility of the IF to see that the assignment is valid as against the debtor under the law of his country.

(7)   The time for payment for approved and unapproved debts by the IF.

20.6   It is important that the EF ensures that his agreement with his client harmonises with these regulations; otherwise he might be left with responsibilities towards his client, without having the equivalent responsibilty to him of the IF. For example, his rights to come off risk for an approved debt, which is disputed, must be equivalent to those in the regulations between factors.

Advantages and disadvantages of the system

20.7   The **advantages** of the two factor system of factoring are that it allows for:

(i)   the factor, who is close to and can monitor his client, to be responsible for the client's compliance with the agreement and warranties given; and

(ii) the factor, who is close to and can monitor the debtor, to be responsible for obtaining payment.

The **disadvantages** are:

(1) there may be delays in the transmission of funds; the funds have to pass through three hands instead of two; and

(2) there may be duplication of accounting.

The first disadvantage may be overcome if, instead of passing on individual payments, the factors in a chain operate a clearing system to set off amounts due to and from each other on a global basis. The second may be overcome by a comprehensive reporting system whereby the EF does not need to keep individual debtor accounts but may rely on returns from the IF.

Other uses of the two factor system

20.8 When a prepayment facility is required and exchange control regulations in the country of the debtor allow it, the two factor system may also be used for the following purposes:

(1) **Exchange risk cover.** If the exporting client is selling in the currency of the IF's country, by making 100% prepayment the proceeds for the exports can be transferred to the EF immediately upon shipment of the goods. If the EF sells the currency immediately upon receipt, he may protect the client against currency fluctuations during the credit period. In such a case, the IF will be protected against any recourse by an indemnity from the EF who will in turn protect himself by the usual retentions on his account with the client (see 8.33–8.34).

(2) **Reduced finance charges.** If the general level of interest rates in the IF's country is lower than that in the country of the EF, the client may be financed at a similarly reduced rate by means of prepayments being made at the agreed level by the IF to the EF. The EF would then pass the benefit on to this client. The IF would be protected by the EF in relation to any recourse as in (1) above.

Direct import factoring

20.9 As an alternative to the two factor system there is a growing use by exporters of a relation with a factor in the country of their customers. The traditional business of American factors, whereby they acted to collect debts in the United States for exporters in Europe and guaranteed them against bad debt losses, survives to this day and is developing. The business, which was originally carried out by factors in their capacity as mercantile agents, is now undertaken by factors in the modern sense. For maturity factoring, in which these two services only are required and no financial facility is provided, it is often considered unnecessary to use the two factor system. Accordingly, when the exports of a merchant or manufacturer to an individual country are of such a volume as to make a factoring agreement worthwhile for sales to that country alone, the client may enter into a maturity factoring agreement *direct with a factor* in that country. The intervention of an export factor in such a case is not essential because:

(a) in the absence of finance, monitoring of the client's financial position is not necessary; and

(b) in the absence of funds in use at risk it is not absolutely essential to ensure that the assignments are free from third party claims according to the law of the country of the exporter. If any debt is so encumbered the factor, not having paid, will not be on risk.

The advantages of direct import factoring are that communications and remittances are not delayed by having to be passed through an extra party.

20.10 Such an arrangement may be made direct between a client, who has approached a member of a chain (see 20.4 above) in his own country, and that member's correspondent factor in the country to which the exports are directed. The factor in the client's country would then be available to help to dispose of any major problems that may arise between the parties to the contract. For this and for the introduction he would expect a small commission; but the arrangement would save the costs of cross-border visits by the acting factor. Furthermore, the cost of this commission is likely to be far less than the remuneration required by an export factor under the two factor system. It is, therefore, likely that the cost of direct import factoring will be less than for the two factor system if the volume of sales is sufficient to make direct import factoring worthwhile.

Direct export factoring

20.11 In order to avoid the duplication of records and the alleged extra administration entailed, some factors have eschewed the two factor system in favour of operating their full factoring, recourse factoring or maturity factoring system for exports in exactly the same way as for domestic business. The rationale is that the two factor system postulates duplication of accounting and records and delays in communications and remittances. The proponents of the two factor system argue that any disadvantages that there may be are outweighed by more efficient collections and credit approvals by the IF. Certainly, where accounting and reporting systems are such that the duplication may be avoided and if proper multilateral clearing systems for the set-off of amounts payable can be evolved, these disadvantages will be outweighed. The two factor system will then be without rival for efficiency if any form of financial facility is included in the arrangements.

20.12 The direct export factor may rely on one of the following for credit approvals:

(*a*) normal bank and status reports; or

(*b*) information from a correspondent agent either of his own or of his shareholding bank; or

(*c*) arrangements on a recourse basis and rights over the client's credit insurance policy (see 3.16–3.19); or

(*d*) the factor's own credit insurance policy.

20.13 For collections the direct export factor may either:

(*a*) deal with them himself until such time as difficulties arise, when he may use either a collection agent or his own or his shareholding bank's agent; or

(*b*) he may appoint an agent to handle all collections.

The disadvantage of (*a*) is that, unless he has expertise in the language of every country to which his clients may sell, many of his letters or telexes sent in English may be disregarded by the debtors. If he uses (*b*), he will not however avoid all the disadvantages of the two factor system.

20.14 Direct export factoring may also be used by members of chains (as above). In such cases the collection agent is often another factor who is a member of the chain (a 'correspondent factor'), and it may also be possible for that factor to provide the exporter's factor with credit information or even to share the risks of the debtor's insolvency. These questions are a matter of policy within the chain's own constitution and the relevant regulations. They do not concern the client who in any case looks only to the factor in his own country for the service to be provided.

Invoice discounting or undisclosed factoring for exports

20.15 Invoice discounting arrangements may often include debts outside the United Kingdom. In such circumstances, the system is normally no different from that which relates to domestic sales. The factor may protect himself by insisting on an Export Credits Guarantee Department policy or other credit insurance cover (see 21.25); the factor's rights should be protected by an assignment of the benefits of the policy and an arrangement by which, should the client become insolvent, claims may be met notwithstanding the vesting of the debts in the factor. (See 3.18–3.21 for private credit insurance.) It is essential, however, that the factor should have a correspondent factor or other agent in each country in which a debtor is located; it may be necessary, in the case of a failing or inefficient client, for the factor to take over the sales ledger and collect for his own account.

20.16 Undisclosed factoring on a non-recourse basis is unlikely. Undisclosed factoring is an alternative to invoice discounting in conjunction with credit insurance (see 3.18). The rationale of the provision of this service is the factor's expertise at credit assessment based on his library of credit information. In this he is unlikely to rival any credit insurance organisation that handles a substantial volume of export credit insurance or any factor in the country where debtors are located. If a factor were to offer such a service for exports, he would probably need to rely himself upon credit insurance or the support of overseas factors or agents.

Back-to-back factoring

20.17   Back-to-back factoring is an extension of the two factor system: its object is to overcome the difficulty created by the channelling by an exporter of all his sales to one country through a distributor. The result is in some cases that the amount of credit required by the distributor is far higher than can be granted by the IF on the normal unsecured basis. In many cases the import of the client's products is the only business of the distributor; and it may often be a subsidiary or associate of the client. The difficulty of accepting the credit risk is overcome by the entry into a factoring agreement by the distributor with the IF and the use of the balance owing by the IF for debts purchased as security for the credit granted.

20.18   A typical back-to-back arrangement works like this:

(1)   The EF enters into a factoring agreement, covering the full service, with the client (exporter) and makes arrangements with IF to act as his correspondent factor.

(2)   The IF enters into a factoring agreement with the distributor for his domestic sales. This agreement may be for any form of factoring in which prepayments are available. However, the normal arrangements will be varied as follows:

(*a*)   Prepayments are not normally taken; they may, however be limited to a very small percentage to cover the distributor's overhead expenses.

(*b*)   The IF and the distributor agree that, at any time at the discretion of the IF, the amount due to the IF for the supplies by the client (indebtedness assigned to him by the EF) may be set off against amounts due to the distributor under the domestic factoring arrangements.

It is thought that this availability of set-off would inure in the insolvency of the distributor. [*Bankruptcy Act 1914, s 31; Companies Act 1948, s 317*].

(3)   The approvals given to the EF by the IF will be made in one of two ways:

(*a*)   on the basis of the position on the distributor's account with the IF; or (*b*) on the basis of firm orders from approved debtors received by the distributor for goods to be shipped.

Alternatively, the IF may accept all debts with recourse but undertake not to exercise any recourse to the extent that he has available rights of set-off.

(4) The exports from the client to the distributor will then be factored through the two factor system in the usual way save that settlement by the distributor to the IF (and consequently the IF to the EF) will depend upon his sub-sales and the position on his account with the IF.

It will be appreciated that the system may be difficult to bring into operation when the distribution arrangement is just starting. Until goods have been imported and sold the IF has no basis for his approvals as he has nothing owing to the distributor. This lacuna can be overcome only by the exporting client accepting that his first sales will be with recourse.

A diagram of a back-to-back factoring arrangement is shown in Appendix IX.

Back-to-back arrangements by a single factor

20.19 An arrangement similar to back-to-back factoring is sometimes entered into without the assistance of an EF. In such a case the factor enters into a domestic factoring agreement with a distributor and agrees to accept instructions to pay a percentage of the purchase price of each invoice to the supplier. The supplier may or may not be in the same country as the distributor. Difficulties have been encountered by factors in accepting such instructions and confirming them to the supplier. The percentage to be paid to the supplier will be the invoice value (less VAT for imports) less the importer's mark-up. The balance payable to the importer may not be sufficient to cover the importer's overheads owing to a high incidence of recourse for returned goods. The importer may allege that the recourse arises from deficiencies on the part of the supplier and should be deducted from payments to him. The purpose of such arrangements is to give the supplier confidence in the granting of credit to the distributor; the factor may, therefore, not be in a position to make such deductions owing to the form of his confirmation to the supplier. If it is part of the proposed arrangements that such confirmation should be given to the supplier, then it is advisable that the instructions should be for all payments to go to the supplier (or to an account under the joint control of the supplier and the distributor). It will then be up to these two parties to divide the amounts so paid. As such difficulties may be compounded when there is more than one supplier these arrangements should be made only with a distributor of the goods of one supplier.

Chapter 21

International Matters for Special Consideration

21.1   In this chapter there are considered three matters which, if not dealt with carefully, may cause problems to factors engaged in factoring transactions across national borders. These are the application of national laws (see 21.2–21.9 below), the transmission of funds (see 21.10–21.15 below), and exchange risks (see 21.16–21.17 below). The efforts of UNIDROIT to deal with the legal problems of international factoring are also described (see 21.18–21.23 below) and finally some comments are given on international factoring from the point of view of the client.

The legal effect of international transactions

21.2   In domestic factoring the relations between the three parties, the client, the debtor and the factor, are governed by one legal system and the legal framework of the relations in the UK has been described in previous chapters. However, in international factoring, the law of at least two countries may affect any of these relations; it may be more than two because a factor may be situated in a country that is neither that of the client nor the debtor.

Conflicts of law

21.3   Which law is to be applied to each of the undermentioned matters is of concern to the factor and, unfortunately, the answers are not, in most circumstances, clear. The matters for consideration are:

(1)   The validity of the assignment as between the factor and the client;

(2)   The factor's rights to the assigned debts when an administrator has been appointed to the business of an insolvent client;

(3)   The validity of the assignment as against any third party seeking to attach the debt;

(4)   The law to be applied in solving a dispute between the factor and his client or a correspondent factor (EF or IF) in another country; and

(5)   The validity of the assignment as between the factor and the debtor and the countervailing rights of the debtor.

186

21.4   It is usually considered by factors that their rights in relation to the debtor and any countervailing claims of the debtor are governed by the law of the country under which the contract giving rise to the debts was entered into. Not only may this itself be difficult to determine, but the rule is not free from uncertainty. In practice, as proceedings to recover the debt usually take place in the country of the debtor, the law of that country will be likely to be applied in all such matters. Although a factor in England may provide in his agreement with his client that English law must apply to his sale contracts, the difficulty, time and expense of showing this to be the case are such that it is usually advantageous to accept the application of the law of the debtor's country without question. To do otherwise may mean lengthy arguments in court and the cost of expert witnesses.

Validity of assignment of debt when insolvent client domiciled in another country

21.5   As regards the validity of the assignment of a debt in relation to administrators of insolvent clients' estates and other third parties' claims, the usual view is that the assignment must be valid in accordance with the law of the country in which the client is domiciled. For a company in the United Kingdom this is considered to be the country in which the registered office is located, because it is under the law of that country that the administration of the insolvency would be regulated. (*Re Anchor Line (Henderson Bros) Ltd [1937] 2 AER 823*). For an unincorporated client one must look to where the main part of the business is conducted. These considerations are the reasons for the special matters to be taken into account in entering into agreement with Scottish clients (see 7.33–7.39). In other jurisdictions other criteria might be adopted; for example, in the United States the law governing registration under the Uniform Commercial Code and priorities depends on the situation of the client's most important executive office. Difficulties may arise if a client has major executive offices in more than one country or state.

21.6   The validity of the assignments under the law of the country in which the client is domiciled will not necessarily prevent a third party, other than the administrator of the insolvent estate, obtaining priority. As long ago as 1900, priority was given to an unsecured creditor of a company in receivership when the creditor had attached a debt owing to that company by a French debtor, notwithstanding that the debt fell within the ambit of the charge in relation to which the receiver had been appointed. (*In Re Maudslay, Sons & Field [1900] 1 Ch 602*). In that case the receiver had been appointed by the court in accordance with the terms of a debenture evidencing a floating charge on all the company's assets. Subsequently the creditor, holding a dishonoured acceptance of the company, complied with the formalities of French law for attachment of the debt. Unlike the position under English law, the earlier crystallisation of the charge, in the absence of the required formalities for an assignment under French law, did not have the effect of vesting the debt in the chargee. The court applied the *lex situs* of the debt to the third party's claim. Although it was argued that a *chose in action* has no locality, the court held that for the purposes of the case the debt was deemed to have, at least, a 'quasi-locality'. The *lex situs* was therefore applied by analogy with immovable property. The case turns on its particular facts. However, it seems that if the creditor himself had been domiciled in France there would have been no doubt that French law would have applied to the conflict as to priorities. In view of the growth of cross-border trading it is not unlikely that an insolvent client may have creditors and debtors in the same overseas country. In such a case, some of the creditors may well seek to attach (in accordance with their own law) debts of the client already assigned to the factor under the domiciliary law of the client.

21.7   A study of the authorities on this subject shows it to be one of great difficulty and much uncertainty. The facts of the cases that can arise have been described as 'bewildering permutations and combinations'. (Lawrence Collins 'Floating Charges, Receivers and Managers and the Conflict of Laws' 1978, International and Comparative Law Quarterly 691, at p 696.) A more recent case now seems relevant to the locality of the debt: 'The general rule is clear that the debt is situate where the debtor resides . . .' per Upjohn J in *Re Claim by Helbert Wagg & Co Ltd* [*1956*] *1 Ch 323*, at p 342. But this is the general rule only and it may in some circumstances be negatived by the terms of the contract out of which the debt arose. A factor buying a series of individual debts of moderate amounts is in no position to determine his probable rights in relation to all the conflicts that may arise in each particular case and should, therefore, have regard to the precautions mentioned below. At least, he should be aware of the risks if he, for commercial reasons, decides to forego these precautions.

Use of two factor system to alleviate the problems

21.8   It is commonly thought that by the use of the two factor system all those problems will be overcome. The general view is that the EF will ensure that his rights to the debts are valid as regards his relations with the client and any administrator and the IF will ensure that the debt is validly assigned as regards his ability to collect. However, it is doubtful if the IF would accept responsibility if the circumstances were similar to those described in the *Maudslay* case mentioned above with the substitution of a factor for the debenture holder. However, the two factor system at least gives the EF the opportunity to be advised regarding the formalities of the law of the countries in which the debtors are situated. These formalities vary widely. For example, in order to ensure priority over a competing third party interest subsequent in time

(*a*) in Germany all that is required is a clear notice on the invoice; whereas (*b*) in Switzerland the original of a written assignment must be delivered to the debtor by registered post.

Direct factoring when client abroad

21.9   If direct import factoring services with a prepayment facility are to be provided, the factor must be careful to ascertain the formalities for valid assignments in the country in which the prospective client is situated. Compliance with English law by a UK factor offering a full direct import service to a client in the United States will not avail the factor if he has not filed his factoring agreement, as a security interest, in the state in which the client has his chief executive office. (Uniform Commercial Code: Articles 9–102, 9–103 and 9 part 4.) It is clear therefore that, unless assignments of debts in international factoring are perfected in accordance with laws of both the country of the client and the country of the debtor, the factor cannot be certain that his assignments will not be successfully challenged. If finance is to be provided by way of prepayments in cross-border factoring, either the two factor system should be used (see 20.3) or one of the following precautions should be taken:

(*a*) In the case of direct import factoring, a certificate of the validity of the agreement should be obtained from a lawyer expert in the particular branch of the law in the client's country.

(*b*) In the case of direct export factoring, the factor should use a first class agent, who may advise on the formalities necessary to perfect the assignments.

Transmission of funds in settlement of debts

Cheque payments in domestic business

21.10   The transmission of funds by debtors in payment of debts for commercial supplies in the UK is made in the majority of cases by the remittance of cheques. The system for clearing cheques in the UK is efficient and rapid and remittances through the bank giro system also take no longer than a few days. The problem is otherwise in most countries overseas and a factor and prospective client, and the prospective client's adviser, must all ensure that, where export factoring is in contemplation, the costs and timing of payments are fully understood by the parties.

21.11   In relation to domestic business the factor pays his client for each debt purchased, in the absence of prepayments, either on a fixed maturity date (i.e. after an agreed period after invoice date or date of the assignments) or on the date when the debtor pays. In the case of a maturity date arrangement the few days for cheque clearance is well understood and accepted by the client; in the case of 'pay when paid', the best practice is for the factor to pay on the date of the receipt of the debtor's cheque in the expectation that the clearance time for his cheque will be equivalent to that of the debtor's cheque. In this way the client's position in relation to this aspect is the same as it would have been had he not employed a factor.

Transmission of funds in international business

21.12 However, cheques sent by debtors overseas may take more than a few days to clear; they may take up to two weeks. Similarly, mail transfers take much longer than in the United Kingdom. Therefore, in the case of a maturity date arrangement the payment date must be adjusted to take account of the extra time for the remittance of funds and in a 'pay when paid' arrangement it would be normal for the factor to pay only when he had cleared funds in his bank. The present system for the transfer of funds telegraphically, known as SWIFT, may be used by overseas debtors sometimes for large transactions, but they are normally considered to be too expensive for the normal run of factoring transactions. Naturally, if SWIFT is used, then the factor may make payment to his client on an equivalent basis. It is important also to ensure that arrangements be made at the outset as to whether any bank charges for the remittance of funds are to be borne by the client or the factor. If it is to be the latter, the client must take these charges into account in assessing the overall cost of the service.

21.13 The delays in remittances from debtors may be aggravated if the two factor system is used. The import factor may not be prepared to remit to the export factor until a debtor's cheque received by him has been cleared and the export factor may wish to see that he has cleared funds before settling with his client. Unless, therefore, the two factor system is organised under a 'chain' in which a multilateral clearing system for payments is in operation, the client may be faced with this extra delay.

21.14 In direct import factoring the additional delay in collections occasioned by the sending of cheques to a client overseas or the payment by mail transfer may well make it worthwhile for both parties that payments to the client should be made by SWIFT. In such an event, unless the transactions are individually very large, it will be likely that a payment once a week by the factor, in respect of cheques received and cleared up to the date of payment, will save sufficient in charges to outweigh the slight delay occasioned by the accumulation of funds for the week. As in export factoring the method of payment and responsibility for costs must be agreed at the outset.

21.15 If finance by way of prepayments is provided for the client these problems of obtaining cleared funds from debtors do not affect the date of the factor's prepayments. However, they affect in similar fashion the calculation of the finance charges. The date of the debtor's payment is usually the date up to which the finance charge is calculated (see Chapter 9).

Currency risks associated with international factoring

21.16 There are necessarily some currency risks associated with exporting. Exporters are often obliged by the force of competition to quote prices and to invoice in the currency of the country of their debtor's domicile. An exporting client of a factor may be protected against the risk of fluctuations in the currency in which he has invoiced between invoice date and payment in one of three ways:

(*a*) He may arrange with his bank to sell the currency forward and with his factor to remit to him, on payment by the debtor, in the currency of the invoice.

(*b*) He may arrange for the factor to credit him in sterling at the rate of exchange ruling on the date when he notifies or offers the currency debt. The exchange risk will then be the factor's responsibility.

(*c*) He may arrange with the factor, under the two factor system, that the IF will make a prepayment immediately upon receipt of the copy invoice. The factor will then sell the currency on the spot market and credit the client with the proceeds in sterling. If the IF is to pay the full invoice value the client will be entitled to sterling at the spot rate for the full invoice amount and the IF will have paid in his own currency. Payments may be made by import factors for this purpose on the security of an indemnity from the export factor.

21.17 To cover against exchange fluctuations for a continuing stream of relatively small transactions is an administrative burden. As a result, although some export factors offer the service indicated in (*b*) above, not all do so. It is obviously administratively impracticable to sell forward the amount of each individual invoice. Accordingly, such an arrangement is likely to be made by a factor who handles a large volume of export transactions by selling the currency forward on a daily or weekly basis in bulk. The factor may do this by accumulating the amounts of invoices notified or offered to him in the particular currency by all his clients. Naturally, clients should be advised not to arrange transactions in currencies other than those of the major trading countries for which facilities for forward cover are available. A factor would be well advised not to accept debts of which the invoices are in other currencies.

The International Institute for the Unification of Private Law

21.18 The International Institute for the Unification of Private Law, more commonly known as UNIDROIT, was set up by the Italian government under the auspices of the League of Nations with the object of promoting the harmonisation of commercial law. It is now financially supported by about 50 countries. The Council of the Institute, which is situated in Rome (Via Panisperna 28), decided in 1974 to include within its work programme for the period 1975 to 1977 a study of the subject of assignments of debts in general and of the contract of factoring in particular. Following a preliminary study and the replies to a questionnaire sent to interested parties, including national factoring associations, it set up a restricted study group of academics and practitioners. The study group considered that owing to the great differences of legal systems the study should in the first place be restricted to the desirability of promulgating rules for international factoring only. It was felt, however, that the adoption of such rules by national governments would eventually influence domestic legislation on the subject. It was also considered undesirable to formulate a standard factoring contract for use between any factor and his client. It was felt that the relationship of the factor with his client, although for international factoring falling within the framework of the proposed rules, should be a matter of freedom to contract between the parties.

21.19 At the outset it was appreciated that although the mechanics of factoring in its various forms are conceptually fairly simple, the converse is true of the law under which factoring arrangements operate in many countries. Furthermore, these problems are aggravated by the wide variations in the legal systems and national laws.

Definition of 'factoring' under UNIDROIT

21.20 In view of the difficulty of defining 'factoring' which in different countries, and even to different people in the same country, means different things (see Chapter 1), it was decided to define 'Factoring Contract' as widely as possible. It was not even possible to lay down that factoring must include some element of taking 'assignments' or the transfer of the ownership of debts, because in some countries factoring does not postulate such a transfer but only a charging of debts. It was therefore agreed that for the purpose of the proposed rules 'factoring' should mean **an agreement to provide on a continuing basis two or more of the following**:

(*a*) finance;

(*b*) maintenance of debtor accounts;

(*c*) collection of debts;

(*d*) protection against credit risks.

It was also agreed that the proposed rules would apply only to factoring in relation to the supply of goods or services:

(i) across national boundaries;

(ii) to trade or professional debtors;

(iii) when notices to make payment to the factor are to be given to the debtors.

It was, however, agreed that the proposed rules would apply to the use of the two factor system even if the factor, or one of them, was not located in the country of either of the parties to the sale or service contract.

21.21 The proposed rules (to be recommended to governments) cover, as regards the validity of assignments:

(*a*) the effectiveness of agreements to assign future debts and debts of a particular character in bulk;

(*b*) the failure of provisions in purchase contracts to prohibit assignments to make the assignment ineffective;

(*c*) the transfer to the factor of ancillary rights;

(*d*) the formalities required for notices to be effective as regards the debtor and the discharge of the debtor's obligations to pay the factor.

The proposed rules also cover the countervailing rights of the debtor. All these proposals, save for the outlawing of the ban on assignments, are broadly in line with the law as it is known in England and described in this book.

21.22 These draft rules have now been approved by the Governing Council of the Institute and circulated to interested parties. It is expected that an international convention will be held to consider these draft rules and it is to be hoped that they will eventually be adopted by the governments of the major trading nations.

Limitations in application of the rules

21.23 It is to be noted that the rules themselves are somewhat limited in their application. They do not cover domestic factoring arrangements nor do they interfere with arrangements between factors and their clients. In particular no attempt was made to propose substantive rules for regulating priorities; this was held to be impossible without impinging on national laws relating to the regulation of companies, bankruptcy, banking and the registration and publicity of security rights. Furthermore, owing to the widely differing national views on the subject, not least between those whose concepts are based on common law and those who live under a civil code system, it was not even possible to formulate rules as to which law should apply in given circumstances – that of the debtor's country or that of the client's. The fact that not even a 'conflict of laws' rule could be formulated is an indication that the uncertainties regarding this aspect described at the start of this chapter have not been exaggerated.

International factoring – the client's viewpoint

21.24 The attention drawn to these difficulties is not to discourage those who provide international factoring services – an invaluable aid to the small exporter. The purpose is to advise care so that the arrangements should be regulated in such a way that the risks are minimised. Only in this way

will it be possible for the service to be provided confidently and
economically. Furthermore, it is essential that a prospective client, who
requires a financial facility with international factoring, and his adviser
should be fully aware of the effects of the uncertainties of the conflicts of
law on international factoring. Only with this understanding is it
possible for the client to conduct his business so as to cause the factor the
minimum of risk and aggravation. These aspects will be reflected in the
factor's charges to the client, so that a well conducted business and co-
operation on the legal aspects are of ultimate benefit to the client. The
greatest advantage to the client of factoring internationally is the
collections included in the full service, recourse factoring and maturity
factoring. Collections by a correspondent factor or a good agent can
outweigh the advantages of credit insurance or other forms of financing
exports where the client is selling to a reasonably large number of
customers in developed countries on open credit terms.

Consideration of political and exchange transfer risks

21.25 If the business includes countries in less developed areas of the world,
consideration must be given to the political and exchange transfer risks
which are unlikely to be covered by the factor except to the extent that he
may rely on an Export Credits Guarantee Department (ECGD) policy.
Such reliance may be on the factor's own policy. Alternatively, the
factor may provide recourse factoring or, if finance is not required,
collections only in conjunction with the client's own ECGD policy and a
factoring endorsement as described earlier (see 3.18–3.21).

The choice between factoring and other assistance for exporters

21.26 In circumstances in which collections are not a problem to the client and
he is selling in relatively large amounts to a small number of customers,
the alternative of credit insurance should be considered. In such a case if
finance is required, in suitable cases, ECGD will provide a financial
guarantee to a bank or finance house on the basis of which the finance
may be provided at preferential rates, or non-recourse finance may be
provided by one of the bank's small exporters arrangements on the back
of the bank's own ECGD policy. These arrangements cover sales on
open credit as well as on bill terms.

21.27 A further aspect to be considered in contemplation of assistance for
exports, whether for protection against bad debts or for finance or for
both, is that a factor with a good correspondent or agent is usually in a
position to give a much quicker response to credit enquiries than one
without.

21.28 In any case in which finance is a major consideration and exports are
made on open credit terms, the question of recourse by the factor or the
bank must be taken into account. A non-recourse factor will refrain
from requiring repayment if a debt remains unpaid when it is seriously

overdue. Even if a bank is supported by a financial guarantee, except under the small exporter's scheme mentioned above, it may require the client to sign a promissory note by which the finance provided against any debt will be repayable if that debt is not paid a specific number of days after due date. In such a case the client may have difficulty in financing the debt whilst awaiting ultimate payment or settlement of a claim on ECGD.

21.29 The choice of method to finance and protect export credit depends on:

(*a*) the pattern of trade;

(*b*) the stability of the countries to which exports are to be made;

(*c*) the terms of payment;

(*d*) which of the three services (collections, credit protection or finance) are required and the importance of each to the prospective client.

Part G

The Future

Chapter 22

The Legal Framework

(The discourse contained in this chapter first appeared in 'Law and Tax Review', Vol 1 No 11 January 1983, published by Oyez Longman.)

22.1 The reason that factors in the UK provide their services by means of an outright purchase of debts from their clients is largely historical. The service was based mainly on the activities of factors in the United States who, before the coming into force of the Uniform Commercial Code, had no way of taking security rights over debts otherwise than by an outright purchase. Furthermore, when the service was first introduced into the United Kingdom, the concept of a fixed charge on book debts of a company had not been developed. A floating charge would not have enabled a factor to be confident of recovering all his funds in use owing to the well-known deficiencies of that form of security including the prior rights of preferential creditors. Finally, the financing of trade debts, whether by means of the full non-recourse factoring service or by simple invoice discounting, was initially undertaken mainly by concerns without banking status. By taking advantage of this distinction it was possible to avoid the then restrictive provisions of the Money Lenders Acts.

An alternative legal form of providing finance by factoring

22.2 It is generally accepted now that it *is* possible to effect a fixed charge on debts of a company so that it may be a specific charge attaching to the debts as they come into existence (see 15.20). It would therefore be possible for factors to provide their services for companies, as far as the finance for trade debts is required, by means of lending money on the security of such a charge. Those provisions of the Money Lenders Acts, that dissuaded factors from providing services in this way, have now been repealed. In order to ensure that a charge on debts will be considered to be fixed, it is essential that the arrangements between the chargor and chargee are such that the chargor is unable to deal with debts other than collect them and pay the proceeds direct to the chargee (see 15.20). A normal lender may have difficulty in ensuring that the chargor cannot so deal with his debts, but a factoring arrangement is specifically designed so that the factor's client does not have a right to do so. The factor, collecting the debts himself, has safeguards to prevent such dealings by the client. Therefore, the finance generated by a factoring agreement could well be provided by way of lending against a fixed charge. This would leave the service of collection, administration of the ledger and protection against bad debts to be provided by means of a service agreement.

22.3   The advantages of the present system by which debts are purchased by the factor are as follows:

(1) *Direct recovery.* In the event that the client becomes insolvent, there is no sudden change in the collection of the debts (otherwise than in invoice discounting or undisclosed) and thus any detraction from efficient collection, by the sudden giving of instruction to pay a receiver, is avoided.

(2) *No requirement to register.* In the past the absence of requirement for a company to register the assignments of its debts for the purpose of raising finance has been considered an advantage.

(3) *Accounting considerations.* The fact that, to the extent of prepayments made by the factor, the assignment removes the debts from the balance sheet of the client may have the effect of decreasing both current assets and liabilities. This may improve the apparent current ratio.

(4) *Gross payment of finance charge.* The discounting charge is payable gross by the client, although it may be payable under an agreement that may last more than a year. The reason is that it is not interest but a discount deducted from the purchase price payable by the factor for the debts. It is analogous to the charge for discounting bills of exchange. The deduction of tax from the finance charge by the client could, it is believed, cause an extra administrative burden to both client and factor.

22.4   On close examination, however, it seems that the advantages of the system by which debts are purchased by the factor set out in 22.3 above are not now of great benefit to either client or factor. First, it is of the essence of a fixed charge on debts that the client should not be at liberty to deal with the debts or their proceeds. If the factor were to take such a charge, an irrevocable power of attorney in favour of the factor enabling him to collect could be included. The factor would then provide his usual collection service which would continue after the insolvency of the client. In this way, the appointment of a receiver would be unnecessary and the disadvantages of an interruption in the flow of receipts avoided. Secondly, registration of charges is no longer seriously considered to detract from the standing of the chargor as regards trade credit from suppliers; and in the case of the smaller and medium sized business it is the consideration of their credit standing that in the past has deterred them from registering charges. Thirdly, the change in the current ratio may not improve the apparent strength of the client's balance sheet in any case in which he is known to be factoring or, where as should be the case, a contingent liability for the recourse is noted. Finally, it might well be possible to structure a loan agreement whereby the interest payable would not be 'yearly interest'. There is no statutory definition of the term and from case law the feature in determining whether or not the interest is yearly seems to be the length of the agreement. If the interest were not to be considered 'yearly' it would be payable gross (see 'Tolley's Focus on Interest and Discounts', 2.27–2.33).

Lending on security of the debts

22.5   As against the rather dubious advantages of continuing to provide factoring on the traditional basis, the following advantages may be adduced for the alternative method of lending on the security of the debts:

(1) *Prohibitions of assignments.* It seems that those who finance trade debtors by lending against the security of a charge, whether fixed or floating, are not troubled by the problems described earlier in Chapter 13. Although a charge on *choses in action* may, in effect, be by way of assignment there is no record of any debtor refusing to pay a receiver appointed to his creditor because the debtor's purchase contract prohibited an assignment of the debt. It is hardly conceivable that a liquidator would impugn the receiver's right to such a debt with an allegation that the assignment was ineffective. In any event the instrument of such a charge would no doubt be drafted in such a way that it would attach to any moneys paid in settlement of the debt.

(2) *Stamp duty.* A lending arrangement avoids any question of stamp duty (see 7.8–7.13) as mortgages and charges are not now subject to stamp duty.

(3) *Conflicts with holders of other charges.* The uncertainty which may arise in a conflict between a factor of debts in the traditional way and the holder of a charge affecting book debts has been dealt with in some detail in Chapter 15. The uncertainty arises mainly because factoring agreements, not being charges, are not capable of registration by companies. If the factor were to take a fixed charge on book debts, it would be registerable and the priority position would be clear.

22.6   From the above analysis there are strong reasons and telling advantages in a change to lending on security. There is, however, one difficulty. The sales ledger, collection and credit control elements of the service may be provided by a routine service agreement; but the protection against bad debts raises a difficulty. It is one thing to buy the debts without recourse and remove them absolutely from the ownership of the client. The relief of risk is the result of the transfer of title. On the other hand, the provision of a guarantee against bad debts might well be considered to be insurance and, as such, it would bring in its train the need for authorisation by the Department of Trade under the provisions of the Insurance Companies Act 1982.

22.7   There is no statutory definition of insurance nor any case law on this aspect of a factoring service. It is, therefore, difficult to determine whether or not the provision of this service as a straightforward guarantee of the solvency of the debtors (as opposed to the purchase of the debts without recourse) would result in the requirement for authorisation. Based on case law it would seem quite possible that the provision of such a credit guarantee would fall within class No 14 in Schedule 2 of the Insurance Companies Act 1982: 'Effecting and carrying out contracts of insurance against risks of loss to the persons insured arising from the insolvency of debtors of theirs or from the failure (otherwise than through insolvency) of the debtors of theirs to pay their debts when due'. (See, for example, the dicta of Sir Robert Megarry VC in *Medical Defence Union Limited v Department of Trade [1979] 2 AER 421*: 'First, the contract must provide that the insured will become entitled to something on the occurrence of some event . . . Second, the event must be one which involves some element of uncertainty . . . Third, the insured must have an insurable interest in the subject matter of the contract.'.) The exemption, in Section 2(4) of the Act, for activities carried on solely in the course of carrying on, and for the purpose of, banking would probably not apply; although the provision of finance by the factor might loosely be considered to be banking, the protection against bad debts is normally given within approved limits on debtors irrespective of any finance required by the client. The protection would continue to apply even when the finance had been recovered.

22.8   Neither the possible difficulty over credit protection nor the inability to obtain security over the book debts of an unincorporated business detract from the advantages of providing the service on the basis of lending on the security of the debts if the arrangement required by a company is:

(*a*) recourse factoring; or

(*b*) bulk factoring; or

(*c*) invoice discounting.

These differences between lending on security and the purchase of debts must now be viewed in the light of the White Paper on Insolvency. The proposed administrator procedure (see 17.17–17.19) may detract from the advantages of lending on security. If an administrator is appointed the realisation of the security will be stayed but there seems little doubt that the factor's rights to the debts vesting in him will be unaffected.

A composite method of factoring

22.9   By the use of a charge combined with a traditional form of factoring agreement (the purchase of debts by the factor), factors may well be able to widen their market. In Chapter 5, limitations on the use of factoring were described: it was argued that a factor could not safely provide the financial part of his service in certain trades and industries in which the debts might not be payable by the debtors without question, on the termination of the business, owing to the very nature of the businesses. The types of business concerned included contractors in the building industry and others whose contracts of sale or service provided for their provision by instalments represented by separate invoices. They included providers of many types of capital equipments. In all such cases, in the absence of back-up from the client itself, the debtors may be unwilling to pay and legally not liable.

22.10   In many instances where a factor has made prepayments to businesses providing services or goods on long term contracts the cost of finishing any contracts on the insolvency of the supplier might be small in relation to the final amount payable by the debtor. However, the factor often does not have the means to finish the contract or deal with warranty claims, rectification or after sales service required by the debtor before payment. The means are often in the hands of a liquidator or receiver or a trustee in bankruptcy; but he will have little incentive to use the property of the business for this purpose in order to allow the factor to recover his funds in use.

22.11   The factor himself may, in suitable cases of corporate clients, consider the advisability of taking a charge on the assets, other than the debts vesting in him under the factoring agreement, in order to secure any recourse in excess of his retention on current account. Such a charge should be a fixed charge on all rights of the client under contracts with his debtors and a floating charge on all other assets; and it should give the factor the right to appoint a receiver with power to manage the business in the usual specified circumstances of insolvency or default. If the factor takes the right to have all the debts vesting in him repurchased by the client on the client's insolvency (and such a provision is not unusual in a factoring agreement), the factor will be able to appoint a receiver having made demand for the repurchase price of the debts. In such circumstances the receiver may well be in a position to complete contracts and provide back-up necessary to ensure the full recovery of debts. The receiver would take over the uncompleted contracts with debtors and may use materials on hand and employ the client's staff to effect completion.

22.12 In suitable cases the taking of such a charge in conjunction with a factoring agreement may enable a factor to provide any form of service, that includes a financial facility, with reasonable safety to a wider range of trades and industries.

Chapter 23

The Influence of the Micro-Computer

Data processing packages for small businesses

23.1   The present trend towards inexpensive hardware and systems for micro-computers, many of which provide comprehensive accounting systems for small businesses, would seem to make such businesses less reliant on service bureaux. Certainly, many of these systems do not require specialist data processing staff for their maintenance.

23.2   The benefit of this much improved, and still improving price/performance ratio of micro-computers is widely recognised as a trend which will enable more smaller businesses to adopt an integrated data processing package to deal with all their financial records. It might seem that, as the removal of one part of these records — the sales ledger — from the package, would not be worthwhile, this tendency towards micro-computers would detract from the potential growth of factoring. On the contrary, full and proper consideration of the main benefits of a full factoring service — the relief from credit control and collections, and the risk of bad debts and the distracting work and worry related thereto — should alone give impetus to the growth of the service. The task of the pure recording of sales ledger items being a matter of routine (although of vital importance) is a less serious concern to the management of businesses.

The response of the factoring industry

23.3   In any event, the factoring industry is alive to these trends and is developing methods of linking its own systems with those of its clients where such systems are compatible for data transmission purposes. The possibilities of such links include the ability of the client to input his invoices and credit notes to the factor's records electronically; it includes feed-back by the factor to the client. This should reduce the factor's cost per transaction and enable him to provide more and better services for lower charges. Such developments may include:

(a) Complete systems covering the whole accounting for the smaller business supplied either by the factor or any approved systems house.

(b) Enquiry facilities provided through terminals in the client's offices connected to the factor's systems by telephone lines.

(*c*) Exchange of information by magnetic tape rather than printouts —
avoiding the duplication of keying.

The provision of sales statistics by the factor

23.4   These developments also include the provision of a full analysis of sales
by product, area, representative or agent according to the client's
requirements. Such analyses are already provided by a number of
factors. However, at present, in most cases, the sales for each period are
based on the factor's accounting period and relate only to copy invoices
received by the factor during any such period. Ideally most businesses
would like such analyses to be based on sales effected during their own
accounting periods which may be lunar or calendar months. There is,
therefore, a compelling case for factors to find a way by which their
systems, as regards accounting with their clients, may be based on the
actual dates of invoices rather than, as at present, the dates on which
copy invoices are received by them. The other advantage of such a
system would be that any periodic returns to the client, such as current
accounts and aged lists of debtor balances, would include all sales up to
the end of the period. The present widely used system of cutting off at the
end of each month means that the aged report excludes a few days' sales,
the totals of debtors are understated and the average period of credit,
based on such totals, is also understated. The difficulty of evolving such
a system arises from the fact that delays in raising invoices and
submitting them differ from client to client. If the cut-off date were to be
based on the slowest client, then the returns might not go out until the
end of the following month. It seems that it will be necessary for factors
to develop a system whereby the periods for accounting with clients will
be tailored for the individual client's requirements. The linking of the
client's micro-computer with the factor's system may provide for this.

Chapter 24

Conclusion: The Growing Acceptability of Factoring

Proved benefits to independent businesses

24.1   There is no doubt that a properly conducted full factoring service, relieving management from the burdensome tasks of monitoring, recording and controlling the credit which they grant to customers, protecting them against bad debts and providing finance that follows from day to day the needs of the debtor portfolio, is a most valuable management aid to the independent businesses which the United Kingdom economy needs at present. The evidence of this value is in the number of successful businesses which have used the service to achieve profitable and rapid growth, soundly and comfortably financed, to an extent that would not have been possible in any other way.

24.2   Unfortunately, owing to the activites of some of the organisations which—although calling themselves factors—provided only finance and no administrative or protective services, factoring came to be regarded in some quarters as an expensive form of finance for businesses that were unable to borrow from the more traditional services. In the last few years the full value of the service in any of its forms has been accorded better recognition. However, a further improvement in the usage and in the services provided and their cost could well be assisted by a more secure and certain background of law in which a factor might operate.

Need for codification of commercial law

24.3   Throughout this book it has been shown that there is a thread of uncertainty in relation to the legal position of the parties to the transactions. This uncertainty has the effect of aggravating the problems that a factor has to face when a client for whom he has provided financial facilities becomes insolvent. The factor may fail to recover all the funds in use, not by reason of the default of debtors, but owing to strange combinations of circumstances in this uncertain legal background. For these losses the factor must provide in his charges. A review of these branches of the law and their codification might enable the factors to provide their services more confidently and, accordingly, more efficiently and economically.

24.4   Whether such uncertainties remain or not, the ingenuity and skill of the factoring companies' staff will enable the factors to overcome these legal problems and develop new and better systems and methods of business. Parallel to these developments a better understanding of factoring in all its forms by the professional advisers to businesses is growing. Thus, the misuse of factoring will be avoided, not only by the factor, but also by the prospective clients and the ratio of successful use will grow. The service will then be regarded as a natural one for many types of business in certain stages of their development.

Appendices

Contents

		Page
I	Glossary of Terms	209
II	Checklist for Adviser	214
III	Checklist for Factor	217
IV	Specimen Facultative Factoring Agreement	222
V	Specimen Whole Turnover Factoring Agreement	230
VI	Client Account: Purchase Price Payable on Collection Date	240
VII	Client Accounts: Purchase Price Payable on Maturity	241
VIII	Export Factoring: 'Two Factor' System	244
IX	Export Factoring: 'Back-to-Back' Factoring	245

207

Glossary of Terms

Administration charge:	Ad valorem charge by the factor on each invoice for the provision of the service.
Advance payment facility:	Agreed level of prepayments.
Advance or advance payment:	Prepayment (q.v.).
Ageing:	Analysis of outstanding invoices representing trade debts by reference to invoice date or due date.
Aged balance report:	A listing of the ageing (q.v.)
Agency factoring:	Factoring through the medium of a company (acting as agent for the factor) owned by the factor but with a name similar to that of the client. This expression has also been used for a service equivalent to bulk factoring with protection against bad debts.
Approved debt (or receivable):	A debt in respect of which the factor has no right of recourse in the event of failure of the debtor to pay by reason of insolvency alone. Alternatively, in the case of recourse factoring or invoice discounting a debt which is eligible for prepayment.
Associate:	A person, firm or company linked with the client either by reason of substantial common control or relationship.
Availability:	The amount of prepayment which the client is entitled to at a particular time.
Average credit period:	The average period of credit taken by all the debtors of a client over a stated period.

Glossary of Terms

Batch:	A bundle of copy invoices sent to a factor as a notification (q.v.).
Bulk factoring:	Notification factoring with full recourse in which the client has responsibility for keeping the sales ledger.
Client:	A business concern making use of a factor's services.
Collection date:	The date on which a debt is deemed to be paid for the purpose of calculation of finance charges.
Commission:	Administration charge (q.v.).
Confidential factoring:	An alternative expression for invoice discounting or undisclosed factoring.
Correspondent factor:	A factor who is prepared to co-operate with a factor in another country in the two factor system as import factor, export factor or both.
Cover or credit cover:	The extent to which a debt or debts may be accepted by the factor without recourse (save for breach of warranty by the client).
Credit approval:	A limit relating to indebtedness outstanding from time to time or of periodic deliveries within which debts (or parts of debts) are approved for credit cover. Alternatively, the approval for credit cover of an individual order.
Credit limit:	The limit fixed for a credit approval.
Current account:	The meaning of this term depends upon the accounting arrangements used (see Chapter 9), i.e: (i) in the maturity date system the account balance represents the amount of prepayments outstanding (Debit) or undrawn payments due on maturity (Credit); (ii) in the collection date system, the balance (Credit) represents the undrawn purchase price of debts sold to the factor including the retention.
Customer:	Debtor (q.v.).
Debtor:	A person, firm or company to which the client has supplied goods or services or to which the client contemplates such supplies.

Debts purchased account:	See Chapter 9. Account on which is recorded all unmatured debts purchased from a client. In some cases the term is used for a record of all unpaid debts purchased from a client.
Debt turn:	Average credit period (q.v.).
Deemed insolvency:	A situation in which a debtor, who has not settled an assigned debt, is untraceable or is not worth the expense of proceedings for official insolvency.
Discounting charge:	The finance charge in consideration for prepayments.
Dispute:	The failure of a debtor to accept the goods or services and the invoice therefor without question.
Eligible debt (or receivable):	A debt in respect of which a client is entitled to a prepayment (in most cases approved debts are eligible except in maturity factoring).
Export factor:	A factor in the country of a client who will provide factoring services for the client's exports either direct or by the use of a correspondent.
Finance charge:	Discounting charge (q.v.).
Full factoring:	Notification factoring substantially without recourse, providing all three elements of the service — finance, administration and credit protection.
Full service factoring:	Full factoring.
Funds in use:	Day to day aggregate of prepayments and charges not recovered by payments from debtors.
Import factor:	A factor who provides services in relation to debtors in his own country for a client in another either direct or through an export factor.
Ineligible debt:	A debt in respect of which the client is not entitled to a prepayment. In some cases this will be a debt for which the client cannot give the usual warranties e.g. because it is subject to set-off by the debtor.
Interest:	Discounting charge (q.v.).

Glossary of Terms

Invoice discounting:	The purchase of debts by the factor from the client without any notice to the debtor usually with full recourse, the client collects the debts as agent for the factor.
Letter of offer:	Schedule of offer (q.v.).
Maturity date:	The final due date for payment by the factor to the client for the purchase price of the assigned debts. This may be the fixed period after invoice date or the date of the submission of copy invoices; or it may be the collection date.
Maturity period:	An agreed period for the calculation of the maturity date; usually fixed by reference to the past average credit period experienced by the client.
Non-notification factoring:	An alternative expression for invoice discounting or undisclosed factoring.
Non-recourse factoring:	The full factoring service or any variant in which the factor accepts the risk of loss arising from failure of the debtors to pay approved debts by reason of insolvency, e.g. maturity or undisclosed factoring.
Notification	(a) the submission of copy invoices to the factor by the client in circumstances in which the debts already vest in the factor by virtue of the factoring agreement; or (b) arrangements for the giving of notice to the debtors to pay assigned debts to the factor.
Old line factoring:	Full factoring (q.v.).
Open item system:	A system of sales accounting by which all outstanding invoices and unallocated cash and credits are shown rather than a simple brought forward balance.
Permitted limit:	Credit limit (q.v.).
Prepayment:	The payment of a substantial proportion of the purchase price of a debt on delivery to the factor of the copy invoice representing that debt.
Purchase price:	The amount payable by the factor for the debts sold to him — normally the invoiced amount less the factor's charges.

Receivable:
Debt to be sold to the factor by the client. Normally any debt arising in the normal course of the client's business.

Record account:
See Chapter 9. This term is sometimes used for debts purchased account (q.v.) when the latter has the second meaning assigned to it in this glossary.

Recourse:
The obligation of the client to repurchase any debt sold to the factor in specified circumstances. It may otherwise be framed as a guarantee by the client to the factor of due payment by the debtor.

Refactoring charge:
An additional charge made by some factors in recourse factoring for refraining from re-assigning a debt which is subject to recourse.

Reserve:
Retention (q.v.).

Retention:
Proportion of the purchase price of debts purchased by the factor withheld to provide for set-off of any recourse.

Schedule of offer:
A list of invoices, prepared by the client, representing debts to be offered to the factor in arrangements in which each debt to be sold is subject to offer by the client and acceptance or refusal by the factor.

Service charge:
Administration charge (q.v.).

Shipping limit:
Limit of deliveries during a specified period (normally each month) that will be approved for credit.

Supplier:
Client (q.v.).

Take on/takeover debts:
Debts in existence at the commencement of factoring to be assigned to the factor.

Unapproved debt (or receivable):
A debt in respect of which the factor may exercise his right of recourse for any reason. In the case of recourse factoring a debt that is not eligible for prepayment.

Undisclosed factoring:
Purchase of debts by the factor from the client with no notices to the debtors so that the client collects as agent for the factor — sometimes provided without full recourse. See, also, non-notification factoring.

Checklist for Adviser
[Name of Company or Firm]

		Paragraphs in book
A. Matters to be considered		
1.	Reason for requirement of factoring	6.1–6.2
	(*a*) financial	
	(*b*) protection	
	(*c*) administrative.	
2.	If finance required	6.4–6.5
	(*a*) Has cash flow projection including use of factoring been prepared?	
	(*b*) Has profit forecast including use of factoring been prepared?	
	(*c*) Is service being sought as last resort for failing business?	5.12
3.	If administration required	4.5–4.6
	(*a*) Have savings been considered?	
	(*b*) Has cost been set against ability to increase business volume without additional overheads?	
4.	If protection only required, advantages and disadvantages against credit insurance.	4.8–4.13
5.	If exports included,	
	(*a*) Are collections an important aspect?	21.24
	(*b*) Consider geographical distribution and advisability of ECGD cover combined with	21.25–21.26, 21.28

    (i)   factoring

    (ii) other forms of finance.

  (*c*) Check on factor's overseas correspondents.   21.27

6. Consider services required and combinations offered by:

    (i) Full service   2.2–2.11

    (ii) Recourse factoring   3.2–3.4

    (iii) Bulk factoring   3.5–3.6

    (iv) Maturity factoring   3.7–3.8

    (v) Invoice discounting   3.9–3.13

    (vi) Undisclosed factoring   3.14–3.15

    (vii) Agency factoring.   3.16–3.17

7. If factoring with recourse, consider ability of client to absorb recourse or use of credit insurance.   5.11, 5.14

8. Is the nature of business suitable for service selected?   5.5–5.6, 5.8–5.10

9. If guarantees are to be given, do they cover the factor's losses: 8.36–8.38

  (*a*) for any reason;

  (*b*) in respect of breach of the client's warranties only.

B. Choice of factor

1. Nature of services provided.   2.2–3.23

2. Reputation and status of factor and reference of existing user.

3. Basis of calculation of administration charge.   9.2–9.8

4. Whether or not a refactoring charge included.   9.6

5. Basis of calculation of finance charges — value dating.   9.9–9.16

Checklist for Adviser

		Paragraphs in book
6.	Responsibility for legal costs.	9.8
7.	Payment of purchase price on maturity date or collection.	9.17–9.23
8.	Basis of and factor's discretion as to financial facility.	2.7–2.8, 6.6
9.	Method of dealing with disputed items.	8.12–8.13
10.	Arrangements for termination.	2.11, 6.6
11.	General review of standard contract.	6.6
12.	Method of dealing with credit approvals.	2.5, 4.8, 6.6
13.	Position on cancellation of credit approvals.	2.5, 4.8, 6.6
14.	Review of factor's systems.	

Checklist for Factor

COMPANY NAME		
SURVEY DATE	CONDUCTED BY	
PERSONS INTERVIEWED		
NATURE OF BUSINESS		
CAPITAL	AUTHORISED	ISSUED

SHAREHOLDINGS AS IN SEARCH **CONFIRMED/CHANGED**	DIRECTORS AS IN SEARCH **CONFIRMED/CHANGED**

NOTE ANY DISCREPANCIES WITH LATEST B/SHEET

ASSOCIATE/SUBSIDIARY COMPANIES

AUDITORS	BANKERS

CHARGES AS IN SEARCH **CONFIRMED/CHANGED**

NOTE ANY DISCREPANCIES WITH LATEST SEARCH

IF IMPORTS PAID BY LETTER OF CREDIT OBTAIN COPY FACILITY LETTER

REGISTERS OF CHARGES INSPECTED **YES/NO**	MINUTE BOOK INSPECTED **YES/NO**

ANY DISCREPANCIES

Checklist for Factor

SALES LEDGER

TYPE OF DEBTOR	OPEN ITEM LEDGER
	YES/NO

NUMBER OF ACTIVE ACCOUNTS	NUMBER OF ACCOUNTS IN LEDGER

LEDGER ANALYSIS

_____ £ _____

_____ £ _____

_____ £ _____

_____ £ _____

AGEING   CURRENT

      1 MONTH

      2 MONTHS

      3 MONTHS

      3 + MONTHS

BAD DEBTS		AMOUNT	NO.
LAST 3 YEARS GROSS LOSSES	1		
	2		
	3		
		AMOUNT	NO.
POTENTIAL LOSSES IN LEDGER			

CREDIT INSURANCE

POLICY HELD

          PREVIOUSLY HELD

          NEVER HELD

COPY OF POLICY OBTAINED **YES/NO**

NUMBER OF NEW ACCOUNTS PER MONTH	REFERENCES TAKEN **YES/NO**
ESTIMATED PERCENTAGE OF PAYMENTS CLEARING BALANCES	LENGTH OF PERIOD
AVERAGE NUMBER OF PAYMENTS PER MONTH	ANY BAN ON ASSIGNMENT **YES/NO**
ANY GOVERNMENT DEPARTMENTS IN DEBTOR LIST	PERCENTAGE OF OUTSTANDINGS

IF I.D. COMMENTS ON CREDIT CONTROL & COLLECTIONS

SUPPLIERS

NAME	GOODS SUPPLIED	UP TO DATE	R.O.T.	% OF P.L.

ANY SPECIAL CONTRACTUAL ARRANGEMENTS WITH SUPPLIERS SHOULD BE NOTED AND COPY CONTRACTS OBTAINED WHERE APPLICABLE.

CREDITOR POSITION AS AT:

	TOTAL	CURRENT	1 MONTH	2 MONTHS	3 MONTHS
INLAND REVENUE					
P.A.Y.E.					
V.A.T.					
TRADE					
OTHERS					
TOTAL					

PRODUCT

POST DELIVERY OBLIGATIONS

    WARRANTIES   LONG TERM CONTRACTS

    GUARANTEES   STAGE PAYMENTS

    TOOLING   OTHERS

    RETURNABLE CONTAINERS

PRODUCT INSPECTED

TERMS OF SALE: 1) STANDARD

              2) EXCEPTIONS

              3) FORWARD DATING

              4) CONSTRUCTIVE DELIVERY

              5) SALE OR RETURN OR REPLACEMENT FOR NON-SALES

              6) POTENTIAL SET-OFF (OBTAIN LIST)

              7) SALES TO INDIVIDUALS

              8) RETROSPECTIVE DISCOUNTS

VALIDITY OF INVOICING

SAMPLE INVOICE OBTAINED **YES/NO**	COPY OF CONDITIONS OF SALE OBTAINED **YES/NO**
SAMPLE HEADED NOTEPAPER OBTAINED **YES/NO**	SEASONAL TURNOVER **YES/NO**
TURNOVER FOR LAST 12 MONTHS TO_____	PROJECTED TURNOVER FOR NEXT 12 MONTHS TO_____
DOMESTIC £_____	DOMESTIC £_____
EXPORT £_____	EXPORT £_____

FINANCIAL

	HOW SECURED	RATE
OVERDRAFT		
MEDIUM TERM LOAN		
OTHERS		

LATEST AUDITED ACCOUNTS OBTAINED IF NOT WHY NOT **YES/NO**	PERIOD ENDED
LATEST MANAGEMENT ACCOUNTS OBTAINED **YES/NO**	PERIOD ENDED

HOW OFTEN ARE MANAGEMENT ACCOUNTS PREPARED

LIQUIDITY STATEMENT AS AT

    FIXED ASSETS   £ _____

    CURRENT ASSETS £

    CURRENT LIABILITIES £ _____ NET CURRENT ASSETS £ _____

                               NET ASSETS £ _____

Checklist for Factor

DEBTOR (Name and Short Address)	CURRENT BALANCE	HIGHEST BALANCE	HIGHEST PAYMENT	PERFOR- MANCE	RATING

COMPANY NAME:

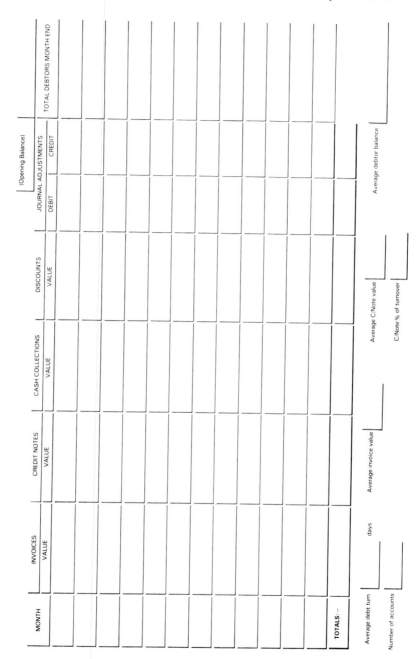

MONTH	INVOICES VALUE	CREDIT NOTES VALUE	CASH COLLECTIONS VALUE	DISCOUNTS VALUE	JOURNAL ADJUSTMENTS DEBIT	(Opening Balance) CREDIT	TOTAL DEBTORS MONTH END
TOTALS:—							

Average debt turn   days

Number of accounts

Average invoice value

Average C/Note value

C/Note % of turnover

Average debtor balance

221

Specimen Facultative Factoring Agreement

THIS AGREEMENT

is made the   day of   19
BETWEEN   of
            (hereinafter called 'the Factor') of the one part and
of
(hereinafter called 'the Supplier') of the other part
WHEREBY IT IS AGREED as follows:

Definitions

1.   In this Agreement the following terms bear the meanings hereinafter set out:

    (i)   'Contract' in relation to a Debt means the document or documents under which the Debt arises;

    (ii)   'Invoice' in relation to a Debt means the document or documents which evidences or evidence the existence of the Debt;

    (iii)   'Credit Note' in relation to a Debt means the document or documents which evidences or evidence a reduction in the amount of the Debt;

    (iv)   'Debtor' means any person, partnership or corporation having a place of business in the defined territories to whom the Supplier in the ordinary course of its business has contracted to supply goods or services for payment other than immediate cash payment;

    (v)   'Debt' means the sum to be paid by a Debtor to the Supplier in respect of any contract for the supply of goods or services;

    (vi)   'Purchased Debt' means a Debt purchased by the Factor from the Supplier under this Agreement;

    (vii)   'Approved' in relation to a Purchased Debt or part thereof means that the Factor has agreed to accept the credit risk thereon in the event of the subsequent financial inability of the Debtor to pay;

    (viii)   'Non-approved' in relation to a Purchased Debt or part thereof means that such Debt or part thereof has not been approved;

    (ix)   'Approved Limit' means the limit to which the Supplier may despatch goods or provide services to a particular Debtor in the knowledge that the resultant Debts purchased by the Factor will be Approved Debts;

    (x) 'Insolvency Event' means:

        (a)   Where the Debtor is a registered company the earliest of the date of commencement of winding-up of the Company (not being a members voluntary winding-up) or the making of an arrangement or composition with creditors other than for the purposes of reconstruction or amalgamation, or the appointment of a receiver or in the case of a foreign corporation any analogous act event or process under the law of any foreign jurisdiction;

        (b)   Where the Debtor is not a registered company the earliest of the commission of any act of bankruptcy or the making of any arrangement or composition with creditors or any analogous act event or process under the law of any foreign jurisdiction.

    (xi) 'Defined Territories' means

    or such other countries as may from time to time be agreed in writing between the Supplier and the Factor.

    (xii) 'United Kingdom' means England, Scotland, Wales, Northern Ireland and the Channel Islands.

Offer of Debts

2.   The Supplier shall offer to sell and the Factor shall purchase upon the terms and conditions hereinafter set out the Debts which during the continuance in force of this Agreement become owing to the Supplier from Debtors in respect of goods or services supplied or contracted to be supplied to such Debtors in the defined territories PROVIDED that the Factors shall not be bound to purchase any Debt so offered.

Credit Cover

3.   (a)   The Supplier will furnish to the Factor for credit approval written particulars in a form approved by the Factor in respect of all orders for goods or services received (save such as the Factor may agree shall not be furnished). The Factor will inform the Supplier in each case whether the resultant Debt, if purchased, will be an Approved Debt, a Non-approved Debt, or a Debt Approved as to part only and Non-approved as to the balance.

        (b)   The Factor shall be at liberty at any time to give notice to the Supplier cancelling or reducing any Approved Limit of a Debtor's indebtedness and such notice of cancellation or reduction shall take immediate effect and shall apply to any invoice in respect of goods or services which have not been despatched or provided at the date of receipt of such notice.

Assignment of Rights

4.   The Supplier will include in every invoice which may evidence a Purchased Debt a clause in the following form or in such other form as may be agreed between the Factor and the Supplier:-

'The amount payable under this invoice has been purchased by to whom you are hereby authorised and requested to make payment at and whose receipt alone shall be a good discharge. This authority and request is irrevocable without the consent in writing of

Facultative Agreement

Invoices

5. (a) The Supplier will at agreed intervals deliver to the Factor copies of all invoices delivered by it to Debtors since the last delivery of invoices together with a schedule thereof in a form agreed by the Factor. The delivery of each such schedule shall constitute an offer by the Supplier to sell to the Factor the Debts to which the invoices in such schedule relate which offer shall be irrevocable for a period of one month from the date of the delivery of each schedule.

(b) The Factor may at its discretion accept an offer in respect of all or some only of the Debts comprised therein and in the latter case it shall be entitled to make such consequential amendments to the documents submitted by the Supplier in connection with the offer as may be necessary. In addition, if the said documents reveal any discrepancies or errors the Factor shall be entitled at any time prior to its acceptance of the offer and at its sole discretion to make such corrections to the documents as it may think fit. All amendments and corrections made by the Factor under this clause shall be deemed to have been made on behalf of the Supplier and shall be binding on the Supplier.

(c) If so required the Supplier shall deliver to the Factor originals of invoices as well as a copy, under which circumstances the Factor shall forward the originals of the invoices to the Debtor.

Warranties

6. By the making of an offer under Clause 5 hereof the Supplier shall be deemed to warrant to the Factor in respect thereof that:

(a) goods have been supplied and/or work and/or services have been or will be done or rendered by the Supplier in accordance with its contract with the Debtor;

(b) The Debtor is liable for the full amount of the invoice without deduction, set-off or counter-claim;

(c) the Supplier has (or had immediately before the property in the goods passed to the Debtor) good, valid and unencumbered title to goods supplied;

(d) each copy invoice delivered to the Factor is a true and correct copy of the invoice delivered to the Debtor and that the invoice to the Debtor has been marked in accordance with the provisions of Clause 4 hereof;

(e) no extension of time for payment has been granted by the Supplier to the Debtor nor will be granted without the prior approval of the Factor;

(f) The Factor has been notified in writing in every case where the Debtor is a subsidiary or associated company of the Supplier, a director or employee of the Supplier or a member of the family of a director or employee of the Supplier;

(g) the Supplier will keep proper books of account;

(h) the Supplier will make all relevant tax payments in relation to goods and services creating Purchased Debts.

Credit Notes

7. If the Supplier issues a credit note or makes any allowance to a Debtor in respect of a Purchased Debt the Supplier will send to the Factor a copy of such credit note or notification of such allowance such note or notification when sent to the Factor to

be accompanied by the Supplier's remittance for the full sum credited or allowed unless the amount is with the consent of the Factor charged to the Supplier's current account herein after referred to.

Acceptance

8. (a) If an offer is accepted by the Factor it will by way of consideration for the purchase of the Debt credit a record account in the name of the Supplier in the books of the Factor with an amount equal to the invoice value of the goods or services comprised in the accepted invoices (as adjusted under Clause 5 (b) if appropriate) and will advise the Supplier of such credits. If the Factor does not accept an invoice it will cancel the direction for payment to it in such invoice.

   (b) If an offer is accepted by the Factor the Debts comprised therein shall be purchased in sterling and where such offer includes Debts that are for payment in a currency other than sterling then the Factor will convert the amount due to the sterling equivalent at a rate of exchange as established by the Factor on the date of acceptance of such offer.

Service Fee

9. (a) The Factor will debit to the Supplier's current account hereinafter referred to and retain an amount equal to   per cent of the gross value of all invoices credited to the record account of the Supplier (or such other percentage as may from time to time be agreed in writing between the Supplier and the Factor) where such invoices relate to sales made by the Supplier to Debtors within the United Kingdom.

   (b) The Factor will debit to the Supplier's current account hereinafter referred to and retain an amount equal to   per cent of the gross value of all invoices credited to the record account of the Supplier (or such other percentage as may from time to time be agreed in writing between the Supplier and the Factor) where such invoices relate to sales made by the Supplier to Debtors within the Defined Territories other than the United Kingdom.

Maturity Period

10. (a) For the purpose of this Clause 'the Estimated Maturity Period' shall mean a period of   days where such invoices relate to sales made by the Supplier to Debtors within the United Kingdom and   days where such invoices relate to sales made by the Supplier to Debtors within the Defined Territories other than the United Kingdom or in each case such other period as may be agreed from time to time in writing between the Factor and the Supplier. Each of the above periods shall be the time estimated on average by the Factor to elapse between the acceptance of offers under Clause 5 hereof and the payment of the Purchased Debts by the Debtor. Any alteration of the relative Estimated Maturity Period shall apply only to Debts purchased after the date of such alteration.

   (b) The Factor will in respect of each Debt on the expiration of the relative Estimated Maturity Period after such Debt is credited to the Supplier's record account transfer to a current account in the name of the Supplier in the books of the Factor the amount previously credited to the Supplier's record account in respect of that Debt.

(c)   The Factor will maintain a Memorandum Interest/Discount Account and record therein the actual payment date of each Purchased Debt and will credit or debit the Supplier's current account with a sum calculated on a daily basis in respect of the time by which the actual payment period of such Debt is less than or exceeds respectively the relative Estimated Maturity Period but no such calculation shall be made in respect of any Approved Debt for any period after the happening of any Insolvency Event.

(d)   The sum referred to in sub-clause (c) of this Clause will be calculated upon the amount credited to the Supplier's current account in respect of the relevant Debt and will be at the rate of   per cent per annum over the Base Rate of   (as from time to time in force) or such other rate as may be agreed in writing from time to time between the Factor and the Supplier.

(c)   (i)   The Supplier will, at the option of the Factor, forthwith re-purchase any Non-Approved Debt previously purchased by the Factor. This right may be exercised by the Factor at any time by debiting the re-purchase price to the Supplier's current account and by sending a notice in writing to the Supplier, provided that prior notice had been given to the Supplier that the Debt is Non-Approved.

        (ii)   The re-purchase price shall be a sum equal to the amount credited by the Factor to the record account under Clause 8(a) above less any sum previously received by the Factor on account of the relevant Debt.

Payments

11. The Supplier may draw on its current account but will not draw in excess of the credit balance from time to time standing thereon unless the Supplier shall previously have entered into a separate advance payment facility with the Factor in relation to such drawings.

Assignment

12. The Supplier will if called upon by the Factor so to do and at the Supplier's expense forthwith execute a legal assignment to the Factor in such form as the Factor shall require of all of the Purchased Debts or any one or more of them and the full benefit thereof and all monies payable or to become payable thereunder by the Debtor the Supplier paying the stamp duty on any such assignment and in consideration of the agreements herein contained the Supplier hereby irrevocably appoints the Factor and each and every Director and Manager of the Factor for the time being to be its attorney to execute in its name and on its behalf such an assignment.

Debtor Information

13. Each copy invoice delivered to the Factor shall be accompanied by such information in writing regarding the commercial and financial position of the Debtor as is in the possession of the Supplier and has not already been imparted to the Factor by the Supplier in writing on the delivery of any previous invoices.

Returns

14. Any goods not accepted or returned by the Debtor to the Supplier for any reason and any proceeds thereof will be held in trust for the Factor under immediate advice and all goods so returned will be plainly marked as belonging to the Factor.

Monies Received

15. All monies or bills of exchange received by the Supplier from the Debtor(s) in purported payment of any Purchased Debt will be held in trust for the Factor and paid over or delivered immediately.

Insurance, etc.

16. The Supplier undertakes in respect of each Debt offered for sale:

    (a)   that any insurance required under its contract has been effected;

    (b)   that any claims thereunder which the Supplier is entitled to make in respect of loss of or damage to goods has been or will be punctually made;

    (c)   that any proceeds of such claims in respect of Purchased Debts are or will be held in trust for the Factor and will be paid over immediately.

Endorsement

17. The Factor is hereby authorised to endorse in the name and on behalf of the Supplier all negotiable instruments received by the Factor in relation to Purchased Debts.

Application of Payments

18. Where Approved and Non-approved Debts owing by the same Debtor shall have been purchased by the Factor, the Supplier agrees to the appropriation by the Factor, as he sees fit, of any payments on account made by a Debtor.

Rights and Authorisation

19. (a)   The Factor may inspect and make copies of or extracts from the books and records of the Supplier at any time and will on request be supplied with evidence of the due performance of a contract.

    (b)   The Factor shall have any right of stoppage in transit which the Supplier is entitled to exercise.

    (c)   If a Debtor declines to pay any Purchased Debt because of any alleged dispute, set-off or breach of contract, the Factor shall be entitled at any time to require the Supplier forthwith to re-purchase the Debt. This right may be exercised by the Factor at any time by debiting the re-purchase price to the Supplier's current account and by sending a notice in writing to the Supplier and the provisions of Clause 10(e)(ii) shall apply thereto.

    (d)   The Factor shall be entitled in any dealings with Debtors to take or refrain from taking any action, proceedings or other steps to enforce payment by a Debtor and to compound with, give time for payment or grant other indulgence to or make any arrangement with a Debtor without affecting the Factor's rights hereunder.

    (e)   The Factor may answer credit enquiries regarding the Supplier and Debtors.

    (f)   All payments received from Debtors within the Defined Territories, made in a currency other than sterling shall be converted to sterling at the appropriate rate of exchange as on the day on which the payment is received by the Factor.

    (g)   All accounts between the Factor and the Supplier shall be in sterling. Any loss or profit as a result of exchange currency differences resulting from Debts purchased in a currency other than sterling shall be debited or credited as appropriate to the Supplier's current account.

(h)   In the event of there occurring civil commotion, war, government action or any other condition arising in that part of the Defined Territories where a Debtor is situate, as a result of which such Debtor is precluded from making payment of all or part of a Purchased Debt or in the opinion of the Factor would be precluded from making such payment then the Factor shall be entitled at any time to require the Supplier forthwith to re-purchase the Debt. This right may be exercised by the Factor at any time by debiting the re-purchase price to the Supplier's current account and by sending a notice in writing to the Supplier and the provisions of Clause 10(e)(ii) shall apply thereto.

Records and Accounts

20. (a)   The Factor will keep proper records of all its dealings with the Supplier and Debtors and render statements at regular intervals to the Supplier and Debtors.

(b)   All statements rendered by the Factor to the Supplier will be accepted as accurate unless the Supplier makes any written objection thereto within seven days of the receipt of such statements.

Termination

21. This Agreement may be determined (but without prejudice to the continuation of the terms hereof in relation to all invoices accepted as aforesaid before such determination) by three months' notice in writing given by either party to the other and may be terminated by the Factor without notice if the Supplier:

(a)   breaks any term of this Agreement;

(b)   goes into liquidation;

(c)   makes any arrangement or composition with its creditors or ceases or threatens to cease to carry on business;

(d)   has a receiver appointed over any of its assets;

(e)   has a distress execution or other process levied on any of its assets which is not paid out in five days;

(f)   is unable to pay its debts within the meaning of Section 223 of the Companies Act 1948.

Provisions

22. (a)   The Supplier shall not be entitled to assign this Agreement or the benefit thereof.

(b)   If by the terms of this Agreement any act would be required to be performed on or within a period ending on a Saturday or Sunday or any day which is a common law or statutory holiday in any part of the United Kingdom the act shall be deemed to have been duly performed if performed on or by the next business day after that day.

(c)   This Agreement is subject to the special provisions, if any, in the Addendum number(s)   attached hereto.

Dear Sirs

ADVANCE PAYMENT FACILITY

We refer to the Factoring Agreement made between us and dated the   and confirm that we are prepared to make available to you a facility whereby we will make advance payment to you of a portion of the purchase price becoming due to you under the Factoring Agreement in respect of the debts purchased by us pursuant to the Agreement.

This facility will be made available on the following terms:

1.   Whenever you wish us to make a payment under this facility you will complete a written request in the form set out in Appendix 'A' or such other form of request as may be agreed between us from time to time.

2.   On receipt of a request as above we may, at our discretion, make an advance payment to you on account of the relative purchased debts. The aggregate amount outstanding in respect of advance payments hereunder shall at no time exceed (or such other percentage as may be notified to you by us) of the aggregate value of debts purchased by us pursuant to the Factoring Agreement and for the time being outstanding to the credit of the Debts Purchased Account opened in your name pursuant to the Factoring Agreement.

3.   The amount of each advance payment made to you pursuant to this facility shall be debited to your Current Account.

4.   Each advance payment made to you pursuant to this facility shall be attributed to the debts for the time being credited to your Debts Purchased Account in such proportions as may be determined by us and in default of any express determination shall be deemed to have been attributed in such proportions that the percentage of the purchase price of each such debt advanced to you is the same.

5.   In respect of any amounts paid to you in advance under the facility a charge will be levied on a day to day basis at   % per annum above the Base Rate of   (as from time to time in force). This charge will be debited to your Current Account on the last calendar day of each month.

Will you please confirm your acceptance of the above terms by signing and returning to us the enclosed duplicate copy of this letter.

Yours faithfully

We hereby agree to the terms of this letter in relation to the Advance Payment Facility which you have agreed to grant to us.

_____

for

Specimen Whole Turnover Factoring Agreement

AGREEMENT FOR THE FACTORING OR DISCOUNTING OF
RECEIVABLES

1. PARTIES: (1) ANGLO FACTORING SERVICES LIMITED
of 1 Palace Place, Brighton BN1 1ET, East Sussex ("the Factor",
which expression shall include the Factor's assigns except where
the context otherwise requires)

    (2)
        of

                                                  ("the Client")

2. DATE

3. DEFINITIONS:

(1) In this Agreement, except where the context otherwise requires, the singular shall
include the plural and vice versa, the masculine shall include the feminine and neuter
and vice versa and the following expressions shall have the meanings assigned to them
below:

"Approved
receivable"

Any receivable which (i) falls within any permitted limit (and
where there are two or more receivables owing by the same Debtor
the receivables shall be treated for this purpose in the order in
which they become due for payment) and (ii) in relation to which
the Client is not in breach of any warranty or undertaking
contained in this Agreement and (iii) is not a receivable or
within a class of receivables specified in paragraph 1 of the
Schedule.

"Associate of
the Client"

A director, shareholder or employee of the Client or a person
whose relationship to the Client is within the meaning of
associate as defined by Section 184 of the Consumer Credit Act
1974.

"Collection date"

(1) As regards a receivable paid in cash, the date of receipt from
the Debtor and as regards a receivable paid by cheque or other
instrument, the date on which the amount of the same is collected
from the drawee or acceptor; or (2) Such other date as may be
specified in paragraph 2 of the Schedule.

"Commencement
date"

The date specified in paragraph 12 of the Schedule.

230

"Date of insolvency"	(1) In the case of bankruptcy, sequestration or winding up by the Court, the date of the ajudication order, sequestration award or winding up order respectively by the Court having jurisdiction.
	(2) In the case of a voluntary winding up, the date of the effective resolution for voluntary winding up by members of the Debtor.
	(3) In the case of the appointment of a receiver, the date of the appointment.
	(4) In the case of any arrangement, the date when the same is made.
"Debtor"	Any person who is or may become indebted in respect of any receivable or prospective receivable.
"Delivery"	(1) In the case of goods, despatch in the United Kingdom to the Debtor or his agent.
	(2) In the case of services, completion of their performance.
"Goods"	Any merchandise and, where the context so admits, any services (and "sale of goods" shall include the provision of services).
"Insolvency"	(1) Bankruptcy.
	(2) Sequestration.
	(3) Winding up by reason of inability to pay debts.
	(4) The appointment of a receiver of any part of the income or assets of the Debtor, or the making of an arrangement, formal or informal, with or for the benefit of the general body of the Debtor's creditors.
"Legal representative"	The Debtor's executor, administrator, trustee in bankruptcy, liquidator or other person for the time being entrusted by law with the management of the Debtor's assets or affairs.
"Notified receivable"	A receivable notified to the Factor under Clause 9(2).
"Permitted limit"	A limit established by the Factor at its sole discretion on application to it by the Client in relation to any Debtor for the purpose of determining the extent to which the aggregate indebtedness of any Debtor at any one time comprises approved receivables.
"Purchase price"	The price payable by the Factor under Clause 5 in respect of a receivable.
"Receivable"	The amount (or where the context so requires, a part of the amount) of any indebtedness incurred or to be incurred by the Debtor under a supply contract.
"Recourse"	The right of the Factor to require the Client to repurchase a notified receivable at a price equal to the amount remaining unpaid by the Debtor in respect thereof.

231

"Supply contract"   A contract for the sale of goods by the Client.

"Unapproved receivable"   A receivable that is not an approved receivable.

(2) Expressions which, in or for the purpose of any proceedings outside England, have no precise counterpart in the jurisdiction in which those proceedings take place, shall be construed as if bearing the meaning of the closest equivalent thereto in the jurisdiction concerned.

4.   TRANSFER OF RECEIVABLES

(1) The Client agrees to sell and the Factor to purchase all receivables, existing at the commencement date or arising thereafter during the currency of this Agreement, in relation to any Debtor of the class or description specified in paragraph 3 of the Schedule. The ownership of each such receivable shall, as regards receivables existing at the commencement date, vest in the Factor on that date and, as regards future receivables, vest in the Factor automatically upon the same coming into existence.

(2) Upon any receivable vesting in the Factor under sub-clause (1) there shall also automatically vest in the Factor all Client's rights under or in relation to the relevant supply contract (including the right to rescind or terminate such contract and/or to accept a return of goods comprised therein), all instruments and real and personal securities taken or held by the Client in connection therewith and the Client's title to all rights in the goods comprised in the supply contract.

(3) The Client shall at the request of the Factor and at the Client's expense execute a formal written assignment or assignation to the Factor of the receivables, rights, instruments and securities referred to in sub-clauses (1) and (2) and deliver to the Factor any such instrument or security with any necessary indorsement or other signature. If in relation to any receivable such formal assignment or assignation should be of no effect at law the Client shall hold such receivable, and the rights, instruments and securities relating thereto, on trust for the Factor.

5.   PURCHASE PRICE

(1) The purchase price of each receivable vesting in the Factor under clause 4(1) shall be such amount (including any tax) payable by the Debtor in respect thereof as notified by the Client under clause 9(2) less (i) any discount or other deduction allowed or allowable by the Client to the Debtor in relation thereto, and (ii) the administration charges provided by Clause 6.

(2) Except as provided by sub-clauses (3) - (5) the purchase price of a receivable shall be paid by the Factor to or for the account of the Client on the collection date thereof or, as regards an approved receivable, on the date of any earlier insolvency of the Debtor.

(3) At any time after the expiry of 24 hours of receipt by the Factor of notification under clause 9(2) relating to an approved receivable, the Factor shall at the request of the Client prepay in whole or in part such percentage of the purchase price of the receivable as is set out in paragraph 4 of the Schedule subject to deduction of the discounting charge specified in paragraph 5 of the Schedule.

(4) The Factor shall not be obliged to make any such payment or prepayment whilst any winding up petition is pending against the Client or whilst any act of bankruptcy committed by the Client remains an available ground for a bankruptcy petition. At any time when the Factor is entitled to terminate this Agreement under clause 20(2) the Factor may, whether or not exercising its right to terminate, withhold all prepayments and recover any prepayment which shall have been made in respect of any receivable then unpaid.

(5) The Factor shall at any time be entitled to set off against any payment due to the Client any amount payable or prospectively payable by the Client to the Factor, whether under this Agreement or otherwise.

(6) Unless otherwise agreed by the Factor at the request of the Client, the purchase price of all receivables shall be payable in Sterling.

(7) Where a receivable is payable otherwise than in Sterling in the United Kingdom, (i) bank charges for collection and/or conversion into Sterling shall be deducted in arriving at the purchase price and (ii) the purchase price shall be computed by reference to the rate of exchange ruling in London on the collection date, or any earlier date of insolvency of the relevant Debtor, but for administrative convenience and for the purpose of computing the administration charge in accordance with Clause 6, the Factor may provisionally apply the rate ruling in London on the date of receipt by the Factor of the notification relating to the receivable, making such adjustments as may thereafter be necessary. Similar provisions shall apply to payment of the repurchase price where the Factor has recourse in relation to a receivable to which this clause applies and such repurchase price shall be computed at the same rate as that applied to the purchase price of the receivable to which it relates.

6.   ADMINISTRATION CHARGES

The administration charge to be deducted in computing the purchase price payable by the Factor under clause 5(1) shall be such percentage as is specified in paragraph 6 of the Schedule (or such other percentage as shall have been agreed by the parties in writing) of the gross value of each receivable notified to the Factor, such gross value to be computed before deduction of any discounts or other deductions allowed or allowable by the Client to the Debtor. Any additional administration charge for which provision is made in paragraph 7 of the Schedule shall be payable to the Factor by the Client as therein provided.

7.   STATEMENTS OF ACCOUNT

The Factor shall send a statement of account to the Client at least once in every month and such statement shall be deemed to be correct and shall be binding on the Client unless the Client notifies the Factor of an error therein within thirty days of the date of its despatch.

8.   WARRANTIES BY CLIENT

The Client warrants:-

(1) that the Client's business is as stated in paragraph 8 of the Schedule;

(2) that the Client has not granted any disposition or any charge or other encumbrance which affects or may affect any of the receivables the subject of this Agreement;

(3) that prior to the making of this Agreement the Client has disclosed to the Factor every fact or matter known to the Client which the Client knew or ought to have known might influence the Factor in its decision whether or not to enter into this Agreement and, if so, the terms of the Agreement, including any term as to recourse, prepayment, establishment of any permitted limit or designation of any receivable or class of receivables as unapproved;

(4) that every Debtor has an established place of business and is not an associate of the Client.

233

9.   UNDERTAKINGS BY CLIENT

The Client undertakes:-

(1) to ensure that the warranties given in clause 8 in relation to the making of this Agreement shall, unless otherwise agreed by the Factor, remain fulfilled in relation to the continuance of the Agreement and throughout the currency thereof, and to perform any outstanding or continuing obligations of the Client to every Debtor under the relevant supply contract or any related contract;

(2) promptly to notify the Factor, in such manner and with such particulars and documents evidencing the receivable as the Factor may from time to time require, of every receivable sold by the Client to the Factor, as soon as the relevant goods have been delivered or, if so required by the Factor, at any other time;

(3) to ensure that except as otherwise approved by the Factor in writing every contract relating to a notified receivable (a) shall be made in the ordinary course of the Client's business; (b) shall provide for terms of payment not more liberal than those set out in paragraph 9(a) of the Schedule; (c) shall be subject to the law of the country or one of the countries specified in paragraph 9(b) of the Schedule; and (d) shall provide for the relevant invoice to be expressed and payment to be made by the Debtor in the currency specified in paragraph 9(c) of the Schedule;

(4) to ensure that every notified receivable shall be payable by the Debtor as a legally binding obligation without defence, cross claim or set-off and that neither the Debtor nor his legal representative will dispute liability in respect thereof;

(5) as regards every notified receivable, to give to the Debtor such written notice of transfer of the receivable to the Factor as may be required by paragraph 10 of the Schedule;

(6) to notify the Factor promptly in writing of any disagreement between the Client and any Debtor relating to any receivable and to supply to the Factor a copy of any credit note issued to a Debtor as soon as such credit note is issued;

(7) to deliver direct to the Factor (or, if so required by the Factor, direct to a bank account specified by the Factor) any remittance received by the Client in payment of or on account of any receivable, and pending such delivery to hold such remittance in trust for the Factor and separate from the Client's own monies;

(8) to cooperate fully with the Factor in the collection of any receivable and the enforcement of payment thereof, whether by proceedings or otherwise, and to indemnify the Factor against all legal and other costs and expenses incurred in connection with such enforcement so far as it relates to an unapproved receivable;

(9) in the case of undisclosed factoring or discounting, to maintain proper credit controls and to act promptly and efficiently in the collection of the receivables;

(10) to comply with any requirement of the Factor that the Factor's prior consent be obtained to the issue of any credit note to any Debtor;

(11) not to rescind, terminate or vary any contract relating to a notified receivable without the prior consent of the Factor;

(12) not to assign, charge or otherwise encumber any receivable the subject of this Agreement, nor enter into any other agreement for the factoring or discounting of any receivables (whether or not the subject of this Agreement) without the prior written consent of the Factor.

10. RECOURSE

As regards (i) each unapproved receivable, (ii) each receivable which comprises solely discount wrongly claimed or deducted by the Debtor and (iii) each receivable which the Debtor is or claims to be unable to pay by reason of legal constraints (other than those created by the Debtor's insolvency) or acts or orders of government, the Factor shall have recourse to the Client on the expiry of notice to the Client of the length specified in paragraph 11 of the Schedule. The Factor will credit the Client with all sums subsequently recovered by the Factor in respect of such receivable as the result of enforcement of rights, title or securities vested in the Factor under clause 4(2). The said receivable, rights, title and securities shall, unless otherwise determined by the Factor, remain vested in the Factor until the repurchase price has been fully discharged, whether by payment to the Factor or by set-off of an amount credited to the Client under the provisions of this Agreement.

11. VALUE ADDED TAX

(1) For the purpose of securing recoupment of value added tax invoiced to a Debtor who becomes bankrupt or suffers sequestration or goes into liquidation the Client agrees:-

(i) that where legal ownership of the receivable is still vested in the Client, the Factor shall be at liberty to lodge a proof of debt in the Client's name for the amount of the receivable exclusive of value added tax;

(ii) that where legal ownership of the receivable has passed to the Factor, the Factor shall be at liberty to re-assign the receivable to the Client (for a nil consideration in the case of an approved receivable);

and that in either such case the Client shall use its best endeavours to recover such value added tax and shall promptly remit to the Factor, and meanwhile hold on trust for the Factor, any dividend received or value added tax recovered by the Client.

(2) Sub-clause (1) shall not apply in relation to any receivable in respect of which the Factor has exercised its right of recourse under clause 10.

12. APPROPRIATION AND DIVISION OF RECEIPTS

(1) In any case in which approved and unapproved receivables may be owing by the same Debtor then, subject to the provisions of sub-clause (2), the Factor shall be entitled (notwithstanding any contrary appropriation by the Debtor) to appropriate any payment or other benefit received in discharge of or on account of receivables owing by such Debtor, and any credit or allowance granted by the Client to the Debtor, in discharge of or on account of any approved receivable in priority to any unapproved receivable.

(2) Any dividend or other benefit received from the estate of a Debtor following the date of insolvency, shall be divided between the Factor and the Client pro-rata to the aggregate amount of approved and unapproved receivables owing by the Debtor at the date of insolvency.

13. CREDIT BALANCES

The Client hereby irrevocably authorises the Factor to make payment in settlement of any credit balance which may arise on any Debtor's account in the Factor's records, whether such credit balance arises from the issue of a credit note by the Client or otherwise.

14. COLLECTION OF RECEIVABLES

Where notice of transfer of a receivable to the Factor has been given to the Debtor, then until a receivable has become revested in the Client in accordance with clause 10, the Factor shall have the sole right to collect the receivable and to enforce payment thereof in such manner and to such extent as it shall in its absolute discretion decide, and to institute, defend or compromise in the name of the Factor or the Client and on such terms as the Factor thinks fit any proceedings brought by or against the Factor in relation to the receivable.

15. CLIENT'S ACCOUNTS AND RECORDS

The Client shall permit the Factor and its authorised agents at all reasonable times to inspect all or any of the Client's records and documents relating to any transaction giving rise to a receivable or relating to the financial position of the Client. The Client shall furnish to the Factor at the Factor's request a copy of any balance sheet, account or statement produced by the Client showing its financial position or the results of its operations.

16. POWER OF ATTORNEY

The Client hereby irrevocably appoints the Factor and the Directors and the General Manager and the Secretary for the time being of the Factor jointly and each of them severally to be the attorneys or the attorney of the Client to execute or sign in the Client's name such deeds and documents, to complete or indorse such cheques and other instruments, to institute or defend such proceedings and to perform such other acts, as the Factor may consider necessary in order to perfect the Factor's title to any receivable or goods or any right, instrument or security taken or arising in connection therewith or to secure performance of any of the Client's obligations under this Agreement.

17. CANCELLATION OF PERMITTED LIMIT

Any permitted limit may be cancelled or varied by the Factor in its absolute discretion by written or oral notice to the Client and such cancellation or variation shall take effect forthwith except in relation to receivables arising from goods sold and delivered before receipt of the said notice by the Client.

18. CHANGE IN CONSTITUTION OF CLIENT

This Agreement shall remain effective notwithstanding any change in the constitution, composition or legal personality of the Client, whether by death, retirement, addition or otherwise.

19. PLURALITY OF CLIENTS

Where two or more persons are named as Client in this Agreement, the undertakings and warranties contained in this Agreement shall be deemed to be given by each of them, their liability hereunder shall be joint and several and the Factor shall be at liberty (i) to release or conclude a compromise with any one or more of them without affecting its rights against the other or others, (ii) to treat a notice or demand by the Factor to any one or more of them or to the Factor by any one or more of them as a notice or demand given to or by the other or others (but the Factor shall not be obliged to treat such notice or demand in the manner aforesaid).

20. COMMENCEMENT AND TERMINATION

(1) This Agreement shall commence on the date specified in paragraph 12 of the Schedule and, subject to the provisions of sub-clause (2), shall continue for the minimum period specified in paragraph 13 of the Schedule and thereafter until terminated by the expiry of any notice specified in that paragraph.

(2) If at any time the Client shall (i) become insolvent (ii) call any meeting of creditors or, being a body corporate, pass a resolution for winding up otherwise than

by reason of insolvency or, being a partnership, be dissolved or (iii) commit any material or persistent breach of this Agreement, or if a garnishee order nisi obtained by any judgement creditor of the Client shall be served on the Factor, or if any of the persons of whom the Client, not being a body corporate, is comprised shall commit any act of bankruptcy, or if any person who has given to the Factor a guarantee or indemnity in respect of the Client's liabilities to the Factor shall give notice terminating the guarantee or indemnity or shall become insolvent, then in any such event the Factor shall be at liberty to terminate this Agreement forthwith by notice.

(3) Upon termination under sub-clause (2), the Client shall become liable forthwith to repurchase at the value notified to the Factor all receivables then outstanding, whether approved or unapproved, but so that none of the said receivables shall revest in the Client until the repurchase price of all such receivables has been paid.

(4) Subject to the provision of sub-clause (3) and of clause 5(4), such termination shall not affect the rights and obligations of the parties hereto in relation to such receivables which came into existence prior to termination, which shall remain in full force and effect until duly extinguished.

21. EXCLUSION OF OTHER TERMS; PRESERVATION OF FACTOR'S RIGHTS

(1) This Agreement, including the Schedule and any Special Conditions set out in paragraph 14 thereof, contains all the terms agreed between the Factor and the Client to the exclusion of any representations or statements made by or on behalf of the Factor, whether orally or in writing, prior to the making of this Agreement.

(2) The Factor's rights under this Agreement shall not in any way be affected by any delay or failure to exercise any right or option, whether under this Agreement or otherwise, nor by the grant of time or indulgence to the Client or to any Debtor, guarantor or indemnifier.

22. NO ASSIGNMENT OR DELEGATION BY CLIENT

The Client shall not be entitled to assign any of its rights or delegate any of its duties under this Agreement without the prior written consent of the Factor.

23. APPLICABLE LAW AND JURISDICTION

This Agreement shall be governed and construed in accordance with English Law and the Client hereby accepts the jurisdiction of the English Courts, but without prejudice to the right of the Factor to bring proceedings in the Courts of any State in which the Client carries on business.

Whole Turnover Agreement

THE SCHEDULE

1. Receivables within permitted limit which are not approved (Clause 3(1)):

2. Collection date otherwise than as defined (Clause 3(1)):

   Not applicable

3. Debtors for inclusion (clause 4(1)):

   All debtors to which goods have been or are to be supplied in the United Kingdom, and any other debtor or debtors to the inclusion of which the parties shall have agreed in writing.

4. Prepayment percentage (clause 5(3)):

   % or such other percentage as shall have been agreed between the parties in writing.

5. Discounting charge (clause 5(3)):

   (a) Rate:

   % per annum over the Base Rate for the time being in force or such other rate as shall have been agreed by the parties in writing. For the purposes of this provision the Base Rate shall be the Base Rate of either Lloyds Bank p.l.c. or Barclays Bank p.l.c. at the option of the Factor as notified in writing to the Client from time to time.

   (b) Method of calculation:

   Daily on the amount, as at the close of business on each day, of the aggregate of outstanding receivables vesting in the Factor after deduction of the aggregate of credit balances on the accounts of debtors and after (i) further deduction of any credit balance on the Client's account with the Factor or (ii) addition of any debit balance on such account, as the case may be. For the purpose of this calculation, a receivable shall be deemed to be outstanding until the collection date thereof or, in respect of an approved receivable, any earlier date of insolvency of the relevant debtor.

6. Administration charge (clause 6) (exclusive of Value Added Tax)

7. Additional administration charges (clause 6):

8. Nature of Client's business (clause 8):

238

9. Client's contract with Debtor (clause 9(3)):

    (a) Terms of Trade

    (b) Governing Law   England

    (c) Currency of invoices   Sterling

10. Notices to Debtors (clause 9(5)):   On each invoice representing a receivable sold to the Factor in a form prescribed by the Factor from time to time.

11. Recourse for receivables unapproved (clause 10)):

    (a) For breach of warranty or undertaking

    (b) For any other reason

12. Date of commencement of Agreement (clause 20):

13. Period of Agreement (clause 20):   One year (minimum period) and thereafter until determined by not less than one month's written notice given by either party to the other.

14. Special Conditions:

IN WITNESS whereof the parties have caused their respective common seals to be hereunto affixed.

THE COMMON SEAL OF
ANGLO FACTORING SERVICES LIMITED
was hereunto affixed on the   day
of   19   in the presence of:

         Director

         Secretary

THE COMMON SEAL OF

was hereunto affixed on the   day
of   19   in the presence of:

         Director

         Secretary

Appendix VI: Client Account

Purchase Price Payable on Collection Date

S & W Supplies Co. Ltd.
98 West River Road
Shoreham By Sea
Sussex
BN4 5EX

ANGLO FACTORING SERVICES LIMITED
A SUBSIDIARY OF ROTHSCHILD INVESTMENT COMPANY LIMITED
1 PALACE PLACE BRIGHTON BN1 1ET
TELEPHONE BRIGHTON (0273) 21177
TELEX 877020
VAT REGISTRATION NO 184632 56

CLIENT STATEMENT

AS AT (DATE): 31 MAR 84
ACCOUNT NUMBER: 7416
PAGE NO: 1

FUNDS IN USE

VALUE DATE	DEBITS	CREDITS	BALANCE
1 MAR	987.56		202,300.00
2 MAR	86.25		203,287.56
3 MAR			203,373.81
4 MAR	17,500.00		220,873.81
5 MAR		57,500.00	163,373.81
6 MAR	40,000.00		203,373.81
8 MAR			
8 MAR			
11 MAR	103.50	47,500.00	155,873.81
12 MAR	17.25		155,977.31
13 MAR			155,994.56
13 MAR	15,000.00		170,994.56
14 MAR		25,500.00	145,494.56
16 MAR	15,000.00		160,494.56
17 MAR	711.56		161,206.12
18 MAR	22,500.00		183,706.12
19 MAR	207.00		183,913.12
20 MAR		15,475.00	168,438.12
20 MAR	15,000.00		183,438.12
21 MAR	7,500.00		190,938.12
25 MAR		10,375.00	180,563.12
25 MAR	1,000.00		181,563.12
26 MAR	3,500.00		185,063.12
27 MAR	557.42		185,620.54
29 MAR		5,850.00	179,770.54
31 MAR	1,919.76		181,690.30

ADMINISTRATION CHARGE	VAT RATE	VAT AMOUNT
2,322.22	15 %	348.32

CURRENT ACCOUNT

RATE	DESCRIPTION	CHARGES	DEBITS	CREDITS	BALANCE
12.250	B/F Balance				101,062.59CR
12.250	Inv Rec 57250.00 Less Chg	987.56		56,262.44	157,325.03CR
12.250	Inv Rec 5000.00 Less Chg	86.25		4,913.75	162,238.78CR
12.250	Prepayment		17,500.00		144,738.78CR
12.250	Debtor Payments		40,000.00		104,738.78CR
12.250	Prepayment Credits 785.61		785.61		103,953.17CR
12.250	Discount		52.50		103,900.67CR
12.250	Debtor Payments				
12.250	Inv Rec 6000.00 Less Chg	103.50		5,896.50	109,797.17CR
12.250	Inv Rec 1000.00 Less Chg	17.25		982.75	110,779.92CR
12.250	Prepayment		15,000.00		95,779.92CR
12.250	Debtor Payments				
12.250	Prepayment		15,000.00		80,779.92CR
12.250	Inv Rec 41250.00 Less Chg	711.56		40,538.44	121,318.36CR
12.250	Prepayment		22,500.00		98,818.36CR
12.250	Inv Rec 12000.00 Less Chg	207.00		11,793.00	110,611.36CR
12.250	Debtor Payments				
12.250	Prepayment		15,000.00		95,611.36CR
12.250	Prepayment		7,500.00		88,111.36CR
12.250	Debtor Payments				
12.250	Prepayment		1,000.00		87,111.36CR
12.250	Prepayment		3,500.00		83,611.36CR
12.250	Inv Rec 32315.00 Less Chg	557.42		31,757.58	115,368.94CR
12.250	Debtor Payments				
12.250	Discounting Charge @12.250 %	1,919.76	1,919.76		113,449.18CR

TOTAL DISCOUNTS	TOTAL INVOICES	TOTAL CREDIT NOTES
52.50	154,815.00	785.61

240

Purchase Price Payable on Maturity

A B C Limited,
1 High Street,
London W1

STATEMENT OF SALES LEDGER CONTROL ACCOUNT

DEBTOR CURRENCY: STERL   Supplier Currency: STERL   Supplier No: 01177   Page: 256

Date	Trans Code	Narrative	Reference	Maturity Date	Debtor Currency	Exchange Rate	Debit	Credit	Balance
02.07.83		B/F BALANCE							381,760.10 DR
05.07.83	606	PAYMENT-DEBTORS			01	1.0000		1,704.04	380,056.06 DR
07.07.83	606	PAYMENT-DEBTORS			01	1.0000		742.34	
07.07.83	650	CREDIT NOTE			01	1.0000		270.20	
07.07.83	700	LETTER OF OFFER	252	25.09.83	01	1.0000	44,669.71		423,713.23 DR
08.07.83	606	PAYMENT-DEBTORS	252		01	1.0000		2,925.20	420,788.03 DR
09.07.83	606	PAYMENT-DEBTORS			01	1.0000		4,017.01	416,771.02 DR

BALANCE AT 09 JUL 83   416,771.02 DR

A B C Limited,
1 High Street,
London   W1

STATEMENT OF DEBTS PURCHASED ACCOUNT

Supplier Currency: STERL

Supplier No: 01177

Page: 256

Date	Trans Code	Narrative	Reference	Maturity Date	Debtor Currency	Exchange Rate	Debit	Credit	Balance
14.04.83	700	LETTER OF OFFER	240	03.07.83	01	1.0000		25,278.72	25,278.72 CR
21.04.83	700	LETTER OF OFFER	241	10.07.83	01	1.0000		29,320.38	54,599.19 CR
28.04.83	700	LETTER OF OFFER	242	17.07.83	01	1.0000		30,679.70	85,278.80 CR
05.05.83	700	LETTER OF OFFER	243	24.07.83	01	1.0000		63,875.75	149,154.55 CR
12.05.83	700	LETTER OF OFFER	244	31.07.83	01	1.0000		37,619.63	186,774.18 CR
20.05.83	700	LETTER OF OFFER	245	08.08.83	01	1.0000		49,439.71	236,213.89 CR
24.05.83	700	LETTER OF OFFER	246	12.08.83	01	1.0000		26,055.51	262,269.40 CR
01.06.83	700	LETTER OF OFFER	247	20.08.83	01	1.0000		48,504.84	310,774.24 CR
09.06.83	700	LETTER OF OFFER	248	28.08.83	01	1.0000		3,000.90	313,775.14 CR
16.06.83	700	LETTER OF OFFER	249	04.09.83	01	1.0000		57,147.70	370,922.84 CR
23.06.83	700	LETTER OF OFFER	250	11.09.83	01	1.0000		35,753.36	406,676.20 CR
30.06.83	700	LETTER OF OFFER	251	18.09.83	01	1.0000		34,113.37	440,789.57 CR
14.04.83	957	MAT LETTER OF OFFER	240	03.07.83	01	1.0000	25,278.72		415,510.85 CR
07.07.83	700	LETTER OF OFFER	252	25.09.83	01	1.0000		44,669.71	460,180.56 CR

BALANCE AT 09 JUL 83   460,180.56 CR

STATEMENT OF CURRENT ACCOUNT

A B C Limited,
1 High Street,
London   W1

Supplier Currency: STERL

Supplier No: 01177

Page: 257

Date	Trans Code	Narrative	Reference	Maturity Date	Debtor Currency	Exchange Rate	Debit	Credit	Balance
01.07.83		B/F BALANCE							178,028.83 DR
01.07.83	905	INTEREST CHARGE- JUNE 83	762				1,144.08		179,172.91 DR
01.07.83	957	ADVANCE PAYMENT	999				105,000.00		284,172.91 DR
14.04.83	650	MAT LETTER OF OFFER	240					25,278.72	258,894.19 DR
07.07.83	710	CREDIT NOTE	252				270.20		
07.07.83	711	SERVICE FEE DOM	252				536.04		
07.07.83		VAT DOM	252				80.41		259,780.84 DR

BALANCE AT 09 JUL 83   259,780.84 DR

243

'Two Factor' System

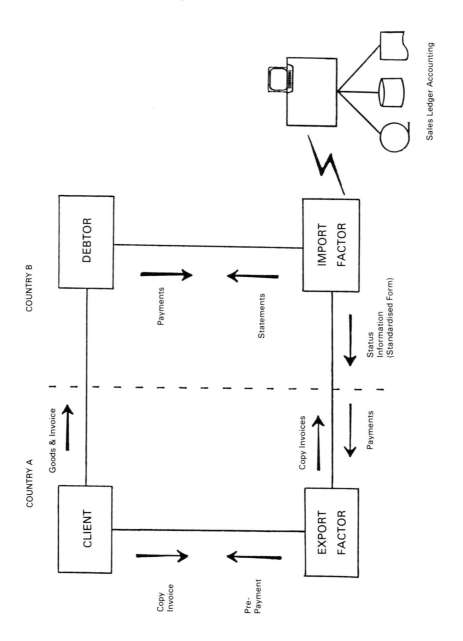

'Back-to-Back' Factoring

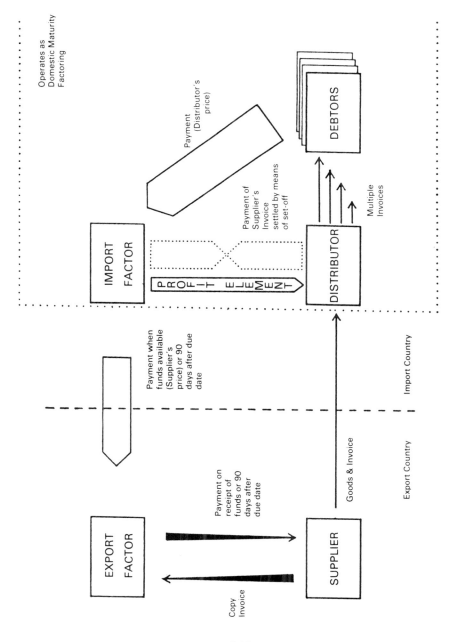

Index

References are to chapters and paragraph numbers of this book.

A

Accountant
  as advisor 6.1–6.7
    choice of factor 6.6
    choice of right service 6.2–6.5
  as auditor 6.8–6.11
Accounting procedures of factor Ch 9
Accounts, client (*see also* Apps VI, VII)
  purchase price payable on
    collection 9.17
    advantages 9.19
  purchase price payable after fixed
    maturity period 9.12
    client current account 9.21(3)
    debts purchased account 9.21(2)
    sales ledger control account 9.21(1)
    typical examples 9.22–9.23
    value added tax, and 9.24–9.25
Accounts receivables financing 3.4
Administration charge 9.2–9.5
Administrative services 4.5–4.7
Administrator, appointment of,
  proposals of White Paper,
  17.17–17.19
  insolvent clients and, 19.3
Agency factoring 3.6, 3.16–3.17
Agreement (*see also* Contract)
  approved and unapproved debts
    8.24–8.26
  basic types 7.12–7.13
  charges on other assets 8.39
  commencement of 2.9
  confidentiality and 3.15
  guarantees, *see* Guarantees
  facultative 7.13, 7.18–7.22 App IV
    advantages 7.19
    disadvantages 7.20
  master 7.12
  termination of 2.11, 8.40–8.43
    client's change of mind 8.42
    insolvency of client 8.43, 18.16
    protection of factor 8.40–8.41
  unincorporated clients, special
    considerations 7.13, 7.29–7.32
  whole turnover 3.10, 7.13,
    7.23–7.28, 7.30, App V
Approval of debts by factor 2.5,
  8.24–8.26 (*see also* Debts)

Assignment of debts 7.2–7.11
  client abroad, validity of when
    21.5–21.7
  equitable assignments 7.6
  legal assignments 7.5, 7.12
    and equitable compared 7.6–7.7
  registration of 7.29–7.30
Assignment, contract terms prohibiting
  Ch 13
  corporate clients in England 13.12
  inclusion of, reasons for 13.8
  overcoming problems of inclusion,
    methods of 13.9–13.11
  position since 'Helstan' case 13.2
  pre 1978 view of effect of terms 13.1
  risk to factor 13.6–13.7
  United States, comparison with 13.5
  use of 'ban on assignment terms'
    13.3–13.7
Attorney, power of 8.15–8.17

B

Back-to-back factoring 20.17–20.19
Banks
  co-operation with 3.22–3.23
  interest of clearing banks 1.18
Bankruptcy
  reputed ownership in, 7.31–7.32
  rights of parties in relation to, rules
    to apply 18.9–18.13
  (*see also* under Liquidation;
    Winding-up)
Benefits of factoring Ch 4
  administrative service 4.5–4.7
  ancillary service 4.7
  non-recourse, and client's balance
    sheet 4.16–4.17
  protection against bad debts 4.8–4.13
    credit insurance and factoring
      compared 4.11
  provision of finance without formal
    limit 4.14–4.15
  sales ledger administration 4.1–4.4
Block discounting 7.18, 15.1
Bulk factoring 3.5
  agency factoring as form of, 3.16–3.17

C

Carrier's liens 16.12–16.14

Chain of factors, *see* International factoring systems

Charges
collateral security, as 8.39
crystallisation of charge upon insolvency 17.2
factor's conflicts with other assignees and chargees Ch 15
position of factor 15.1
creation of other charges 15.2–15.4
priority of charges 15.5–15.9
importance of early notice by factor 15.9
registration of 8.5
types of conflicting charges 15.14–15.24
prior fixed charge 15.20–15.22
prior floating charge 15.14–15.16
subsequent fixed charge 15.23–15.24
subsequent floating charge 15.17–15.19
waivers from third party: a safeguard 15.10–15.13
form of 15.11–15.13
(*see also* Floating charge)

Charges for factoring services, *see* Factor; Payment

Choses in action (*see also* Debts) 7.3, 7.6, 7.31

Cheque payments, *see* Payment

Clearing House Automated Payments System (CHAPS) 9.15

Client 1.2
administration of sales records by 10.6
assessment of by factor Ch 10
credit risk 10.8–10.9, 10.15–10.18
factor's rights on winding-up or bankruptcy 18.14–18.19
financial position of business 10.5
insolvency of, *see* Insolvency of client
nature of business 10.3
reassignment of disputed debts to 8.12–8.13
recourse to, *see* Recourse factoring
sales ledger—source documents 10.7
statutory books 10.11
supplier's terms of business 10.12–10.13
terms and conditions of sale 10.4

Codification of commercial law 24.2–24.4

Collection from debtor Ch 11
contractual set-off 11.29
crown set-off 11.44–11.47
debtor's defences and counterclaims 11.23–11.30
equitable set-off by debtor against factor 11.25–11.27
factor's liability for credit balances 11.35–11.38
factor's position if client insolvent 11.39–11.43
factor's position if failure of consideration 11.32–11.34
legal remedies as final resort 11.14–11.22
debts assigned in equity only 11.15
instructions to solicitors and pre-court steps 11.17–11.19
interest 11.22
which court and enforcement of judgment 11.20–11.21
no positive liability of factor to debtor 11.31
normal procedures 11.2–11.13
action when normal collection methods fail 11.8–11.10
benefits of efficient collection service 11.12
examination of client's terms of business 11.2–11.3
factor's collection procedures 11.4–11.7
not applicable 11.11
precaution before legal proceedings 11.13
security to factor by notice to debtor 11.30
set-off in insolvency 11.28
special circumstances 11.11

Collection service 2.3, 4.5–4.7

Combination of services 3.18

Commencement of agreement 2.9

Company, collateral security from 8.36–8.39

Computers, *see* Future of factoring

Confidential factoring 1.14, 3.9 (*see also* Invoice discounting)

Conflict of laws 21.3–21.9
alleviating problems of 21.8

Construction industry 5.5(3)

Consumer Credit Act 1974, position of factors under 1.28–1.32

Contract of sale, variation of, 8.7
Contract, for 'sale or return' or 'sale on approval' 14.9–14.10
Contract of sale, terms affecting factor Ch 14
  long term contracts 5.5(2), 14.2–14.8
    cut-off clauses 14.6–14.7
    for services 14.2–14.3
    for supply of goods 14.4–14.5
    undertaking from debtor direct 14.8
Continuation of arrangement after appointment of receiver, 17.14
Credit insurance 4.11–4.15, 8.28
  combination of credit insurance and recourse factoring 3.18
  assignment of benefits of policy only 3.20
  methods of 3.21
  factoring, comparison with 4.11–4.15
Credit notes 2.6, 4.3, 4.4, 8.8
  insolvency and 19.3
Credit Protection Element (CPE) 10.15
Credit risk, assessment of 10.8–10.9, 10.15–10.18
Credit, trade 5.1 et seq.
Currency risks, *see* International factoring Ch 21

D

Dearle v Hall, rule in: priority of charges 15.5–15.9
Debtor, recovery of funds from 8.20–8.23 *and see* Collection from debtor; Insolvency of debtor
'Debt turn' 10.9
Debts
  after appointment of receiver, factors position 17.12
  approved and unapproved 2.5, 8.24–8.26, 12.11–12.14
  assignment of 7.2–7.11 (*see also* Assignment of debts)
  bad
    major debts 4.9
    protection against 2.5, 4.8–4.13, 4.17
    small debts 3.18
  'ban on assignment' terms 13.3–13.7
  capital equipment, resulting from sale of, 5.5(1)
  choses in action 7.3, 7.6, 7.31
  conflicting claims to debts Ch 16
  contingent liability for 6.11

  disputed, reassignment to client 8.12–8.13
  encumbrances on 10.10–10.13
    subsequent 8.5
  excluded from agreement 10.14
  existing and subsequent debts, factors position regarding, on receivership 17.8–17.13
  goods released on trust receipt 10.11, 16.11
    liens of a carrier 16.12–16.14
    rights of a mercantile agent 16.15
    'Romalpa' clauses 16.2–16.10
    effect on factors 10.11, 16.4
    position of factor summarised 16.9–16.10
    position in Germany 16.7
    priority of claims 16.5–16.6
    question of inferred knowledge 16.8
  notice of 8.20
  ownership, transfer of 2.3, 7.2–7.11
  purchase of 1.24, 7.14–7.17
  proof of, provided by client (seller) 8.30
  reserves for 6.8
  retentions 2.7, 2.8,
  transfer of all other rights in relation to 8.28
  trusts—creation of in relation to debts sold, 8.18
  validity of 8.2 (*see also* Warranties)
  value, reduction of 8.9
    counter-claim and 8.10
    dispute over 8.10
  vesting, methods of, 7.32–7.34
Deductions 8.21, 8.27
Developments in factoring in Europe and UK 1.11–1.18
  interest of clearing banks 1.18
  invoice discounting in early post-war years 1.12–1.14
Disclosed factoring, Table: factoring variants in Ch 3
Disclosure, clients duty 8.4
Disputes as between client and debtor 2.6
  notification of factor by client 8.11
Documents
  administration of sales records by client 10.6–10.7
  clients undertaking to execute 8.14
  inspection of 8.31
  power of attorney 8.15–8.17
  source 4.3

Index

E

Encumbrances, debts on, 10.10–10.13
  subsequent 8.5
Exchange transfer risks 21.25
  (*see also* International factoring)
Export Credits Guarantee Department
  3.21, 20.15, 21.25–21.26, 21.28

F

Factor
  accounting procedures 9.17–9.20
  administration and special service
    charges 9.2–9.8
  administrative duties 2.3
  administrative service 4.5
  advantages to small businesses
    4.5–4.7, Ch 23
  charges and accounting procedures
    Ch 9
  finance charges 9.9–9.16
    memorandum account 9.14
    'value dating' of payments and
      collections 9.15–9.16
  payment upon proof of delivery of
    goods by client 8.30
  power of attorney 8.15–8.17
  retention by 2.8
  time for payment of purchase price of
    debts sold to factor 9.21–9.23
  title to debts, perfecting, 8.14
  value added tax 9.24–9.25
Factoring
  acceptability of,, Ch 24
  agreement, *see* Agreement
  benefits of Ch 4
  composite method of, 22.9–22.12
  definition 1.19–1.22
  effects of misuse 5.8–5.17
  full service 1.22, Ch 2
  future of Ch 22–24
  inspection of clients accounts and
    records, provision for, 8.31
  independent businesses, benefits,
    Ch 24
  international Ch 20, 21
  legal framework Ch 22
  limitations on use 5.3–5.6
  nature of Ch 2, 3
  origin of 1.3–1.10
  overtrading and, 5.18–5.20
  suitability 5.5–5.7, 5.11
  UNIDROIT and, 1.20, 21.20–21.22

Facultative agreement 7.18–7.22,
  App IV
  winding-up and, 18.2–18.4
Fees for services Ch 9
Finance, alternative means of
  providing, 22.2–22.9
Finance, provision of, Table: factoring
  variants in Ch 3, 2.7, 4.14–4.15, 5.10
  charges for, *see* Factor
Floating charges 7.20–7.21, 12.2, Ch 15
  crystallisation 17.2
Full factoring service 1.22, 2.2–2.11
Future of factoring Ch 22–24
  growing acceptability Ch 24
    need for codification of commercial
      law 24.3–24.4
    proved benefits to independent
      businesses 24.1–24.2
  legal framework Ch 22
    alternative form of providing
      finance 22.2–22.4
    composite method 22.9–22.12
    lending on security of the
      debts 22.5–22.8
  micro-computer, influence of Ch 23
    data processing packages for small
      businesses 23.1, 23.2
    provision of sales statistics by
      factor 23.4
    response of factoring industry 23.3

G

Garnishee order, insolvency, 19.6–19.8
Germany 13.8, 16.7, 21.8
Glossary of terms App I
Goods, proof of delivery by client 8.30
Government departments 11.44–11.47
Guarantees, company, 8.28, 8.36–8.38,
  11.18

H

'Helstan' case 1978 13.2

I

Indemnity 8.37–8.38
Insolvency of client Ch 17–19 (*see also*
  Winding-up)
  appointment of receiver—effect of,
    17.2
    factors rights on, 17.3–17.7
  debts coming into existence after
    appointment 17.12

250

existing debts, factors rights
regarding 17.8–17.11
miscellaneous problems Ch 19
attachment of balance by client's
creditor, factor's position
19.5–19.8
credit balances on debtor's
account, factor's position
19.2–19.4
termination of agreement and, 8.43,
18.16
Insolvency of debtor Ch 12
approval of debts while receiver
running company 12.4
conflicts between execution auditors
and administrators of insolvent
estate 12.7–12.11
factors liability for credit balances on
debtors account 11.34–11.37,
19.2–19.4
procedures in liquidation 12.5
proof of debts 12.10
recourse the unapproved debts
12.11–12.14
recovery remedies 12.3–12.6
recovery of value added tax
12.15–12.18
reservation of title by client
12.19–12.22
Insurance 22.6, 22.7 (*see also* Credit
insurance)
International factoring: matters
requiring special consideration Ch 21
client's viewpoint 21.24–21.29
choice between factoring and other
assistance for exporters
21.26–21.29
political and exchange transfer
risks 21.25
currency risks associated with
21.16–21.17
legal effect of international
transactions 21.2–21.9
conflicts of law 21.3–21.7
direct factoring when client
abroad 21.9
use of two factor system to alleviate
problems 21.8
validity of assignment of debt when
insolvent client domiciled in
another country 21.5–21.7
transmission of funds in settlement of
debts 21.10–21.15
cheque payments in domestic
business 21.10–21.11
transmission of funds in
international business
21.12–21.15
International factoring systems Ch 20
back-to-back factoring 20.17–20.19
App IX
by a single factor 20.19
direct export factoring 20.11–20.14
direct import factoring 20.9–20.10
invoice discounting or undisclosed
factoring for exports 20.15–20.16
two factor system 20.1–20.8
advantages and disadvantages 20.7
chains (groups of factors) 20.4–20.6
characteristics 20.3, App VIII
exchange risk cover 20.8
reduced finance charges 20.8
International Institute for the
Unification of Private Law, *see*
UNIDROIT
Invoices 4.3
Invoice discounting 1.12–1.14, 3.9–3.13
with credit insurance by client
3.18–3.21
example of, 3.10
factors protection in cases of
insolvency 3.11
inspection of ledgers 3.12
undisclosed factoring, applied to,
3.14–3.15

L

Law, need for codification of, 24.3–24.4
Legal framework of factoring Ch 22
Licences 1.30
Liquidation or bankruptcy of debtor
conflicts between execution creditors
and administrators of insolvent
estate 12.7–12.10
factor's procedures in 12.5–12.10
Long term contracts, *see* Contract of
sale

M

Master agreement 7.12
Maturity factoring 3.7–3.8
trend towards 1.25–1.27
Maturity period 3.7
Memorandum account 9.14
Mercantile agents, 1.6–1.8
rights of 16.5
Micro-computer, influence of Ch 23
Misuse of factoring 5.8–5.17

Index

N

Nature of factoring Ch 2, 3
  the full service 2.1 et seq
  commencement and termination
    2.9–2.11
  finance for trade credit 2.7–2.8
  (*see also* Table: factoring variants in
    Ch 3)
Non-recourse factoring, Table: factoring
  variants in Ch 3, 4.16–4.17, 5.20
Notice to debtor 1.14, 3.9, 8.20, 11.30,
  15.9
Notification factoring, Table: factoring
  variants in Ch 3
Novation 7.3, 17.15

O

Overtrading, factoring and, 5.18–5.20
'Own Service Factoring' 3.5

P

Partnerships 7.29–7.32
Payment
  against proof of debt 8.30
  cheque 21.10–21.11
  delays in, 21.13–21.15
  transmission of funds in
    international business 21.12
Percentage of retention 2.8
Plant and machinery 5.4
Power of attorney 8.15–8.17

R

Receiver, factor's position on
  appointment, 17.3–17.7
  continuation of agreement for
    factoring after appointment of,
    17.14
  position of, subsequent to winding-up
    order 17.16
Receivership Ch 17 (*see also* Ch 12)
  appointment of administrator
    proposed in White Paper on
    Insolvency 17.17–17.19
  continuation of factoring
    arrangement by receiver 12.4,
    17.14–17.15
  debts, effect on 17.8–17.13
  factor's position regarding existing
    and subsequent debts 17.8–17.13
  factor's rights on appointment of
    receiver 17.3–17.7
  receiver's position after winding-up
    order 17.16
  relations between receiver and factor
    17.1–17.2
  effect of appointment of
    receiver 17.2
Recourse factoring 3.2–3.4, 3.18, 5.11,
  8.27
Recourse of factor for unapproved
  debts 12.11–12.14
Recovery proceedings 8.6
  funds paid by debtor to creditor
    8.20–8.23
Refactoring charge 6.6, 9.6
Registration of charges 8.5
Remuneration Ch 9
Reservation of title by client
  12.19–12.22, 16.2–16.10
Retention 2.7, 2.8, 8.33, 8.34, 17.4 (*see
  also* Debts)
Rights to ownership of debts 1.24
Romalpa clauses 16.2–16.10

S

Sales ledger administration 4.1–4.4
  sales accounting 4.3(2)
  source documents 4.3(1)
Scotland 7.33–7.39, 8.3, 8.14, 16.10
Security, lending on, 7.14–7.17,
  22.1–22.8
Security rights 8.5
Seller, *see* Client
Sole traders and partnerships 7.29
Stamp duty 7.7
  agreements in avoidance of 7.12–7.13
Survey by factor 10.2 et seq.

T

Termination of factors agreements, *see*
  Agreements
Title to debts, factor's 8.14–8.17
Transfer of ancillary rights 8.28–8.29
Trade credit, true nature of 5.1–5.2
Tripartite client/factor/bank
  arrangements 3.22–3.23
Trustee, constructive 8.23
Trusts
  creation of 7.33–7.39, 8.18, 8.19

U

Uberrimae fidei 8.4
Undisclosed factoring 3.14–3.15 (*see
  also* Invoice discounting)

UNIDROIT 21.18–21.23
  definition of factoring 1.20,
    21.20–21.22
  limitations in application of the
    rules 21.23
USA, origin and growth of factoring in,
  1.3–1.20
  Uniform Commercial Code 1.7, 7.14
Use and misuse of factoring Ch 5
  businesses highly suitable for
    factoring 5.6
  limitations on factoring use 5.3–5.5
    from client's point of view 5.3
    from factor's point of view 5.5
  misuse, effects of, 5.8–5.16
    client's failure to achieve profits
      5.12
    disregard of responsibility to accept
      recourse 5.11
    finance used for capital
      expenditure 5.10
    high incidence of after sales
      service 5.13
    position of poor quality debtors
      5.14–5.16
    recognition of, 5.17
Undertaking, *see* Warranties

V

Validity of debts 8.2
Value dating payments and collection
  9.15
Value of debt 8.2

Value added tax 9.24–9.25
  recovery of 12.15–12.18
Variation of contract of sale 8.7

W

Warranties
  client by 8.2–8.13
  disputes and counterclaims 8.10
  factor's rights on breach by client
    8.32–8.35
  notification of disputes by client 8.11
White Paper on Insolvency, Preface
  7.20, 7.32, 17.17–17.19,
Whole turnover agreement 3.10,
  7.23–7.28, App V
  winding-up and, 18.2–18.4
Winding-up Ch 18
  bankruptcy of client 18.9–18.13
  debts in existence at time of,
    18.7–18.8
  effect of voluntary winding-up
    18.5–18.8
  effect of winding-up by the court
    18.1–18.4
  factor's rights on winding-up or
    bankruptcy of client 18.14–18.19
  co-operation of administrator of
    client's insolvent estate 18.15
  exercise of rights to terminate or
    have debts repurchased
    18.16–18.19
  receiver's position subsequent to
    winding-up orders 17.16